FAMILY ISSUES IN THE 21ST CENTURY

PARENTAL INVOLVEMENT

PRACTICES, IMPROVEMENT STRATEGIES AND CHALLENGES

FAMILY ISSUES IN THE 21ST CENTURY

Additional books and e-books in this series can be found on Nova's website under the Series tab.

FAMILY ISSUES IN THE 21ST CENTURY

PARENTAL INVOLVEMENT

PRACTICES, IMPROVEMENT STRATEGIES AND CHALLENGES

NURIT KAPLAN TOREN
AND
GERTINA J. VAN SCHALKWYK
EDITORS

Copyright © 2020 by Nova Science Publishers, Inc.

All rights reserved. No part of this book may be reproduced, stored in a retrieval system or transmitted in any form or by any means: electronic, electrostatic, magnetic, tape, mechanical photocopying, recording or otherwise without the written permission of the Publisher.

We have partnered with Copyright Clearance Center to make it easy for you to obtain permissions to reuse content from this publication. Simply navigate to this publication's page on Nova's website and locate the "Get Permission" button below the title description. This button is linked directly to the title's permission page on copyright.com. Alternatively, you can visit copyright.com and search by title, ISBN, or ISSN.

For further questions about using the service on copyright.com, please contact:
Copyright Clearance Center
Phone: +1-(978) 750-8400   Fax: +1-(978) 750-4470   E-mail: info@copyright.com.

NOTICE TO THE READER

The Publisher has taken reasonable care in the preparation of this book, but makes no expressed or implied warranty of any kind and assumes no responsibility for any errors or omissions. No liability is assumed for incidental or consequential damages in connection with or arising out of information contained in this book. The Publisher shall not be liable for any special, consequential, or exemplary damages resulting, in whole or in part, from the readers' use of, or reliance upon, this material. Any parts of this book based on government reports are so indicated and copyright is claimed for those parts to the extent applicable to compilations of such works.

Independent verification should be sought for any data, advice or recommendations contained in this book. In addition, no responsibility is assumed by the Publisher for any injury and/or damage to persons or property arising from any methods, products, instructions, ideas or otherwise contained in this publication.

This publication is designed to provide accurate and authoritative information with regard to the subject matter covered herein. It is sold with the clear understanding that the Publisher is not engaged in rendering legal or any other professional services. If legal or any other expert assistance is required, the services of a competent person should be sought. FROM A DECLARATION OF PARTICIPANTS JOINTLY ADOPTED BY A COMMITTEE OF THE AMERICAN BAR ASSOCIATION AND A COMMITTEE OF PUBLISHERS.

Additional color graphics may be available in the e-book version of this book.

Library of Congress Cataloging-in-Publication Data

ISBN: 978-1-53616-828-0

Published by Nova Science Publishers, Inc. † New York

CONTENTS

Preface		vii
Chapter 1	Involving Parents in Curriculum: Expectations, Supports and Challenges *Robin Averill*	1
Chapter 2	Parent-Child Homework Interactions: Beginning an Assignment *Francesco Arcidiacono and Esther González-Martínez*	33
Chapter 3	Exploring Parent-Teacher Trust and School Involvement: A Finnish Perspective *Viola Penttinen, Eija Pakarinen and Marja-Kristiina Lerkkanen*	65
Chapter 4	Processes and Pathways of Parental Involvement in Education in Israel *Nurit Kaplan Toren and Revathy Kumar*	91
Chapter 5	The Determinants of Paternal and Maternal Involvement in Childcare *Mariana Pinho and Ruth Gaunt*	115

Chapter 6	Teachers' Perspectives of the Parent Involvement Hexis in Under-Resourced Urban Schools *Nyna Amin*	143
Chapter 7	Primary School Teachers' Experiences of Parental Involvement in a Township School: A South African Case Study *Mantsose Jane Sethusha*	171
Chapter 8	Immigrant Teachers in Schools: A Strategy to Improve Parental Involvement of Immigrant Parents *Florence Nyemba*	193

About the Editors	223
About the Contributors	225
Index	231
Related Nova Publication	241

PREFACE

Parental involvement in child care and the success of their children in school and in life has become a major topic of interest for researchers, educational policy makers, and teachers around the world. Multiple demands and social changes in many countries of the world pose challenges to parental involvement given in part to dual-income families, globalization, increased mobility and access to the electronic media. These social changes, including historical and political transformation in some many low- and middle-income countries, as well as added demands for academic achievement add further challenges to the psychological wellbeing and academic achievements of the youth of the twenty-first century. Given these challenges and diversities, many researchers have identified parental involvement as central to the child's success in school and in life. The focus is on finding the best practices for promoting school success in children by examining the boundaries previously observed between parents and educators, and to derive policies that would serve the best interests of the youth.

In this book, we collated a series of papers focusing on different challenges and practices to obtain greater parental involvement in the schooling of children and youth. The authors espoused, to varying degrees, the unique and complex patterns of parent-school relationships pointing out two significant areas where parental involvement does and should occur, namely home-based and school-based. In their exposition of these two areas, the authors of the various chapters point out both macro and micro antecedents of how parents are involved both at home (home-based) and at school (school-based) supporting their children towards achieving success. At the macro-level, the authors who contributed to this book reflected upon policy issues whereby the Ministries of Education in various countries (i.e., New Zealand, Israel, Finland, South Africa and the United States) instigated strategies for parental and varying degrees of success. There is also evidence of cultural perspectives and teachers' ethnic and professional identities impact on their attitudes towards parental involvement both at school and at home. As claimed by the authors of the various chapters, there are many barriers, obstacles and challenges towards enabling parents for greater involvement in their children's educational achievements, and a need for more consistency across home and school systems. For the most part, however, the authors espouse the belief that strengthening parent-teacher relationships will promote the child's development and success in school and in life.

Achieving both home-based and school-based parental involvement depends, however, on how both parents and teachers perceive each other and the degree of consistency and coherence across systems. On one hand, parents need to perceive the teachers as trustworthy and pursuing the child's best interest at all times, while on the other hand teachers need to perceive the parents as sufficiently knowledgeable to engage effectively in helping the child at home. These perceptions are reflected in the chapters explicating robust strategies, data and rationales across different dimensions of the parent-teacher relationship and the complexities cultural/multi-ethnic diversity, culturally responsive pedagogy, asset-based approaches to education, as well as gender differences and the child's age or level at school. Following the developmental trajectory of children from infancy to adolescence, the authors of the various chapters espouse their most up-to-date findings and viewpoints pertaining to parental involvement from the perspective the parents themselves, the perspective of the teachers, and the views of students both in the home and at the school.

Uncovering processes and pathways of home-based parental involvement, Pinho and Gaunt (Chapter 5) investigated the determinants of paternal and maternal involvement in early childhood care, particularly focusing on the changes pertaining to traditional gender ideology. Parental involvement starts already at a very early age during infancy when parental care forms the basis for early childhood (informal) education in the home. Claiming that the father's role has in the past been overlooked in early childhood (home-based) education, the authors highlight the importance that parental involvement by both parents should begin early to ensure the child's wellbeing and academic success in later life. Although these researchers found only partial support for the gender ideology model amongst a group of Israeli parents, there seems to be similar findings about gender inequality in Finland, where researchers have found gender differences in parental involvement.

Home-based parental involvement in most cases imply the ways in which the parents engage with their children around school-related issues such as homework and assignments. Using a rather unique multi-modal methodology that involved video-recording and ethnographic analyses of parent-child interactions, Arcidiacano and González-Martínez (Chapter 2) explored the various dimensions of parental involvement when helping their primary school children with a homework assignment. Their study shed light on how homework tasks are achieved and present teachers and parents with insights regarding how to improve strategies for home-based parental involvement. Kaplan-Toren and Kumar (Chapter 4) search for answers about both home-based and school-based parental involved during the adolescent years espousing differences and similarities between Arabs and Jews in Israel. It turns out that not only are there cultural differences in home-based parental involvement—for example, authoritarian vs. authoritative parenting and a potential generation gap amongst Arab parents and their adolescent children—but also that school-based parental involvement showed a beneficial effect on adolescents' scholastic competence and academic achievements.

Exploring the parent-teacher trust relationship and school involvement in primary schools in Finland, Penttinen, Pakarinen and Lerkkanen (Chapter 3) found that parents—that is, both mothers and fathers—of boys and girls in the Grade 1-6 age group (i.e., ages 6-12 years) did not differ in the trust they have in teachers but that fathers of boys were more involved in later primary school years than fathers of girls. Mothers, on the other hand, did not really distinguish their trust in the teachers and involvement with the school based on the gender of their children. Nevertheless, trust in the teacher and the education system predicted the school-based involvement of parents across the board, posing the question as to how teachers and educators should strategize in order to generate parental involvement in the interest of the child's success. Observing the cultural diversity amongst Arab and Jewish families in Israel, Kaplan-Toren and Kumar (Chapter 4) reflect upon the parent-teacher trust relationship espousing that trust, mutual respect and commitment are essential foundations for a satisfactory partnership between the school, the teachers and the parents. The authors comment also on the cultural diversity found in other regions of the world, while Nyemba (Chapter 8) comment on the plight of immigrant parents experiencing distrust in teachers who present with cultural insensitivity towards their children thus minimizing the prospects of a parent-teacher partnership.

School-based parental involvement, apart from establishing a trusting relationship between parents and teachers, poses a host of different challenges when engaging with parents from minority groups or from culturally diverse backgrounds. Averill proposes new ways to think about engaging parents in curriculum development with the aim of forging links between what is taught in school and the child's everyday life experiences. Focusing specifically on the indigenous groups in New Zealand, Averill explores culturally responsive and sustainable practices for parental involvement that might have meaning for other regions where parents feel excluded from the schooling of their children based on their background. Amin (Chapter 6) and Sethusha (Chapter 7) focused on the viewpoints of teachers pertaining to parental involvement in secondary and primary schools respectively in South Africa. In both these chapters the authors espouse the complexity of cultural and demographic differences between teachers and parents adding a further dimension to understanding and strategizing for greater parental involvement both at home and at school.

Preface

Amin (Chapter 6) explicated the rather negative attitudes of teachers towards parents in their school community. The teachers, who are of a different socio-cultural background apparently have limited insights into the hardships that parents face becoming more involved in the schooling of their children. Although compelled by the Department of Education in South Africa, these teachers seemingly transfer their discontent with the government onto the parents as a means of coping with the challenging educational settings in which they work. On the other hand, Sethusha (Chapter 7) espouse the socio-economic challenges and lack of parental education in townships and informal settlements in South Africa that seem to call for innovative strategies if teachers want to engage the parents in the schooling of the children. As with the situation in Israel (Kaplan-Toren & Kumar, Chapter 4) and the immigrant population in the United States (Nyemba, Chapter 8), cultural diversity amongst teachers, teachers and children, and teachers and parents seem to be key challenges when it comes to generating parental involvement in the schooling of children and youth in different parts of the world. Traditional theories and studies espousing the value of parental involvement both at home and at school do not seem to hold much ground when it comes to engendering parental involvement in these culturally diverse settings.

The studies presented in this book raise the voice of parents, teachers and students. There are many thought-provoking insights and information as well as recommendations for further research and new theories expresses by the different voices represented in these chapters. Nonetheless, we need to emphasise that the viewpoints presented by the chapter authors are their own and based on their respective frames of reference, and do not necessarily reflect our viewpoints as editors of this book. Of course, we respect the voice of research and therefore wish to put forth these viewpoints as a stimulating eye-opener and to encourage researchers and educators around the world towards seeking out viable practices pursuing greater parental involvement in best interest of all the children and youth of the world.

Nurit Kaplan Toren and Gertina J. van Schalkwyk
Editors

In: Parental Involvement
Editors: Nurit Kaplan Toren et al.
ISBN: 978-1-53616-828-0
© 2020 Nova Science Publishers, Inc.

Chapter 1

INVOLVING PARENTS IN CURRICULUM: EXPECTATIONS, SUPPORTS AND CHALLENGES

*Robin Averill**
Victoria University of Wellington, Wellington, New Zealand

ABSTRACT

Research on culturally responsive and culturally sustaining practice, asset-based approaches, and funds of knowledge indicates the importance of teaching approaches being consistent with and linked to the out-of-school knowledge, beliefs, and priorities of learners and their communities. Many curricula, related policy, and research call for involvement of parents in the learning of their children to enhance achievement and help forge links between curriculum content and everyday life experiences. In many contexts, school and teacher practice in relation to parental involvement in learning is not yet strongly aligned with the expectations of policy and calls from research. In relation to international research and Epstein's model of parental involvement, this chapter explores supports and challenges in relation to schools and teachers in Aotearoa New Zealand enabling their

---

* Corresponding Author's Email: robin.averill@vuw.ac.nz.

learners to enjoy powerful parental involvement in their learning and securing strong learning partnerships between parents and teachers. Particular focus is given to policy expectations of practice regarding, and responsiveness to, Indigenous Māori and Pasifika learners and their communities, groups persistently underserved in New Zealand's Eurocentric school system. A synthesis of ideas from the literature on parental involvement in learning and culturally responsive and sustaining practice is used to frame recommendations for practice and research.

Keywords: parental involvement, curriculum, education policy, culturally sustaining pedagogy, indigenous

INTRODUCTION

Parental involvement in the school curriculum is advocated in many countries for enhancing students' learning, achievement, and schooling experiences and reducing barriers to learning (Desforges & Abouchaar, 2003; Pomerantz, Moorman, & Litwack, 2007). For the purpose of this chapter, 'parental' is taken to include parents, family, and care-givers; those in children's homes responsible for care and support. The term 'policy' is used broadly to encompass documents and resources provided by government bodies to guide school and teacher practice; and the 'school curriculum' refers to learning programmes as implemented by schools. Known benefits from parental involvement in the school curriculum include children experiencing increased motivation to learn, stronger achievement gains, and greater school attendance (e.g., Anthony & Walshaw, 2007; Biddulph, Biddulph, & Biddulph, 2003; Castro et al., 2015; Harris & Goodall, 2008; Robinson, Hohepa, & Lloyd, 2009; Sheldon & Epstein, 2005; Tuuta, Bradnam, Hynds, Higgins, & Broughton, 2004). There is some evidence that different styles and amounts of parental involvement are of benefit to different groups of students (Education Review Office, 2018). For example, a U.S. study found that school-based parental involvement was of more benefit to lower socio-economic students and students with limited prior achievement than for higher socio-economic learners and those with stronger prior achievement, for whom parental involvement more generally was of benefit (Benner, Boyle, & Sadler, 2016). It is likely that children in minority groups may depend on parental involvement and support for their education and for their academic progress more than those whose cultural capital is closer to that of their teachers, school leaders, and society (Kerbaiv & Bernhardt, 2018). Parental involvement in learning can increase parental understanding of the curriculum (Anthony & Walshaw, 2007; Civil, 2006), enhance their relationships with their children, and increase their confidence in their capabilities both to interact with the school and to assist their children (Bernie & Lall, 2008).

This chapter draws on a literature review into how parental and family involvement in school learning programmes can be developed (Averill, Metson, & Bailey, 2016) to explore supports and challenges for parental involvement in curriculum. First, a framework commonly used for considering parental involvement (Epstein, 2001) is outlined. The New Zealand policy and teaching and learning context and key themes of culturally responsive and sustaining practice and parental involvement in relation to these are then discussed. The chapter concludes with considerations for teachers and schools, teacher educators, parents, and policy implementation, in light of identified supports for, and challenges to parental involvement in learning.

A MODEL OF PARENTAL INVOLVEMENT

A model commonly used to describe partnerships between families and schools is Epstein's (1995, 2001, 2011) three overlapping spheres of influence, with the family, community, and school the three 'spheres' that students exist within and are influenced by. Epstein (2001) describes six areas of involvement between parents and schools: parenting, communicating, volunteering, learning at home, decision making, and community collaboration. The three areas most relevant to involving parents with the school curriculum and hence to this chapter are communicating, learning at home, and decision making. Epstein (2011) provides useful descriptors for each area, with 'communicating' referring to two-way interactions about the learner, learning, and what is happening at school between home and school. 'Learning at home' describes school curriculum related activities outside school and teachers and schools assisting parents to help their children with their curriculum learning, and 'decision making' refers to parents having input into school and curriculum decisions.

Epstein's (2001) model is a good fit for New Zealand education in relation to curriculum and other policy guidelines. Epstein's model is learner-centred as is our national curriculum (Ministry of Education, 2007), a curriculum which affords a high level of teacher and school autonomy in its implementation (Sheehan, 2017). Consistent with Epstein's 'communicating' area of parental involvement, New Zealand policy and research emphasize that relationships between teachers and parents must be respectful, non-judgmental, and suit the community, and that two-way communication best supports student learning (Biddulph et al., 2003; Bull, Brooking, & Campbell, 2008; Education Review Office, 2008). Important for enabling home-based learning support, such communication can include discussions focused on the school curriculum and curriculum change (Fisher & Neill, 2007, 2008).

Consistent with Epstein's 'learning at home' category, a range of literature advocates parental involvement in children's learning outside of school (e.g., Bull, et al., 2008; Fan & Chen, 2001; McNaughton, 2016; Ministry of Education, n.d., a,b), including through parents holding high expectations of their children's achievement, discussing learning and school activities with them, and assisting with reading development (Boonk, Gijselaers, Ritzen, & Brand-Gruwel, 2018; Castro et al., 2015). Out-of-school learning activities can include parents and children playing games, shopping, cooking, and reading together, and parents helping their children with homework (e.g., Epstein 2001; Ministry of Education, n.d., c; Van Voorhis, 2003, 2011). Research and policy support material are available to New Zealand teachers in relation to 'communicating' and 'learning at home' (e.g., Education Review Office, 2008, 2015a; Ministry of Education, n.d., ab,c,d). Less material is available, however, to assist New Zealand teachers and schools to develop strategies and processes for supporting parental involvement in school curriculum-based 'decision making', despite policy increasingly expecting such involvement (e.g., Ministry of Education, 2011a, 2018).

Also useful to consider when focussing on parental involvement in learning are factors that can support or hinder parents' decisions to become involved in their children's learning in the first place. Factors that influence such decisions include how parents see their role as parents in relation to schoolwork, how confident they feel in knowing how to contribute in ways the school is open to, how well they feel they will be able to support their child's learning, and the opportunities for involvement afforded by the school and their child (Hoover-Dempsey & Sandler, 1997). Practical considerations, such as the extent to which parents can afford to take time out of work and other commitments, or to travel to attend meetings are also important factors impacting on parental involvement. All of these factors can inform understanding of the supports for, and barriers to parental involvement in decision making in school curricula.

CULTURALLY RESPONSIVE AND CULTURALLY SUSTAINING TEACHING

Culturally responsive pedagogy helps ensure the "cultural knowledge, prior experiences, frames of reference, and performance styles of ethnically diverse students" both enable learning (Gay, 2010, p. 31) and empower students "intellectually, socially, emotionally, and politically" (Ladson-Billings, 2009, p. 20). Culturally sustaining pedagogy (McCarty & Lee, 2014; Paris, 2012; Paris & Samy Alim, 2014) builds on the ideas of culturally responsive pedagogies towards further safeguarding, nurturing, and reflecting learners' cultural practices and identities in their learning experiences. Culturally sustaining pedagogy is intended to foster "multilingualism and multiculturalism in practice and perspective" to "perpetuate and foster – to sustain – linguistic, literate, and cultural pluralism as part of the democratic project of schooling" (Paris, 2012, p. 95).

However, culturally responsive and sustaining teaching are challenging to develop, particularly for teachers and student teachers of ethnicities and cultural heritages different to those of their students (Hindle, Hynds, Averill, Meyer, & Faircloth, 2016). Surprisingly, parental involvement in curriculum seems to have been less frequently explored in the literature on culturally responsive and sustaining practice than teacher practice. As parents can be more deeply engaged with their heritage culture/s than their children, they are likely to have knowledge and insights valuable, even critical, for informing curriculum decision-making.

The depth of knowledge, critical thinking, and commitment to change in teaching decisions intended to be culturally responsive or sustaining can be considered in light of descriptors used in environmental sustainability education: accommodation, reformation, and transformation (Bateson, 2000; Renert, 2011; Sterling, 2004). The three response type descriptors can also be used to describe demonstration of understanding about culturally sustaining practice (Averill & McRae, 2019). Considerations of these three levels of responsiveness are used throughout this chapter to help interrogate policy, research, and practice in relation to supports for and challenges to establishing parental involvement in learning.

Decisions that involve comparatively minor changes from usual practice can be considered accommodation type responses in that they typically do not challenge the status quo or the values of the teacher or learners. More major changes to practice involve reorganising learning in ways that fit largely within usual structures (reformation) and those that are paradigm shifts from usual practice (transformation). Reformation and transformation type responses include decisions that involve substantive change from the status quo. These responses to the ideals of culturally sustaining practice are preferable to accommodation type responses as they necessitate deeper understanding and greater capacity to innovate. Hence, while all levels of response can enhance experiences for marginalised learners, such changes are more likely than accommodation level responses to enhance learners' values and capabilities.

THE NEW ZEALAND CONTEXT

Aotearoa New Zealand is an ethnically diverse country founded on a treaty agreed between Indigenous Māori and the British crown in the mid-1800s. The treaty, commonly understood to ensure principles of protection, participation, and partnership in relation to the treaty partners (Ritchie, Skerrett, & Rau, 2014), is increasingly reflected in law and practice. Deep commitment to the treaty is expected in the teaching of all students including through incorporating the Māori language and reflecting Māori customs in teaching and learning decisions (Education Council, 2017). Māori make up approximately 24% of the school age population, students with heritage of Pacific Nations constitute roughly 10%, and New Zealand European and Asian students make up roughly 50% and 12% respectively (Education Review Office, n.d.). There are as yet relatively small numbers of New Zealand primary and secondary school teachers claiming either Māori or Pacific heritage, approximately 13% and 4% respectively, in comparison to roughly 82% of teachers claiming New Zealand European heritage (Education Counts, 2019). In addition, the proportions of Māori children and children of Pacific Nations heritage (Pasifika) in the school-age population are increasing at a faster rate than for other ethnic groups.

Despite these legal and professional expectations, many Māori learners are not yet experiencing culturally sustaining teaching (Bishop & Berryman, 2006; Hynds, Averill, Hindle, & Meyer, 2017). Persistent achievement differences on traditional measures exist by ethnicity and socio-economic status (Gilmore & Smith, 2011). Enhancing the learning opportunities, achievement, and school experiences of learners of Māori, Pacific Island, and low socio-economic backgrounds are current education system-wide priorities (Ministry of Education, 2012). Demonstration of cultural competencies is expected in relation to the teaching of both our learners of Māori heritage (Ministry of Education, 2011a) and Pasifika learners (Ministry of Education, 2018). All response types (accommodation, reformation, and transformation) are represented in these documents in the cultural competence indicators provided as guides to teachers (Ministry of Education, 2011a; 2018).

However, mismatches between the cultural backgrounds of many teachers and these students and between many teachers' own experiences of learning at school and current expectations challenge policy implementation.

Further challenges exist in relation to the use of the broad terms 'Māori' and 'Pasifika' to describe groups of great diversity. 'Māori' is used to describe all with Indigenous Māori heritage, with differences in language, custom, and practice existing between iwi (tribes) and variation across Māori in relation to knowledge of, and the importance placed on the Māori language and cultural heritage. The term 'Pasifika' is used to describe all those in New Zealand who have cultural heritage linked to diverse Pacific Island nations. Hence, extensive variation exists amongst Pasifika in relation to heritage language and customs and engagement with these, and in terms of how long families have been living in New Zealand.

As in many countries, involving parents in all children's learning towards enhancing learning and motivation to learn is expected in New Zealand (Ministry of Education, 2007, 2011a, 2018):

> Educational success requires a child's community to be actively involved. Responsibility must be shared across these communities and by early childhood educators, schools and teachers, families
> Effective partnerships between parents and education professionals will improve the well-being, behaviour and achievement of children right into adulthood (Ministry of Education, 2014, pp. 13-21).

The school curriculum is intended to connect with children's "wider lives" and engage "the support of their families, whānau [Māori families], and communities" (Ministry of Education, 2007, p. 9). Teachers are to "provide clear statements of learning expectations ... stated in ways that help teachers, students, and parents to recognise, measure, discuss, and chart progress" (Ministry of Education, 2007, p. 39). Clear statements expecting parental involvement in learning are also present in policy specifically relating to the teaching of Māori learners, for example:

Learning is more effective when whānau are valued partners in the education process and when educators and whānau are open to learning from and with one another." (Ministry of Education, 2008, p. 29)

Tātaiako (Ministry of Education, 2011b), a policy implementation resource that outlines factors important for teaching that is culturally responsive and sustaining to Māori learners, states that parents "should feel able to contribute information based on their knowledge of their child" in discussions with their child's teachers "aimed at improving student learning" (p. 28). Two-way agentic parent-school communication about learning is expected, through the inclusion of words such as 'partnership', 'actively involved', and 'shared'.

Active partnership amongst teachers, schools, and parents and parental involvement in learning are inherent in the concepts of 'ako', 'wānanga', 'whanaungatanga', 'manaakitanga', and 'tangata whenuatanga', *Tātaiako's* five 'cultural competencies' needed by teachers of Māori students (Ministry of Education, 2011a, pp. 2-14). For example, indicators of the competencies include that teachers will be engaging with "Māori [family] in open dialogue about teaching and learning" (p. 4), actively seeking "ways to work with [families] to maximise Māori learner success" (p. 6), and actively facilitating "the participation of [family]… to support classroom teaching and learning programmes" (p. 10). Examples of parent voice used to illustrate desirable thoughts and feelings of parents associated with teachers demonstrating the cultural competencies are also consistent with Epstein's (2001) areas of parental involvement. In relation to Epstein's area of 'communicating', examples of parent voice include "our perspectives and our values are respected" (p. 11) and "we talk with teachers regularly about our children's learning" (p. 15). "They do a good job of linking what they teach to things our kids can relate to" (p. 13) and "we know what our children are learning at school and can support them at home" (p. 15) link well to 'learning at home', and the area of 'decision making' is represented through examples such as "we determine the type of information we want to receive about our children's learning and also how that information is provided" and "we can make decisions about the teaching and learning programme" (p. 15).

Factors likely to impact on strategies that could help foster such parent voice include subject content, teacher and parent content and pedagogical knowledge, school values and culture, and teachers' knowledge of the lives of their students. Whether such examples of parent voice represent responsiveness to change at accommodation, reformation, or transformation levels depends somewhat on the existing practices of each school, classroom, or teacher.

Similar policy expectations of parental involvement corresponding to accommodation, reformation, and transformation type responses are included in the areas of 'communicating', 'learning at home', and 'decision-making' in relation to the teaching of Pasifika learners, both in the *Pasifika Education Plan* (Ministry of Education, 2013) and the cultural competencies framework of *Tapasā* (Ministry of Education, 2018). Both the *Pasifika Education Plan* (Ministry of Education, 2013) and *Tapasā* (Ministry of Education, 2018) emphasise key Pasifika values of family, belonging, reciprocal relationships, and intergenerational interaction throughout. The importance of family is represented by Pasifika learners, parents, families, and communities being placed together in the centre of 'the Pasifika Success Compass' (Ministry of Education, 2018, p. 4) and in statements about Pasifika student outcomes:

> Data and information will be used to increase the knowledge and voice of Pasifika learners, parents, families and communities, so they can demand better outcomes and influence the education system from within." (Ministry of Education, 2013, p. 3)

Many indications of practice important for involving Pasifika parents in learning are found in indicators of the cultural competencies described in *Tapasā* (Ministry of Education, 2018). Many indicators focus on building teacher awareness, fostering relationships, and pedagogical development. For example, in relation to building awareness of the needs of Pasifika learners, beginning teachers are expected to understand "the socio-economic, demographic, historical as well as contemporary profiles of Pacific learners, their parents, families and communities" and the impact of these "on learning and wellbeing from a Pacific perspective" (p. 10). Experienced teachers should demonstrate "strengths-based practice" that "builds on the cultural and linguistic capital Pacific learners, their parents, families and communities bring" (p. 11), and education leaders are expected to prioritise "resources, training and support for teachers, school leadership and governance to strengthen their capability and capacity to work and engage effectively with Pacific learners, parents, families and communities" (p. 11). Advocated for fostering effective relationships and professional behaviour are indicators such as beginning teachers understanding "the notion of teu le va ... where engagement is negotiated and agreed with Pacific learners and their parents, families and communities" (p. 12) (see also Reynolds, 2016), and educational leaders demonstrating "strong collaborative and respectful relationships and reciprocal partnerships with Pacific leaders, parents, families and communities that [are] linked to learning outcomes and achievement" and having "strong relationships with Pacific communities and cultural leaders" (p. 13).

Policy is clear that to foster academic progress and student wellbeing, teachers of Māori and Pasifika learners need to be able to strongly enact the relevant cultural competencies relating to interacting with parents with respect and care about student learning. Such interactions involve demonstrating awareness and understanding of the socio-cultural contexts of learners and parents, engaging in dialogue with parents about learning priorities, setting collective goals for children's learning, and teachers being able to ground learning tasks within the experiences and knowledge of learners and parents (Ministry of Education, 2011a; 2018). Such practice contrasts sharply with much current teaching and school practice (Alton-Lee, 2003; Chu, Glasgow, Rimoni, Hodis, & Meyer, 2013; Hynds et al., 2013), hence many of the indicators in both *Tataiako* and in *Tapasā* (Ministry of Education, 2018) are consistent with reformational and transformational practice. Indeed, language indicating change is integrated into both policy support documents. For example, indicators include teachers "consciously [using] and actively [encouraging] the use of local Māori contexts (such as whakapapa (genealogy), environment, tikanga (custom), language, history, place, economy, politics, local icons, geography) to support Māori learners' learning" (Ministry of Education, 2011a, p. 10) and "actively seek and adopt different, ethnic-specific ways of instruction and working with Pacific learners, parents, their families and communities" (Ministry of Education, 2018, p. 14). Such expectations on teachers and schools are high and their implementation is particularly challenging given the Euro-centric nature of society and school traditions and practice (Averill & Rimoni, 2019).

New Zealand schools are encouraged to establish strong home-school partnerships to help align teacher and parental support for children's learning (Alton-Lee, 2003; Education Review Office, 2015a; Taleni, Macfarlane, Macfarlane, & Fletcher, 2018). One-way after-the-event communication with parents, such as sending home written reporting on students' academic progress, is the most common type of interaction with parents about their child's education within New Zealand, as in many contexts. To develop strong parental involvement in learning, however, moving well beyond such communication is needed, such as through regular school-community meetings or weekly home-school journaling of ideas, thoughts, feedback, and concerns about recent and upcoming curriculum topics and student learning. Calls for reformational and transformational change in school and classroom practice in relation to parental involvement are also becoming more prevalent in research. For example, understanding Pasifika concepts such as 'brotherhood', and how leadership and service are developed through customary practices is advocated for enhancing teacher responsiveness to culture and help teachers reduce inconsistencies between students' experience of in and out-of-school lives (Fa'avae, 2017).

Developing a sense of family connection with learning and ensuring schools and parents are working towards shared goals have been achieved in some New Zealand schools (Education Review Office, 2015a,b). However, such initiatives can be challenging to set up (e.g., Fisher & Neill, 2007, 2008). New Zealand schools with strong parental involvement have used school-wide initiatives in which parents and teachers work towards common goals. Typically, in these contexts parents, teachers, and school leaders understand their rights and obligations, and teachers view themselves as part of the school's wider community (e.g., Education Review

Office, 2015a,b). However, although parental involvement policies have been promoted for some time, relatively few New Zealand English-medium schools have yet managed to establish and maintain strong sustained school-parent curriculum partnerships, particularly at the secondary school level. The mismatch between policy intent and practice indicate that schools or parents have been unable or unwilling to prioritise parental involvement in learning, that such policy is challenging to implement, or that practical support, incentives, further guidance, or resources are needed. Care in planning, implementing, and monitoring efforts to involve parents in curriculum learning are essential as poor teacher-parent relationships and poorly informed parental input with homework tasks can undermine learning (Robinson et al., 2009).

In summary, Epstein's (2001) area of 'communicating' is strongly emphasised in New Zealand's education policy, and parental involvement in 'learning at home' and 'decision making' are either stated or implied in many policy documents, particularly in policy relating to the learning of Māori and Pasifika children. For implementation to be straightforward, education policies must align well with society's knowledge and values, research, and informal school-based evidence and beliefs. In addition, culturally-specific policies need to align with the desires and values of their respective groups, which is particularly challenging when the policy focusses on highly diverse groups such as Pasifika. Guidance, supports, and resources are needed to assist with educational policy implementation, particularly for policy in relation to Indigenous and marginalised learners and when there is a mismatch between the out-of-school lives and knowledge of teachers and their students, both of which are pertinent issues in many New Zealand schools.

CONSIDERATIONS - DIVERSE INTERPRETATIONS

Over and above considerations of the complexities of culturally linked understandings of terms, challenges to examining parental involvement in the curriculum include the diversity of terms used across policy, resources, and research, differing interpretations of these terms, and that much work on parental involvement to date has been carried out at the school rather than the classroom level (Bakker & Denessen, 2007; Bernie & Lall, 2008; Desforges & Abouchaar, 2003; Fan & Chen, 2001). Terms used in relation to parental involvement range from 'partnership', commonly accepted as implying families and schools are on an equal footing with both contributing to student learning (e.g., Anthony & Walshaw, 2007; Bull, 2009; Bull et al., 2008; Epstein, 2011; Hornby & Lafaele, 2011), to 'involvement', 'engagement', and 'participation'. Interpretations of the latter terms can vary widely (Goodall & Montgomery, 2014), with very different expectations of little to large amounts of parental interaction and input into children's learning possible across schools, teachers, parents, and children. An additional confounding factor particularly relevant in New Zealand is the diversity of understandings of what constitutes parental roles, families, and family attributes and processes (Biddulph et al., 2003).

Further challenges to research and practice in relation to parental involvement include the wide scope of types of activities used to involve parents. For example, in a meta-analysis of 25 studies, Fan and Chen (2001) found 'parent involvement' referred to a very wide range of activities and values across the studies, making comparisons difficult. Various continua have been used to help discuss such varied results. For example, to describe the examples supporting parental involvement found across studies, Fan and Chen (2001) use a continuum related to the focus of the involvement, from involvement directly related to school (e.g., parents communicating with teachers, assisting with homework, or being involved in school governance), involvement related to both school and homes (e.g., learning journals for students, teachers and parents), to involvement targeted solely at students' homes (e.g., supporting parenting and encouraging ensuring home environments are supportive of learning). In contrast, Goodall and Montgomery (2014), who also draw from a wide range of literature on parental involvement, focus on parental engagement with their children's learning as opposed to involvement in the school more widely. Their continuum ranges from their ideal of teachers incorporating parent-devised and parent-led discussions and activities related to children's learning into the curriculum, to parent involvement being at the school rather than class or student level.

Given the diversity of terms relating to parental partnership, involvement, engagement, and participation in children's learning and the diversity across potential understandings of these, shared discussion, clarification, and understanding of what is being meant by the terms and what is expected in relation to parental involvement for parents, teachers, students, and schools is essential. Next, we look to strategies that have been used within and outside New Zealand to involve parents and families in the school curriculum and factors that have supported and hindered such involvement.

SUPPORTS FOR PARENTAL INVOLVEMENT IN CURRICULUM

Parental involvement in the curriculum is supported by treating families with respect and dignity, contacting parents as a group as well as individually, building on rather than undermining usual family practices, and providing specific suggestions (Biddulph et al., 2003). Partnerships between schools and families are supported by school leadership prioritising these, shared goals for the partnership between parents and schools, and a school culture that supports teachers to involve parents (Education Review Office, 2008; 2015a; 2018; LaRocque, Kleiman, & Darling, 2011; Mutch & Collins, 2012; Taleni et al., 2018). Successful approaches used in low socio-economic New Zealand schools for nurturing parental involvement included that they:

- fully and honestly shared assessment information about the child
- listened to parents' ideas about how they could help and what support they needed
- provided details about the language, strategies and approaches the child used at school

- provided materials and internet links for parents that needed them
- regularly communicated with parents to share and hear what was working and what they all (the child, parent and teacher) should do next. (Education Review Office, 2018, p. 6)

Strong school commitment to integrating parent involvement within the day-to-day school culture and structure is essential for forming powerful school-parent partnerships (Crozier & Davies, 2007; Fisher & Neill, 2007, 2008; Harris & Goodall, 2008; Robinson, et al., 2009). Also important for successful school-parent partnerships are parents knowing the specific ways in which they can be involved in the school and in their child's learning (Hoover-Dempsey & Sandler, 1997; Parkinson, Doyle, Cowie, Otrel-Cass, & Glynn, 2011; Rodriguez, Collins-Parks, & Garza, 2013). For example, school commitment to parental involvement targeted at improving student achievement can be demonstrated through building home-school relationships, holding workshops for parents and students, and setting homework tasks for which parents have particular roles (Bernie & Lall, 2008; Flavell, 2017).

Looking to supports specific to New Zealand, *Tātaiako* (Ministry of Education, 2011a), discussed above, provides ways in which parents can be involved in their child's learning. Schools can use the extensive examples of family and learner voice that accompany each cultural competency to inform their practice. For example, the sentiments: "I have good discussions with the teachers about my child's learning" (p. 7), and "The school/ECE service respects and embraces Māori language and culture" (p. 11) show clearly what is required of teachers for nurturing relationships with Māori parents. Similarly, *Tapasā* (Ministry of Education, 2018) describes competencies and values important to Pasifka peoples (reciprocal relationships, service, family, belonging, leadership, spirituality, love, and inclusion). Both the values and competencies are useful for teachers and schools to use to critique and develop their teaching to strengthen parental involvement. The descriptors of practice within these documents can also be useful as a starting point in considering informing teaching and parental involvement in relation to students of all cultures.

The nature of the national curriculum provides a further consideration. For example, high-autonomy national curricula, such as the New Zealand curriculum, provide space and opportunity for schools to design local classroom and school curricula to capitalise on student and parent knowledge, experiences, and priorities. However, such flexibility in curriculum delivery can also be problematic. For example, incorporation of learning around historical and other societal events and activities which may be uncomfortable for teachers and parents to consider, such as matters relating to colonisation, are at risk of being left out of the enacted curriculum in efforts to maintain strong school community relationships (Sheehan, 2017).

Turning back to Epstein's (2001) areas of parental involvement, 'communication', 'learning at home', and 'decision making' provide powerful focus areas for parents and schools working to establish conditions for developing shared goals and carrying out shared work towards these. Supports for such work include curriculum, school leadership, teachers, and parents prioritising home-school links.

CHALLENGES TO PARENTAL INVOLVEMENT IN CURRICULUM

Challenges to parental involvement in the curriculum include inconsistencies amongst policies and the national curriculum, limited guiding and support materials, particularly at secondary school level, varied teacher beliefs about the usefulness of parental involvement for student learning, varied expertise, language and cultural barriers, and variation in parental views of education and their role in it. Barriers to developing effective school parent partnerships can include inconsistencies across education legislation (Hornby & Lafaele, 2011). For example, policies that set up competition for students or resources between schools can result in efforts being directed away from engaging parents with their children's learning. Challenges include that while there are frequent messages in policy regarding parental involvement (e.g., Ministry of Education, 2011a), further guidelines for schools for establishing and maximising the effectiveness of parental involvement in curriculum or teachers having more time to deeply engage with these would be beneficial. Teachers carry the responsibility of involving parents, while related initial teacher education and professional development focussing specifically on parental involvement in general and in curriculum decision-making in particular, is often limited. Teachers' beliefs about their role, tensions between school and parental agency in relation to teaching and engagement, and differing perceptions of suitable locations for parental involvement, are further challenges to parental involvement in curriculum (Goodall & Montgomery, 2014).

Advancing practice through professional development can also be challenging, particularly when focussed on substantive changes to traditional and current practice. Barriers to nurturing parental involvement in school decision making found in an extensive New Zealand professional development project included school leaders and teachers having difficulty describing implications of specific policy statements for their teaching and community involvement practices (e.g., Averill et al., 2014; Hindle et al., 2016). Difficulties were experienced by teachers in establishing relational trust and a sense of shared responsibility for student learning between schools and parents. The establishment of new mechanisms for strengthening school-community engagement also proved problematic (Hynds et al., 2013). Despite the professional development being focussed on implementing policy for enhancing teaching of Māori learners, teachers and school leaders identified that they needed greater personal understanding of Māori language and custom (Averill, Hynds, Hindle, & Meyer, 2015).

Differences between home languages and cultures and the dominant language and culture of the school and teacher also pose barriers to involving parents and interacting with them about student learning and the school more widely (Crozier & Davies, 2007; Fisher & Neill, 2007; Sheldon & Epstein, 2005; Taleni et al., 2018). In particular, parents whose first language is not used at the school may have difficulty communicating with the school both in terms of language and if their perceptions of school processes, curriculum, or societal norms differ from school practice. Such cultural mismatches of perceptions and beliefs between teachers and parents can be problematic when trying to nurture parental involvement. For example, teachers can expect parents to hold much the same beliefs, priorities, and ideas as they do themselves (Reay, 1998). In a United Kingdom study involving Bangladeshi and Pakistani students and parents, the parents saw their key role in their children's learning as providing a supportive home environment (Crozier & Davies, 2007). The parents said that their children's school had not made their expectations of parents explicit and that they did not think they were expected to have any direct involvement with their child's learning. In a compounding factor, student interviews from the same study showed that students often did not want their parents to be involved in their learning.

Further barriers to parental involvement in their child's learning can include parental confidence and capability with the curriculum content. For example, parents who did not have positive experiences with a particular subject in their own schooling can be reluctant to attempt to support their child with this learning (Fisher & Neill, 2007, 2008; Muir, 2012; Rodriguez et al., 2013). As curriculum content becomes more advanced, some parents feel unable to continue to assist their children as they may lack confidence in their own knowledge and understanding (Bryan, Burstein, & Bryan, 2001; Sheldon & Epstein, 2005). Further tensions include that teaching methods may be different to those they experienced or parents may be uncomfortable with current methods (Civil, 2006; Gal & Stoudt, 1995; McNaughton, 2016; Muir, 2012).

INVOLVING PARENTS IN CURRICULUM - EXAMPLES

A key reason for involving parents in curriculum is that parents know and understand their children better than teachers do, particularly when the teacher is not of the same cultural group as the family. Data from a current study into the reflection of Pasifika values in classrooms (Averill & Rimoni, 2019) highlight that non-Pasifika teachers do not always understand Pasifika children well, whereas "[Pasifika] teachers understand where our kids are coming from" (Teacher Aide). Pasifika teachers in the study gave examples of linking key curriculum ideas to contexts they knew their Pasifika children experienced outside school, such as comparing classroom and church experiences and expectations. Parents can be empowered to make such links for children, or to help the teacher make these links, in situations where the teacher is unaware of such contexts. Parents were invited to one school in the same study to share a meal with teachers and discuss with them ideas for cultural contexts suitable for helping develop understanding of the current mathematics topic (algebraic patterning) and how these ideas would be most appropriately shared with children. Teachers were very enthusiastic about this experience, commenting that it "honoured parents' knowledge," enabled them and the parents to get to know each other better, and that they "learnt a lot that they could use with learners." Parents are often involved in teaching cultural performance student groups in New Zealand schools. Rich opportunities for parent involvement in curriculum exist through parents and teachers discussing classroom learning that can be linked with these cultural group activities. The cultural performance activities can provide powerful contexts for exploring traditional classroom curriculum topics, such as pattern analysis, dance, choreography, uniform design, fund raising, measurement, geometry, and story-telling (Taeao & Averill, 2019).

PRINCIPLES FOR PROMOTING PARENTAL INVOLVEMENT

Reflecting on the ideas from the literature shared in this chapter, principles necessary for promoting parental involvement in curriculum must attend to attitudinal, behavioural, and structural dimensions. The fundamental principle is that positive relationships and development of practice are in place through all stakeholders strongly demonstrating respect for others, their experiences and knowledge. Schools, teachers, and school communities must value, prioritise, and celebrate opportunities to work together for children's learning and achievement, and to know each other well. Schools, teachers, and parents need to be open to the development of shared goals and new ideas and sufficiently flexible to accommodate these.

Schools, teachers, and parents must commit their efforts to the learners and each other by advancing into practice the strategies and activities that their shared decision-making has brought to light in timely fashion. School and classroom structures and processes must encourage, serve, and protect, rather than restrict, parental involvement.

CONCLUSION

Policy, research, and theory all advocate for parental involvement in children's learning towards enhancing achievement and wellbeing. Further benefits of parental involvement include increased student motivation and strengthened school community links. Barriers to securing parental involvement in learning include the use of varied terminology, inconsistencies across policies, and confusion regarding policy implementation, diverse perspectives on purposes of and strategies for parental involvement, language and cultural differences between teachers, parents, and students, insufficient professional development, and varied parental confidence in relation to curriculum content, teaching methods, or understanding the school's expectations of them.

Schools, teachers, and students can all help ensure that parents understand ways in which they can be involved in their child's education. In turn, parents can communicate with teachers and schools to share their own expectations in relation to parental involvement. Factors that support parental involvement include school leadership, teachers, students, and parents prioritising, welcoming, and utilising parental input, shared parent-school goal setting, respectful school community relationships, and using processes that fit well with usual family practices. Teachers need to be able to make opportunities for parental involvement relevant and suitable for the parents and children of their classes. As indicated by policy expectations of teachers and schools (Ministry of Education, 2011a; 2018), essential for these strategies in relation to advancing learning of Māori and Pasifika students for many teachers is making their personal development of culturally-linked knowledge and understandings a priority. Without sound culturally-linked understanding and partnership with parents and community members of target cultural groups, teachers are unlikely to be able to enact and institute reformational and transformational responses to culturally sustaining policy expectations.

New Zealand educational policies, including those relating to the teaching and learning of Māori and Pasifika students, are strongly consistent with Epstein's (2001) areas of two-way home-school communication, learning at home through curriculum-related activities, and ensuring parental input into curriculum decision-making. Policy expectations of parental involvement in learning are yet to be fully realised in many New Zealand schools. Guidelines for fostering parental links and practical resources including information for schools to use with families, teacher development time, and school funding, could help foster implementation. While policy support documents convey clear ideals for parental involvement in learning, few current professional development projects specifically target enhancing the achievement of priority learners. Despite policy expectations and existing support material (Ministry of Education, 2011a, 2018), there is to date little research that has focussed on how teachers and schools can develop parental involvement with children's learning in general, and with Māori and Pasifika children's learning in particular. To enable the ideas of policy to be realised, investigation into ways to nurture parental involvement in learning and the impacts of such involvement on achievement, affect, and wellbeing within New Zealand contexts is essential. Themes from the national and international literature discussed in this chapter can help inform teachers and schools in relation to consultation with Māori and Pasifika students and parents about developing and sustaining classroom and school-wide practices for parental involvement in curriculum, and related research.

This chapter has summarised policy and research considerations useful for establishing and maintaining efforts to maximise parental engagement in school-based curriculum decision-making, with a focus on the New Zealand context. What is clear is that establishing strong parental involvement in children's learning is not a straightforward task, particularly in relation to Indigenous learners and parents and those with cultural heritages different from many who inform, lead, and teach in schools. While this chapter has focussed on the New Zealand context, much of the discussion is of relevance to contexts internationally in which parental involvement in their children's learning is not yet strong and where Indigenous or other groups of learners are underserved by schools and the schooling system.

For parental involvement in curriculum to be expected and commonplace, societal change is needed so that it is normal for all school leadership members, teachers, students, parents, and community members to prioritise this. In addition, improved cross-cultural understandings and the provision of resources, suggested strategies, and widespread discussion about co-construction and other practices likely to promote parental involvement would be helpful. Such practical support is necessary in order that all can see such involvement as normal and valuable and that all involved can learn from and enjoy facilitating children's learning together.

REFERENCES

Alton-Lee, A. (2003). *Quality teaching for diverse students in schooling: Best evidence synthesis.* Wellington, New Zealand: Ministry of Education. Retrieved from https://www.educationcounts.govt.nz/_data/assets/pdf_file/0019/7705/BES-quality-teaching-diverse-students.pdf.

Anthony, G., & Walshaw, M. (2007). *Effective pedagogy in mathematics/pāngarau: Best evidence synthesis iteration.* Wellington, New Zealand: Ministry of Education. Retrieved from https://www.educationcounts.govt.nz/_data/assets/pdf_file/0007/7693/BES_Maths07_Complete.pdf.

Averill, R., & McRae, H. (2019). Culturally sustaining initial teacher education: Developing student teacher confidence and competence to teach Indigenous learners. *The Educational Forum, Special Issue, 83*(3), 294-308. doi:10.1080/00131725.2019.1599657.

Averill, R., & Rimoni, F. (2019). Policy for enhancing Pasifika learner achievement in New Zealand: Supports and challenges. *Linhas Criticas, 25*, 549-564. doi: 10.26512/lc.v25i0.23780

Averill, R., Hindle, R., Hynds, A., Meyer, L., Penetito, W., Taiwhati, M., Hodis, F., & Faircloth, S., C. (2014). "It means everything doesn't it?" Interpretations of Māori students achieving and enjoying educational success 'as Māori'. *set: Research Information for Teachers, 2*, 33–40.

Averill, R., Hynds, A., Hindle, R., & Meyer, L. (2015). "Every teacher has to come on board for our Māori students": He wero mō ngā kaiarahi wāhanga ako - The challenge for curriculum leaders. *set: Research Information for Teachers, 3*, 3–11. doi: 10.18296/set.0021.

Averill, R., Metson, A., & Bailey, S. (2016). Enhancing parental involvement in student learning. *Curriculum Matters, 12*, 109–131. doi:10.18296/cm.0016.

Bakker, J., & Denessen, E. (2007). The concept of parent involvement: Some theoretical and empirical considerations. *International Journal about Parents in Education, 1*(0), 188–199.

Bateson, G. (2000). *Steps to an ecology of mind: Collected essays in anthropology, psychiatry, evolution and epistemology*. Chicago, IL: University of Chicago Press.

Benner, A. D., Boyle, A. E., & Sadler, S. (2016). Parental involvement and adolescents' educational success: The roles of prior achievement and socioeconomic status. *Journal of Youth and Adolescence, 45*(6), 1053–1064. doi: 10.1007/s10964-016-0431-4.

Bernie, J., & Lall, M. (2008). *Building bridges between home and school mathematics: A review of the Ocean Mathematics Project*. London: Institute of Education, University of London.

Biddulph, F., Biddulph, J., & Biddulph, C. (2003). *The complexity of community and family influences on children's achievement in New Zealand: Best evidence synthesis iteration*. Wellington, New Zealand: Ministry of Education. Retrieved from https://www.educationcounts.govt.nz/publications/series/2515/5947.

Bishop, R., & Berryman, M. (2006). *Culture speaks*. Wellington, New Zealand: Huia.

Boonk, L., Gijselaers, H. J., Ritzen, H., & Brand-Gruwel, S. (2018). A review of the relationship between parental involvement indicators and academic achievement. *Educational Research Review, 24*, 10–30. doi: 10.1016/j.edurev.2018.02.001.

Bryan, T., Burstein, K., & Bryan, J. (2001). Students with learning disabilities: Homework problems and promising practices. *Educational Psychologist, 36*(3), 167–180. doi:10.1207/S15326985EP3603_3.

Bull, A. (2009). *From community engagement in education to public engagement with education* (Working paper). Retrieved from http://www.nzcer.org.nz/research/publications/community-engagement-education-public-engagement-education.

Bull, A., Brooking, K., & Campbell, R. (2008). *Successful home-school partnerships.* New Zealand: Ministry of Education.

Castro, M., Expósito-Casas, E., López-Martín, E., Lizasoain, L., Navarro-Asencio, E., & Gaviria, J. L. (2015). Parental involvement on student academic achievement: A meta-analysis. *Educational Research Review, 14*, 33–46. doi:10.1016/j.edurev.2015.01.002.

Chu, C., Glasgow, A., Rimoni, F., Hodis, F., & Meyer, L. H. (2013). *An analysis of recent Pasifika education research literature to inform improved outcomes for Pasifika learners* (Report to the Ministry of Wellington). Wellington, New Zealand: Ministry of Education.

Civil, M. (2006). Working towards equity in mathematics education: A focus on learners, teachers, and parents. In S. Alatorre, J. L. Cortina, M. Sáiz, & A. Méndez (Eds.), *Proceedings of the Twenty Eighth Annual Meeting of the North American Chapter of the International Group for the Psychology of Mathematics Education* (Vol. 1, 30–50). Mérida, Mexico: Universidad Pedagógica Nacional.

Crozier, G., & Davies, J. (2007). Hard to reach parents or hard to reach schools? A discussion of home-school relations, with particular reference to Bangladeshi and Pakistani parents. *British Educational Research Journal, 33*(3), 295–313. doi:10.1080/01411920701243578.

Desforges, C., & Abouchaar, A. (2003). *The impact of parental involvement, parental support and family education on pupil achievement and adjustment: A literature review* (Research Report Number 433). London: Department of Education and Skills.

Education Council. (2017). *Our code our standards: Ngā tikanga matatika ngā paerewa.* Wellington, New Zealand: Author.
Education Counts. (2019). *Teaching staff: Information on teaching staff in schools from 2004-2017.* Wellington, New Zealand: Ministry of Education. Retrieved from: https://www.educationcounts.govt.nz/statistics/schooling/teaching_staff.
Education Review Office. (2008). *Partners in learning: Schools' engagement with parents, whānau and communities.* Wellington, New Zealand: Author.
Education Review Office. (2015a). *Educationally powerful connections with parents and whānau.* Wellington, New Zealand: Author.
Education Review Office. (2015b). *Accelerating student achievement.* Wellington, New Zealand: Author.
Education Review Office. (2018). *Building genuine learning partnerships with parents: Teaching approaches and strategies that work: He rautaki whakaako e whai hua ana* [An effective teaching strategy]. Wellington, New Zealand: Author.
Education Review Office. (n.d.). *Ethnic diversity in New Zealand state schools.* Wellington, New Zealand: Author. Retrieved from https://www.ero.govt.nz/footer-upper/news/ero-insights-term-1/ethnic-diversity-in-new-zealand-state-schools/.
Epstein, J. L. (1995). School/family/community partnerships: Caring for the children we share. *Phi Delta Kappan, 76*(9), 701–712. doi.org/10.1177/003172171009200326.
Epstein, J. L. (2001). *School, family and community partnerships: Preparing educators and improving schools.* Boulder, CO: Westview Press.
Epstein, J. L. (2011). *School, family and community partnerships: Preparing educators and improving schools* (2nd ed.). Boulder, CO: Westview Press.
Fa'avae, D. (2017). Family knowledge and practices useful in Tongan boys' education. *set: Research Information for Teachers, 2*, 49–56.
Fan, X., & Chen, M. (2001). Parental involvement and students' academic achievement: A meta-analysis. *Educational Psychology Review, 13*(1), 1–22. doi: 10.1023/A:1009048817385.

Fisher, J., & Neill, A. (2007). Exploratory study of home-school partnership: Numeracy. In *Findings from the New Zealand numeracy development projects 2006* (pp. 139–153). Wellington, New Zealand: Ministry of Education.

Fisher, J., & Neill, A. (2008). Evaluation of home-school partnership: Numeracy. In *Findings from the New Zealand numeracy development projects 2007* (pp. 157–174). Wellington, New Zealand: Ministry of Education.

Flavell, M. (2017). Listening to and learning from Pacific families: The art of building home–school relationships at secondary level to support achievement. *set: Research Information for Teachers, 2,* 42–48.

Gal, I., & Stoudt, A. (1995). *Family achievement in mathematics: NCAL connections*. Philadelphia: National Center on Adult Literacy, University of Pennsylvania.

Gay, G. (2010). *Culturally responsive teaching: Theory, research, and practice* (2nd ed.). New York, NY: Teachers College Press.

Gilmore, A., & Smith, J. K. (2011). *NEMP writing, reading and mathematics report 2010.* Dunedin, New Zealand: Education Assessment Research Unit. Retrieved from http://nemp.otago.ac.nz/report/2010/NEMP%20Report%202010.pdf.

Goodall, J., & Montgomery, C. (2014). Parental involvement to parental engagement: A continuum. *Educational Review, 66*(4), 399–410. doi: 10.1080/00131911.2013.781576.

Harris, A., & Goodall, J. (2008). Do parents know they matter? Engaging all parents in learning. *Educational Research, 50*(3), 277–289. doi:10.1080/00131880802309424.

Hindle, R., Hynds, A., Averill, R., Meyer, L., & Faircloth, S. (2016). An ontological perspective on the development of home-school partnership relationships with Indigenous communities, *The Australian Journal of Indigenous Education, 46*(1), 92-103. doi:10.1017/jie.2016.16.

Hornby, G., & Lafaele, R. (2011). Barriers to parental involvement in education: An explanatory model. *Educational Review, 63*(1), 37–52. doi:10.1080/00131911.2010.488049.

Hoover-Dempsey, K. V., & Sandler, H. M. (1997). Why do parents become involved in their children's education? *Review of Educational Research, 67*(1), 3–42. doi:10.3102/00346543067001003.

Hynds, A., Averill, R., Hindle, R., & Meyer, L. (2017). School expectation and student aspirations: The influence of schools and teachers on indigenous secondary students. *Ethnicities, 17*(4), 546–573. doi:10.1177/1468796816666590.

Hynds, A., Meyer, L., Penetito, W., Averill, R., Hindle, R., Taiwhati, M., & Hodis, F., with Faircloth, S. (2013). *Evaluation of He Kākano professional development for leaders in secondary schools: Final report.* Wellington, New Zealand: Ministry of Education. Retrieved from: http://www.educationcounts.govt.nz/publications/91416/english-medium-education/144630.

Kerbaiv, D., & Bernhardt, A. (2018). Parental intervention in the school: The context of minority involvement. In B. Schneider & J. S. Coleman (Eds.), *Parents, their children, and schools* (pp. 115–146). New York: Routledge.

Ladson-Billings, G. (2009). *The dreamkeepers: Successful teachers of African American children* (2nd ed.). San Francisco, CA: Jossey-Bass.

LaRocque, M., Kleiman, I., & Darling, S. M. (2011). Parental involvement: The missing link in school achievement. *Preventing School Failure: Alternative Education For Youth, 55*(3), 115–122. doi:10.1080/10459880903472876.

McCarty, T., & Lee, T. (2014). Critical culturally sustaining/revitalizing pedagogy and Indigenous education sovereignty. *Harvard Educational Review, 84*(1), 101–124. doi:10.17763/haer.84.1.q83746nl5pj34216.

McNaughton, S. (2016). *Empowering parents to support their child's learning of mathematics: Investigating the effects of an acadmically focussed home-school partnership* (Masters thesis). The University of Auckland, New Zealand.

Ministry of Education. (2007). *The New Zealand curriculum.* Wellington, New Zealand: Author. Retrieved from http://nzcurriculum.tki.org.nz/The-New-Zealand-Curriculum.

Ministry of Education. (2008). *Ka Hikitia - Managing for success: Māori education strategy 2008-2012.* Wellington, New Zealand: Author. Retrieved from http://www.minedu.govt.nz/theMinistry/PolicyAnd Strategy/KaHikitia.aspx.

Ministry of Education. (2011a). *Tātaiako: Cultural competencies for teachers of Māori learners.* Wellington, New Zealand: Author. Retrieved from http://www.teacherscouncil.govt.nz/required/tataiako.stm.

Ministry of Education. (2011b). *Ministry of Education position paper: Assessment.* Wellington, New Zealand: Author.

Ministry of Education. (2012). *Statement of intent 2012-2017.* Wellington, New Zealand: Author. Retrieved from http://www.minedu.govt.nz/~/media/MinEdu/Files/TheMinistry/2012SOI/2012StatementOfIntent.pdf.

Ministry of Education. (2013). *Pasifika education plan 2013-2017.* Wellington, New Zealand: Learning Media. Retrieved from http://www.minedu.govt.nz/NZEducation/EducationPolicies/~/media/MinEdu/Files/EducationSectors/PasifikaEducation/PasifikaEdPlan2013To2017V2.pdf.

Ministry of Education. (2014). *Ministry of Education statement of intent 2014-2018.* Wellington, New Zealand: Author.

Ministry of Education. (2018). *Tapasā: Cultural competencies framework for teachers of Pacific learners.* Wellington, New Zealand: Author.

Ministry of Education. (n.d.a). *Families.* Retrieved from http://nzmaths.co.nz/families.

Ministry of Education. (n.d.b). *Home-school partnership: Numeracy.* Retrieved from http://nzmaths.co.nz/node/1373.

Ministry of Education. (n.d.c). *Home-school partnership: Numeracy activities.* Retrieved from https://nzmaths.co.nz/home-school-partnership-numeracy-activities.

Ministry of Education. (n.d.d). *Engaging parents, whānau, and community.* Retrieved from http://nzcurriculum.tki.org.nz/Middle-schooling/Engaging-parents-whanau-and-community.

Muir, T. (2012). Numeracy at home: Involving parents in mathematics education. *International Journal for Mathematics Teaching and Learning, 13*. Retrieved from http://www.cimt.plymouth.ac.uk/journal/muir.pdf.

Mutch, C., & Collins, S. (2012). Partners in learning: Schools' engagement with parents, families, and communities in New Zealand. *School Community Journal, 22*(1), 167–188.

Paris, D. (2012). Culturally sustaining pedagogy: A needed change in stance, terminology and practice. *Educational Researcher, 41*(3), 93–97. doi:10.3102/0013189X12441244.

Paris, D., & Samy Alim, H. (2014). What are we seeking to sustain through culturally sustaining pedagogy? A loving critique forward. *Harvard Educational Review, 84*(1), 85–100. doi:10.17763/haer.84.1.9821873k2ht16m77.

Parkinson, A., Doyle, J., Cowie, B., Otrel-Cass, K., & Glynn, T. (2011). Engaging whānau with children's science learning: Home learning books. *set: Research Information for Teachers, 1*, 3–9.

Pomerantz, E. M., Moorman, E. A., & Litwack, S. D. (2007). The how, whom, and why of parents' involvement in children's academic lives: More is not always better. *Review of Educational Research, 77*(3), 373–410. doi:10.3102/003465430305567.

Reay, D. (1998). *Class work: Mothers' involvement in their children's primary schooling*. London: UCL Press.

Renert, M. (2011). Mathematics for life: Sustainable mathematics education. *For the Learning of Mathematics, 31*(1), 20–26.

Reynolds, M. (2016). Relating to Va: Re-viewing the concept of relationships in Pasifika education in Aotearoa New Zealand. *AlterNative: An International Journal of Indigenous Peoples, 12*(2), 190–202. doi:10.20507/AlterNative.2016.12.2.7.

Ritchie, J., Skerrett, M., & Rau, C. (2014). Kei tua i te awe māpara [Beyond the influence of cultivation]: Counter colonial unveiling of neoliberal discourses in Aotearoa New Zealand. *International Review of Qualitative Research, 7*(1), 111–129. doi:10.1525/irqr.2014.7.1.111.

Robinson, V., Hohepa, M., & Lloyd, C. (2009). *School leadership and student outcomes: Identifying what works and why: Best evidence synthesis iteration.* Wellington, New Zealand: Ministry of Education. Retrieved from http://www.educationcounts.govt.nz/__data/assets/pdf_file/0015/60180/BES-Leadership-Web-updated-foreword-2015.pdf.

Rodriguez, A. J., Collins-Parks, T., & Garza, J. (2013). Interpreting research on parent involvement and connecting it to the science classroom. *Theory Into Practice, 52*(1), 51–58. doi:10.1080/07351690.2013.743775.

Sheehan, M. (2017). A matter of choice: Controversial histories, citizenship, and the challenge of a high-autonomy curriculum. *Curriculum Matters, 13*, 103–114.

Sheldon, S. B., & Epstein, J. L. (2005). Involvement counts: Family and community partnerships and mathematics achievement. *The Journal of Education Research, 98*(4), 196–207. doi:10.3200/JOER.98.4.196-207.

Sterling, S. (2004). *Sustainable education: Re-visioning learning and change.* Foxhole, United Kingdom: Green Books.

Taeao, S., & Averill, R. (2019). Tu'utu'u le upega i le loloto [Cast the net into deeper waters]: Exploring dance as a culturally sustaining mathematics pedagogy. *Australian Journal of Indigenous Education.* doi.org/10.1017/jie.2019.17

Taleni, T. O., Macfarlane, S., Macfarlane, A. H., & Fletcher, J. (2018). Tofa liuliu ma le tofa saili a ta'ita'i Pasefika [Farewell and farewell search guide to the Pacific]: Listening to the voices of Pasifika community leaders. *New Zealand Journal of Educational Studies, 53*(2), 177–192. doi:10.1007/s40841-018-0114-7.

Tuuta, M., Bradnam, L., Hynds, A., Higgins, J., & Broughton, R. (2004). *Evaluation of the Te Kauhua Māori mainstream pilot project.* New Zealand: Ministry of Education.

Van Voorhis, F. L. (2003). Interactive homework in middle school: Effects on family involvement and science achievement. *The Journal of Education Research, 96*(6), 323–338. doi:10.1080/00220670309596616.

Van Voorhis, F. L. (2011). Adding families to the homework equation: A longitudinal study of mathematics achievement. *Education and Urban Society, 43*(3), 313–338. doi:10.1177/0013124510380236.

In: Parental Involvement
Editors: Nurit Kaplan Toren et al.
ISBN: 978-1-53616-828-0
© 2020 Nova Science Publishers, Inc.

Chapter 2

PARENT-CHILD HOMEWORK INTERACTIONS: BEGINNING AN ASSIGNMENT

Francesco Arcidiacono[*] *and Esther González-Martínez*
University of Teacher Education BEJUNE, Biel/Bienne, Switzerland

ABSTRACT

Homework acts as a critical interface between school and families, and results in frequent parent-child interactions related to assignments. To satisfy a teacher's requirements, families deal with complex questions such as when and how to do homework. In this chapter, we present a set of activities that contribute to the undertaking of homework completion at home. We then focus on how parents and children begin doing an assignment and describe two common situations: a) the child begins doing the assignment without discussing its content with the parent; and b) the child begins doing the assignment after discussing its content with the parent. We examine the interplay of the multimodal resources, including language, gaze, gestures and movements, that are deployed when the participants engage with the pedagogical material and produce an initial

---

[*] Corresponding Author's E-mail: francesco.arcidiacono@hep-bejune.ch.

action tangibly contributing to the completion of the larger task. The data is drawn from a corpus of audiovisual recordings of eight Italian families' daily activities at home. The analysis contributes to a better understanding of how homework tasks are practically achieved and could be of interest to the teachers who assign them.

Keywords: parent-child interaction, homework, assignment completion, video ethnography, multimodal conversation analysis

INTRODUCTION

Doing homework at home is an ordinary activity that acts as an interface between the school and family domains (Pontecorvo, Liberati & Monaco, 2013). Interactions related to homework feature prominently in the everyday life of families and are often the focus of discussions between parents and children. Parents strive to juggle their professional lives with raising children and to integrate homework among other educational and leisure activities, the more basic childcare tasks and the practical organization of family life (Jecker & Weisser, 2015; Wingard & Forsberg, 2009). Moreover, parents must adjust their own perspectives on homework to those of their partners, children and other family members and make sure that these also correspond to the expectations of the school (Corno, 2000). There are tensions in particular between entitlements to parental control and to children's autonomy (Forsberg, 2007). Parents feel that homework is useful and would like to receive additional help from teachers, but are concerned about the school "colonizing" the home (Keogh, 1999; Rayou, 2010). In this context, "how to" materials and offers to outsource proliferate (Meirieu, 2004). Moreover, homework is much more than a practical educational task - it is also an opportunity to "do family" (Morgan, 1996) and to build identities, relationships and expectations for the future.

We conducted a study to better understand how homework features in everyday family life. The investigation is based on audiovisual recordings of the activities of eight Italian families in their homes. In this chapter, we first present a set of activities that parents and children engage in and that are part of the general undertaking of homework completion. We then focus on how parents and children begin doing an assignment - namely, how they transition from preparing for the task to producing an initial action tangibly contributing to its actual completion. We rely on the multimodal conversation analytic approach (Stivers & Sidnell, 2005) to examine the interplay of talk and bodily conduct, and the sequential and temporal organization of the participants' courses of action.

In the field of school-family relations (Iannaccone & Arcidiacono, 2014), homework activities feature as a clear case in which social aspects affect both processes and outcomes. Studying families' homework activities *in situ* improves our understanding of the complexities of family life (Arcidiacono & Pontecorvo, 2004), documents the diversity of socio-cultural contexts in which children strive to succeed, acknowledges parental involvement in educational tasks and informs the teachers who assign them.

In the academic field of school-family relations, parental involvement research has made important contributions to the study of homework activities. Epstein (1992) distinguishes different types of parental involvement in child education that are directly connected to homework, like securing the physical conditions that support learning, and monitoring and assisting children as they engage in learning activities at home. Research has also focused on factors that determine parental involvement in school-related activities. Hoover-Dempsey and Sandler (1995) found that parents become involved if they consider it part of their parental role, have a positive sense of efficacy when helping their children and perceive opportunities to help and requests for assistance coming from their children and the school.

Hoover-Dempsey and Sandler (1995), as well as Hoover-Dempsey et al. (2001), summarize different ways in which parents help their children with school activities and homework in particular. For instance, parents engage with schools and teachers about the assignments and their expectations, establish physical and psychological structures that are supportive of homework completion and set up rules and procedures to shield children from distractions. Parents can also check children's understanding of the homework goals, oversee and assist with assignment completion, teach children learning strategies and respond to their performance. Most of the reported research on family involvement in homework is based on surveys and interviews (Jecker & Weisser, 2015; Kakpo, 2012; Rayou, 2009 for studies on French families), addressing questions like the extent to which children are helped, the family members most frequently in charge of homework monitoring, the match (or mismatch) between school and parental standards and procedures and the assistance received depending on the children's educational stage, the parent's level of education and the family's socioeconomic status, among other factors. A large body of studies, which often have experimental and longitudinal designs, address the disputed issue of homework's effects on school achievement and the specific question of how parental involvement influences achievement-related outcomes (see Cooper, Robinson & Patall, 2006 for a review).

Another approach to homework activities is adopted when the research aims to capture the children's own perspective and experiences. Hutchison (2011) collects homework video-diaries made by primary school students that reveal the children's and families' identity-building practices, educational values and aspirations for the future. Farrell and Danby (2015) interview children who draw up their daily timelines and convey that homework is a time-consuming activity that adults impose on them and that they must comply with before engaging in more pleasant endeavors.

A more naturalistic approach consists of observing homework activities and interactions inside the children's homes, as they happen on the spot and in real time, and making audio and video recordings of them. McDermott, Goldman and Varenne (1984) examine video recordings of working-class American families who succeed, or do not succeed, in blending homework-completion into the flow of household activities. Choi, Kim and Lee (2012) study children who are Korean native speakers doing their homework with their immigrant mothers who lack fluency in the language used at the school. Their analysis focuses on discursive features such as how the mothers prompt children to do homework and provide feedback and how the children respond to their mothers' linguistic challenges. Foster and Goodwin (2006) attest to the relationships between the directives that American families use in homework interactions, the children's behavior and the way obligations and duties are defined in the household. For Wingard and Forsberg (2009),

American and Swedish families orient to homework as "one more task to fit into the busy daily schedule" (p. 1592). The authors identify two forms of parental involvement: anticipating and planning homework activities on the one hand, and engaging directly in the completion of the homework tasks on the other. The parents stand out as "taskmasters" and "surrogate teachers at home," presenting a "united front" to ensure that the homework is completed in spite of their children's resistance. Homework obligations are often mentioned as soon as parents and children meet after school (Wingard, 2006). Inquiring about homework allows parents to assess the amount of time needed to complete the assignments and to schedule them in the day's agenda. Wingard (2007) examines two verbal practices parents and children deploy when planning homework: adding a high-priority activity to already established ones and inserting a high-priority activity into the agenda ahead of previously established ones. According to Pontecorvo, Liberati and Monaco (2013), when dealing with homework, Italian parents perform organizational, pedagogical, emotional and moral work with their children and socialize them to time management.

METHODS

This chapter presents part of a study realized on the basis of a larger research project conducted on "The everyday life of working families in Italy, Sweden and the United States".[1] The main goal of the original project was to learn how families organize and develop their everyday life activities and deal with the challenges they face. The original project documented the everyday lives of working families in the United States as well as in northern and southern European countries. It showed that despite cultural and political differences in terms of childrearing, parents generally had similar

---

[1] The original research project involved scholars from three institutions: The University of California-Los Angeles (United States), the 'Sapienza' University of Rome (Italy), and the University of Linköping (Sweden), supported by the Alfred P. Sloan Foundation, New York (United States). The data collection was made possible by the participating families' cooperation and willingness to allow the research team into their homes.

experiences. North American families considered that their children's upbringing and the organization of their family life should be a private affair, but the wives recurrently reported "not having a life" as a result of family obligations. In both Sweden and Italy, in spite of relatively family-friendly policies, parents often felt alone in juggling the demands of work and family life (Ochs & Kremer-Sadlik, 2013; Pauletto, Aronsson & Arcidiacono, 2017; Wingard & Forsberg, 2009).

In the original project, three research teams, one in each of the countries, selected the participating families according to similar criteria: middle-class dual-income families, paying a monthly rent or mortgage for their apartment/house, with at least two children (at least one of them between 8 and 12 years old) living at home with the parents. The families were recruited through flyers in schools and teachers who were personally acquainted with the research team. After an initial meeting, both parents (and children over eight years of age) signed participation consent forms and discussed the particulars of the data collection that would take place at their home with the team. To capture the complexity of family life, the project adopted several analytical approaches from the disciplines of cultural and linguistic anthropology, psychology, applied linguistics and education sciences. In terms of methods, the project was designed as a video ethnography in which audiovisual recordings of the families' daily activities were supplemented by *in situ* observations and activity-tracking and maps and photographs of the living spaces as well as audio/video tours, questionnaires and semi-structured interviews with family members (Arcidiacono & Pontecorvo, 2004; Ochs, Graesch, Mittmann, Bradbury & Repetti, 2006). The semi-structured interviews with parents revolved around family history, the organization of daily life, childrearing and school-based education. The research team also audiotaped tours in which one family member described the home spaces to a researcher. The team furthermore asked individual family members to perform video-tours without the presence of a researcher, presenting the most meaningful objects and spaces in the house from their perspective. The observations and video-recordings of daily activities at home were carried out simultaneously by two researchers, in the morning and evening, on both weekdays and the weekends. The team also performed systematic tracking of family activities at regular 10-minute intervals.

PARTICIPANTS FOR THE STUDY

For this chapter, we have relied on the research conducted in the Italian context. The study is based on a corpus of 83 hours of audiovisual recordings of eight families at their homes (see Appendix 1 for details about the participants). A few general characteristics of the Italian participants suffice. They were middle-class families with stable family organizations sustained by both parents. The parents placed high value on the education of their children and on attending high-quality schools. The weekdays were structured around school time for children (from 8 am until 2-3 pm) and full-time work activities for the parents (from 8 am until 6-7 pm). The children's schedules also included after-school activities (e.g., sports, music, learning foreign languages) that the parents' work schedules needed to accommodate. Several families relied on baby-sitters and relatives for childcare when the parents were not available. The weekends were mainly devoted to meals with relatives and friends, and other common activities outside the home. The recordings were collected by the original project's Italian research team. Two team members, each operating a camera, simultaneously recorded the family's activities while a third one kept track of the activities in written form. Each family was recorded over the course of seven days, on both weekdays and the weekend, for a total of approximately 20 to 25 hours per family. The recordings were transcribed in their entirety and supplemented by ethnographic notes (Arcidiacono & Pontecorvo, 2004).

ANALYTICAL APPROACH

The original research project deployed several analytic approaches. The idiographic, local approach (Arcidiacono, 2015; Salvatore & Valsiner,

2009) aimed to access the participants' sense-making procedures. Conversation analysis (Sacks, Schegloff & Jefferson, 1974) was deployed to understand how participants organized and understood their own interactions, as exhibited by the turn-by-turn unfolding of talk. Discourse analytic approaches inspired chiefly by discursive psychology (Edwards & Stokoe, 2004), were deployed to determine how representations, beliefs and attitudes were handled through talk.

For the study presented in this chapter, we examined the audiovisual recordings of the Italian families, along with the corresponding transcripts, and identified a non-exhaustive set of passages revolving around homework ($N = 56$). We then proceeded to describe the activities taking place and identified temporal and sequential patterns of production. We each examined the data separately and then discussed our analyses together until we reached an agreement. This phase of the study led to the results presented in the section below titled "A complex set of activities." We present our observations on particularly frequent practices and sometimes provide indications on their distribution among the participants. In this regard, we were however limited by the purely qualitative nature of our study, which involved only a small number of families, and by the analysis of very different and complex situations. This prevented us, for example, from establishing whether the observed practices were determined by the parents' socio-economic level or factors such as age or gender.

The second phase of the study concentrated on the moments in which the parents and the children actually began carrying out an assignment ($N = 13$). For this phase of the study, we deployed a multimodal conversation analytic approach (Stivers & Sidnell, 2005). Accordingly, we transcribed the excerpts following the Jeffersonian conventions (Jefferson, 2004) and annotated them to describe the interplay of talk, gaze, gestures and other body movements. We then performed case-by-case and comparative analysis of the excerpts and discussed it until agreement was reached. The analysis follows the sequential and temporal organization of participants' actions, as well as their own orientations as displayed *in situ*. It aims to identify the participants' actions and the constitutive detail of the multimodal practices deployed to produce them (Stivers & Sidnell, 2005).

In this phase of the study, we focused on the transition between preparing for homework in material terms (for instance opening an exercise book) and actually beginning to do the assignment, in the sense of producing an initial action tangibly contributing to its completion.

FINDINGS AND DISCUSSION

In this study, we were interested in understanding how the parents and their children deal with what needs to be done and how to do it when engaging in homework assignments. We were particularly inspired by ethnomethodological and conversation analytic research on children's collaborative instructional activities (Amerine & Bilmes, 1988)—for instance, studies on how students working in groups get acquainted with their task, plan for it and engage in its completion (Hellermann & Pekarek Doehler, 2010; Pochon-Berger, 2011). The "Beginning the assignment" section below presents some results of the second phase of the study. We conventionally use the terms "mother" and "father" to refer to the two individuals in the couple, but we acknowledge that they also have other identities such as wife and husband, including when interacting with their children. For reasons of confidentiality, we replaced the original names of individuals and families with fictional ones.

A COMPLEX SET OF ACTIVITIES

Examination of the recordings of Italian families showed that homework-related issues occupy a large share of both the time parents spend with their children and the talk they engage in with them. Families very frequently devote time to homework, including on the weekend and sometimes even in the morning before the children leave for school. The mother of the Giti family, for instance, helps her eldest daughter with her math homework in the morning. She points out an error her daughter has made and the father says, "In the morning she always has one number too many or too few. Then, during the day, she becomes more focused," which suggests that doing math exercises before leaving for school is a common occurrence for her. Homework-related discussions may involve the mother, father and siblings of the child who needs to do the homework. One Saturday morning, the Mari family is in their living room. The father helps the son do his math homework and the mother reviews English exercises with her daughter. In the Quadri family, the daughter reviews an essay written by her older brother, upon his request. Overall, the mothers are more active than the fathers when it comes to asking questions about homework, urging children to do them and helping them. The corpus does however contain several long sequences in which fathers help their children do their homework.

The family handles homework issues in many different living spaces: in various rooms of the home, at a parent's workplace, over the telephone or in the car. One Wednesday morning, the mother of the Cali family is caring for her three-year-old daughter in the bathroom, accompanied by her eight-year-old daughter who is doing her homework. It is very rare for young children to work at a table or desk reserved only for them, with all the materials available on it from the beginning. They work in the kitchen, the living room or the dining room, moving sometimes from one room to another. The mother of the Quadri family says to her son, "Do me a favor, Leonardo, and try to find the stapler. I don't know where it is in this mess." The son goes to look for it in his mother's bedroom. Meanwhile, the mother decides to break off a piece of tape with her teeth, since she has no scissors, and the daughter wonders where a binder containing her documents is. Homework is in fact a complex undertaking composed of multiple activities that can sometimes extend over several hours or even days (see Wingard, 2006 on homework-related inquiry, planning and completion phases). Moreover, these activities very often take place at the same time as other family activities such as caring for younger children, preparing dinner, tidying the house or answering telephone calls. Over the space of 20 minutes, the father of the Pico family makes multiple trips between the kitchen, where he helps his wife make dinner and set the table, and the living room, where he

Parent-Child Homework Interactions: Beginning an Assignment

monitors his two daughters as they do their homework. Moreover, when he is in the kitchen, he also discusses the homework with the mother.

An initial activity that is part of the complex homework undertaking consists of determining whether the child has homework and how much, as well as identifying the school subject the homework belongs to. This activity is mainly initiated by the parents and is repeated several times in a single day. It is the most common homework-related activity that both parents and children are involved in, far more common than joint completion of homework. The activity involves calculating the time it will take to do the homework, assessing its difficulty and identifying the child's attitude toward it. It has an influence on the creation of the family schedule, for which parents must determine the homework and other work-related and family activities that need to be done, as well as their children's plans and wishes. It also involves anticipating what the child will need to complete the homework and ensuring that these resources are available when the time comes. The mother and children of the Quadri family (alias), for example, spent a good part of their Tuesday evening organizing things to ensure that the homework will get done despite the family's departure for a few days to the countryside, where they will have no encyclopedia, computer or printer.

Another activity consists of a parent urging a child to get started on the homework. During dinner, the daughter of the Mari family says that she does not want to do her homework. The parents try to convince her, offering to have her father help. The youngest son of the Ripe family says, "I don't know how to study on my own." The mother urges him to get started, promising that she will come to keep him company later. The participants and resources used vary, but the activity often requires reminders and juggling of several competing activities - for example homework vs. leisure time or homework vs. tidying -, the transition rarely taking place all at once. The youngest son of the Ripe family, for instance, is asked to do his homework but volunteers to put the dishes away. The father drily comments that it is "better to help than to go off and study."

Yet another activity involves ensuring that all the physical conditions and individuals necessary for the doing of the homework are present. An appropriate space must be cleared, the school materials must be on hand, the child must be seated, and the parent must be free. This activity also includes managing issues of cleanliness, silence and attention. Parents do this mainly with their youngest children. This is the case with joint completion of homework tasks too, as teenagers usually do their homework more independently, in their own rooms, while the parents are in the kitchen or living room. The parents and children furthermore need to determine what the homework consists of exactly and to identify the way it is to be done. Parents and children identify the content of the assignment, namely, what it involves (for instance, answering questions about goldfish), the work required (reading a text, then the questions and finally writing down the answers), and the specific pedagogical materials (a section of a book and a worksheet) that are to be used. Sometimes, this activity is completed without talk and the participants immediately set about doing the homework. More often, they talk about the content of the assignment, referring to the teacher's instructions and examining the school materials. There is often a reversal of roles: the child tells the parent what needs to be done and how to do it. The father of the Pico family, for example, has to ask his youngest daughter to explain her homework several times because she switches between several textbooks that are open at the same time.

The actual doing of the homework requires knowledge and skills that the parent sometimes lacks. The parent sometimes wonders what method the teacher wants the child to use to do an exercise or admits to not knowing the required answer and to being unable to help the child. In some cases, several members of the household work together to find it. The mother of the Cali family helps her eight-year-old daughter with her math homework. She asks her, "What did the teacher teach you?" and "Did she teach you to do it like this or not?" In the end, she says, "I'll have to go speak with your teacher so she can explain it to me… I don't want to confuse you." Later, she admits that she herself was confused with the "more than" and "less than" symbols and calls the father over to take her place. The daughter tells her father, "No, you need to explain it to her (the mother); I already understood it."

Sometimes, parents limit themselves to giving instructions about the general attitude the child should adopt (sit up straight, concentrate, think, look carefully, read the sheet). One challenge in this activity is to keep the child focused only on completing the task, while the child uses it as a pretext to do something else. The son of the Mari family, for example, begins imitating the characters of a TV show when his homework requires only providing the title. Another major challenge is managing the extent to which the parent is involved and finding some balance between monitoring the child's progress and participating in the actual completion of the assignment. It is also necessary to harmonize the respective criteria of the child, the parent and the school. The mother of the Giti family tells her eldest daughter to finish coloring a picture, and the girl replies that snow is white, meaning that the task is already finished. The father of the Pico family criticizes a sentence in his youngest daughter's exercise book. As he sees it, the fact that birds have no teeth poses a problem not for digestion but for chewing.

The conclusion of the homework session calls for verifications and corrections and putting the materials away. The mother of the Quadri family reads her daughter's essay about a story aloud, pointing out mistakes she has made and parts that are hard to read. This leads the child to read her the original story. The mother uses this as an opportunity to ensure that the child has correctly understood certain expressions ("What does it mean that he did not agree to settle for less than desired?") and her daughter asks her for clarifications ("What does 'forge' mean?").

Later on, the daughter shows her the grammar homework she has done, which she is especially proud of. But even after the assignments have been completed, homework is often a topic of discussion between parents and children, and between the two parents. During dinner, for example, parents may ask their children about what they have done, reassuring them about their preparedness or reprimanding them. At dinner, the father of the Ripe family for example asks his eldest son "Was your geometry homework difficult, or am I mistaken? What was so complex about it that it took longer than usual?" Next, the mother asks the child how far he has gotten in his geography homework. When he answers ("Africa of the South"), the mother corrects him: "You mean South Africa?" The family then moves on to the topic of the documentaries on different countries of the world that are available to the children at their home.

BEGINNING AN ASSIGNMENT

In this section, we focus on how parents and children start doing an assignment. By this we mean specifically how they engage with the pedagogical materials and perform an initial action tangibly contributing to the actual completion of the larger task. For instance, writing the first number of a calculation or the first words of an answer or a composition. We are particularly interested in examining whether the parent and the child discuss the content of the task, what it is about and what is being asked of the child. Moreover, do they read the directions, either silently or aloud, before actually beginning to do the assignment? What are the first actions directly related to the concrete completion of the larger task and who does them? See Hellermann and Pekarek Doehler (2010), Lerner (1995) and Pochon-Berger (2011) on shaping collaboration in instructional activities.

We have identified two common situations, differing by whether or not the parent and the child discuss the content of the assignment. In the first, the child begins doing the assignment without discussing its content with the parent. In the second, the child begins doing the assignment after discussing its content with the parent. In most cases, the parents and children begin doing the actual homework task without feeling the need to first discuss its content. On one hand, the parents and children often speak about homework that is to be done, about the subject in question and the specific topic of an exercise before sitting down together to look at the materials. On the other hand, the parents often manage to quickly grasp what needs to be done as soon as they look at an exercise. In other cases, the instructions are read for the first time after the task has already begun, once difficulties are encountered. The parents and children nevertheless do sometimes discuss the content of a specific task before beginning.

We could have shown how each of the extracts in our collection relates to this difference, comparing the extracts in which the child begins doing the assignment without first discussing its content with the parent with those in which the child does discuss it with the parent before starting. However, to fit into this chapter, this presentation needed to be extremely concise. Deploying the multimodal conversation analytic approach (Stivers &

Sidnell, 2005), we therefore decided to present how exactly these two situations took shape in two interactions in particular. Thus, we illustrate two of these situations—beginning to do an assignment without discussing its content or after doing so showing in detail the associated organizational features. The two excerpts are from recordings made at the Mari family's home. This family is composed of the father (Leo), the mother (Ada), a 13-year-old daughter (Pia) and an 8-year-old son (Ivo). Excerpt 1 corresponds to an interaction whose main participants are the mother and the son. Excerpt 2 corresponds to an interaction between the father and the son. We considered it interesting to show how in the same family, assignments can be started in different ways with the same child. Appendix II provides a list of the Jeffersonian transcription symbols used (Jefferson, 2004). For each excerpt, we provide some key images extracted from the corresponding video clip. We have inserted superscript references in the transcription at the points corresponding to the images reproduced alongside it. In the body of the article, the indications I-1, I-2, I-3, etc. refer to the images. The numbers in parentheses refer to the lines of the excerpt.

The Child Begins Doing an Assignment without Discussing Its Content with the Parent

Excerpt 1 is from the Sunday evening recording of the Mari family. While they are in the kitchen, the mother tells the father and the son that the son must do his homework before dinner. As the mother leads the child toward the living room for this purpose, he warns her that the "homework is a little bit difficult because you must try to remember from now till I was born." The child produces an evaluation of the task based on its difficulty, which he justifies by referring to its content. He also assigns what is to be done to his mother. The mother's response is to prompt the child to go get his bookbag. The two begin looking for the bookbag, which the mother finds in the son's bedroom. While the mother is placing the bookbag on a chair facing a table in the living room, the father calls to her from the kitchen (Excerpt 1).

48   Francesco Arcidiacono and Esther González-Martínez

```
Excerpt 1:  R44_52-158
 1  Leo:   Ada
           Ada
 2  Ada:   <si Leo arrivo subito. un attimo °che- (.) metto lui
           yes Leo I'm coming right now just a moment so I can get him
 3          a faᴵ⁻¹re il compito di storia,° vieni
           started on the history homework come
 4         (1.2)ᴵ⁻²
 5  Ivo:   ·hh ·hh io volevo rivedere un attimo ·hhh la mia: collezione:
           I would like to look a bit at my collection
 6  Ada:   di minerali la [guardiamo dopo.]
           of rocks we will look at it after
 7  Ivo:                  [     °<di mine]rali>°
                                of rocks
 8  Ada:   e di conchiglie ci mettiaᴵ⁻³mo anche quelle nuove. però intanto
           and we'll even add the new shells but in the meantime
 9         facciamo
           let's do
10         (...)
11  Ada:   <ma come non c'e(h)ro £con te oggi (<se siamo stati ogni>)
           but how come I was not with you today if we were
12         ·hh insieme ( )£=
           together
13  Ivo:   =-mamma
            mom
14         (2.4)
15  Ada:   [si ]
            yes
16  Ivo:   [pri]ma domanda:ᴵ⁻⁴
            first question
17  Ada:   <quando ho cominciato a ᴵ⁻⁵mangiare da solo.> °amore tu hai
           when I started to eat by myself
18         cominciato molto presto a mangiare da solo°=
           darling you began to eat by yourself very early on
19  Ivo:   =asᴵ⁻⁶petta ·h [ho ]
           wait I began
```

Figure 1. (Continued).

Parent-Child Homework Interactions: Beginning an Assignment 49

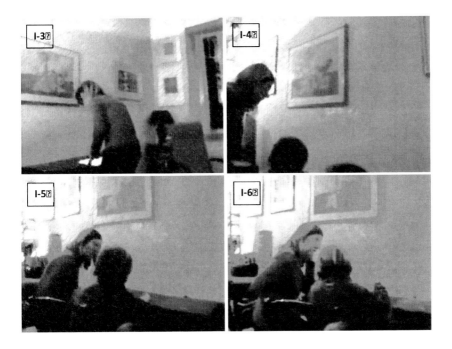

Figure 1. Excerpt 1 and the images.

At the start of the excerpt, the mother asks the father to wait, and, by way of explanation, indicates in a lower voice what she is preparing to do: get the son started on his history homework (lines 2-3). In doing this, she displays that she knows the subject of the homework that is to be done. At the same time, she quickly pulls a book out of the bookbag, which shows that she also knows which school materials need to be used for the homework (Images I-1, I-2). The mother opens the book, flips through the pages and, once she reaches the page where the homework is to be done, places the open book on the table. While doing this, the mother examines the page in question for less than 2 seconds before again turning to the bookbag (Image I-3) in search of a pencil case, which she takes a pencil from. As the mother prepares the materials, he moves away and expresses his desire to look at his rock collection. The mother tells him that he can do that, adding another activity of interest to the child (putting the new shells in the collection) to the agenda, but places the activity at a later time, implying that it will take place after the homework is finished (see Wingard,

2007 on parents' and children's practices for prioritizing activities). After this (line 10, not transcribed), the mother continues the activity of preparing for the homework session by taking the child to the bathroom and then bringing him back to the living room.

As the child is about to sit down at the table, he reproaches his mother for not having been with him during the day. The mother rejects the reproach in a playful tone, giving her own description of the day (lines 11-12). At the same time, she looks for a chair so that she can sit down herself. The child does not pursue this discussion but looks at the book that is open on the table and moves on to make a summons, calling for his mother's attention ("mom", line 13). He then produces a formulation ("first question", line 16), which refers to an initial part of the homework, and says what it entails (the first question in a list). In doing this, he introduces the activity of carrying out the homework task and urges his mother to get involved by assigning an initial action to her: reading the question and answering it. At the same time, the mother places her chair next to her son's and looks toward the open book on the table (Image I-4). The mother reads the question rapidly (in under 2 seconds) and reproduces it aloud as she takes her seat ("when I started to eat by myself", line 17). She does this in part from memory since, starting from "mangiare" the mother is no longer looking at the book but at her son (Image I-5) and then orients her gaze at an object on the table that she moves to one side. At the same time, she begins to answer the question ("you began to eat by yourself very early on", line 18). The child, who has begun writing, tells her to wait (Image I-6) and starts formulating the answer aloud, in the first person ("I began", line 19).

This excerpt shows one way of beginning to do a homework task. As they walk toward the living room, the son warns the mother of the task's difficulty, justifying this with a reference to its content, but the mother does not reply. The mother is oriented toward doing everything that needs to be done before the homework session can begin: taking the child to the living room, notifying the father, bringing the bookbag over, placing the book and pencil on the table, taking the child to the bathroom, seating the child at the table, bringing over a chair for herself. At the same time, she prioritizes the homework over another activity that her son wants to do (look at his rock collection), while reassuring him that this activity will be performed, and in an interesting way (adding the new shells to the collection as a bonus). She also circumvents her son's reproach about the time she has spent on him during the day. The two begin carrying out the task without first discussing its content. A quick examination (lasting just a few seconds), first of the book and later on of the first question, is all the mother needs to acquaint herself with the homework task. The child looks at the book and urges the mother to read the first question and she does so. The question represents the child speaking ("when I started to eat by myself") but the mother is the one who voices it. The mother also answers the question, thereby accepting the role that her son has given her in the completion of the homework ("you must try to remember"). The child holds the pencil, starts writing the answer down, paces his mother's response and verbalizes the first words of the answer. He thus produces an initial action that is directly oriented toward the concrete completion of the task.

The Child Begins Doing an Assignment after Discussing Its Content with the Parent

Excerpt 2 is from the Saturday late morning recording of the Mari family, when they are in the living room. The eldest daughter enters the room, greets her family, leaves again and begins playing the piano in another room; the mother is talking on the telephone (not transcribed). The father is seated at the table, upon which the son's books, notebooks, pencils and other school supplies are spread out. The son is playing in front of a cupboard. Before the excerpt begins, the father asks the son what homework they still need to do. The child lists the subjects—science and math—and the father urges him to begin. The child goes over to the table and picks up one of the books that are lying open there. Probably guided by the son's choice of book, his father asks him what math homework he is supposed to do and urges him to sit down (line 1, Image I-1).

```
Excerpt 2:  R57_327-640
 1  Leo:    >che devi fare in matematica?< siediti.^I-1
                what do you have to do in mathematics sit down
 2  Ivo:    ( ) tanto: ( )^I-2 °ormai la maestra di matematica ci dà ·h
                much now the teacher of mathematics gives
 3          compiti del primo sia de(h)l te(h)rza:°
                homework for both first and third grades
 4          (6.1)^I-3
 5  Ivo:    (in colonna) (1.6) ( )=
                in row
 6  Leo:    =che stai facendo? la: (1.3) i numeri romani?
                what are you doing the the Roman numerals
 7          (1.0)
 8  Ivo:    sì <ce li hanno insegnati fino ·hh al mille guarda^I-4
                yes they have taught them to us up to one thousand look
 9          (0.6)
10  Leo:    be:ne
                all right
11          (0.8)
12  Ivo:    un- u- (0.5) quest- la i vuol dire [uno]=
                en  o thi the i means one
13  Leo:                                        [uno]=
                                                 one
14  Ivo:    =·hh i i romani facevano le lettere che erano come i numeri
                the the Romans made letters that were like numbers
15          ·hh poi la v come ( )
                then the v like
16          (1.0)
17  Ivo:    e poi qua ci sono tutte le regole di come contavano
                and then here there are all the rules about how
                they counted
18          [( )              ]
19  Leo:    [(va benissimo)] che devi fare in questo esercizio?
                very good what do you have to do in this exercice
20  Ivo:    questo [e::     ]
                this and
21  Leo:           [scrivere] in romano?
                    write in Roman
22  Ivo:    °questo°^I-5
                this
23  Leo:    questo lo scrivi in romano?
                this you write in Roman
24  Ivo:    non in rom(h)ano=
                not in Roman
25  Leo:    =eh eh eh:=
                heh heh heh
26  Ivo:    =>£i miei compagni ( )£< glielo chiedevano
                my classmates asked whether we needed to do
27          se ci faceva fare i compiti ·hh con i numeri [romani,    ]
                the homework in Roman numerals
28  Leo:                                                  [eh perché no]
                                                           huh why not
29          (1.0)
30  Ivo:    però la maestra diceva che era meglio di no
                but the teacher said that it was better not to
31          (0.5)
32  Ivo:    ·hh li faremo in quarta
                we'll do it in fourth grade
33          (26.3)
34  Ivo:    °due: cen:to:°^I-6
                two hundred
```

Figure 2. (Continued).

Parent-Child Homework Interactions: Beginning an Assignment

Figure 2. Excerpt 2 and the images.

While producing the directive "sit down", the father pulls his son's chair out and removes the bookbag from the seat. The child then puts the open book on the table, facing his chair and near his father (Image I-2), and seems to begin talking about the homework ("much"), although his first words are barely audible. The father pulls the book toward him and examines the pages it is open to while the child continues presenting the homework ("now the teacher of mathematics gives homework for both first and third grades", 2-3) and picks up a pen (Image I-3). The child again mumbles something about the homework while handling a large pencil case and the father continues examining the pages in front of him. In line 6, the father asks his son what he is currently working on, then offers a candidate answer ("the Roman numerals"). The child agrees, tells the father what he was taught in class, turns ahead a page and urges his father to look at something (line 8) on the right-hand page that he indicates with a pointing gesture (Image I-4). The child then presents the way that the Roman numerals are written—his phrasing reverses the terms ("the Romans made letters that were like numbers", line 14)—and tells the father that the rules are given in the book. The child sits down and turns back one page to the section of the book that he had shown first. The father then asks him what he needs to do in the exercise (line 19). The child indicates something on the right-hand page, touching it with his finger, that he refers to as "this" (line 22). He then flips the page forward and shows the father another section of the book, that he refers to as "and this" (lines 20-22, Image I-5). At the same time, the father suggests a candidate answer to his question about what he needs to do in the exercise: "to write in Roman" (line 21). The father supports the son's gesture as the child turns the page back, points at what seems to be the exercise's directions and again suggests the candidate answer: "this you write in Roman" (line 23). This could be a reference to his son saying in line 14 that the Romans wrote letters like numbers. More plainly, the father may be referring to the fact that the exercise involves making regular calculations in Arabic numerals. The son perceives the humor of the suggestion and rejects it, laughing and the father also laughs (line 25). The son justifies the rejection, as the father insists, referring to the directions the teacher had given in class (lines 26-32). The child then begins looking attentively at the page in front of him and begins writing on it, ending, after a long silence, by verbalizing a number that is part of his exercise ("two hundred", line 34, Image I-6).

Excerpt 2 shows a way of beginning to do an assignment that is very different from the one at work in Excerpt 1. Here, the child begins carrying out the task after discussing its content with his parent, at least in part. In this excerpt, the parent asks the child about the homework he still needs to do, urges him to begin and to sit down, and removes an object from a chair for him. He remains seated throughout the activity and attentively examines the pages of the book that his son shows him. He focuses on questioning the child about what he has done at school and the content of the exercise. He actively tries to elicit a description of the assignment's content from his son, for instance performing calculations with Arabic versus Roman numerals. It is the son who comes to him, picks up the book, places it in front of the father, picks up the pencil, sits down and turns the pages to show him both what he has done at school and what he needs to do. The talk remains focused on the work previously completed at school and the homework that remains to be done. The son answers the father's questions, even though he does not produce an actual description of the exercise's content (he does not say "performing calculations with Arabic numerals"). At no time does he introduce an alternative activity. He also engages in performing the calculations on his own initiative, without shaping and soliciting the participation of the parent. This contrasts strongly with Excerpt 1, in which the mother does most of the preparation for the concrete completion of the homework (while the child introduces other activities and does not talk about the content of the homework task), examines it rapidly and begins producing the answer herself in accordance with her son's request.

CONCLUSION

In this chapter we present a study showing how homework is done in two Italian families, in concrete terms, in real situations and time, during parent-child interactions at home. Our goal is to contribute to the scientific study of family homework interactions while providing useful information to the teachers who create and assign this homework. Wingard and Forsberg (2009) identify two forms of parental involvement: anticipating and planning homework activities on the one hand and engaging directly in the completion of the homework tasks on the other. Our results confirm that doing homework is a complex undertaking to which parents contribute via different activities that are also performed in different ways. The parents engage in activities like making inquiries, planning, physical organization, content discussion, monitoring, actual completion, checks and post-completion discussions. These activities are often carried out discontinuously and stretch out over long periods of time. Several activities can be carried out simultaneously, for example discussing homework and looking for the materials needed to do it or doing other family activities such as tending to a baby or making dinner. Furthermore, it is not always easy to distinguish moments that are devoted to anticipating and planning homework from moments devoted to its actual completion. For example, a request for information from a parent on the amount of homework to be done can lead to explanations about the specific way to perform a task if the child shows fears of being unable to do it. The actual completion of the assignment is therefore not an activity with clearly defined starting and ending points. An assignment is also rarely done all in one session but more often stage by stage, with breaks when it is necessary to respecify what needs to be done, to motivate the child and create the right conditions. As for spatial organization, it is extremely rare for young children to work at a table or desk reserved only for them, with all the materials already in place. In terms of knowledge and skills, the study also shows the range of challenges families encounter, the efforts they make to overcome them and the resources they use for this. These observations confirm the findings of many studies in a wide range of national and socio-cultural contexts (McDermott, Goldman & Varenne, 1984; Rayou, 2010; Wingard & Forsberg, 2009).

Our study focuses specifically on the way that children and parents approach beginning an assignment. To what extent do parents adopt didactic methods for teaching children (Popkewitz, 2003) and how much "schoolification" (Petrie, 2005) is there in family homework completion? Macbeth (2011) underscores that learning the lessons "entails learning how to speak of them" (p. 449). Do parents and children read the directions and discuss them before getting started on a task? What practices do parents use to get their children to talk about an assignment's content? What is the interactional production of the homework's content like, and how is it done (Macbeth, 2011)? How do the participants orient to and organize the tasks (Hellermann & Pekarek Doehler, 2010)? How do parents and children divide up the work? What place do children reserve for their parents in these activities? Breen (1989), makes a distinction between task-as-workplan and task-as-process. Coughlan and Duff (1994), show that students may engage in activities that are very different in response to the same task. Our study contributes to research in multimodal conversation analysis that underscores the interactional, situated and contingent character of learning tasks (Hellermann & Pekarek Doehler, 2010). It shows that an understanding of what homework is about is achieved through both discussion and orientations of the body and to objects (Pochon-Berger, 2011).

Our observations nevertheless go beyond the way homework is done because at these moments, children and parents talk about school in general (Pontecorvo, Liberati & Monaco, 2013; Rayou, 2010). Children describe the teachers and talk about things they have experienced in class, specifying what they like and what is problematic for them. Parents make comments about the methods the teachers or textbooks use to explain ideas that they themselves learned differently. These comments often reveal the parents' positive or negative rapport to school and knowledge. While talking about homework, parents also convey an evaluation of their children's skills as well as expectations placed upon them that go well beyond academic performance (Corno, 2000; Hoover-Dempsey & Sandler, 1995). The study involved a small number of expeditiously described families, events and excerpts and does not aim to identify practices that are representative of other people's behavior. But scholars have already discussed some of the practices we are focusing on and these may be familiar to readers/parents/former school children. This may suggest some relevance in our observations for understanding family homework interactions beyond the specific studied setting. Of course, significant differences are predictable depending on the socio-economic situation of the parents, the family composition, the ages of the children, the types of homework they are doing, and so forth.

Regardless of their particular circumstances, what parents may take away from our study is that discussing homework with their children means spending time with them, reaching a better understanding of their experiences at school and meeting the institution's requirements as a family. Moreover, they may wish to discuss the content of an assignment with their children before engaging in its actual completion, for as long as time allows. For teachers, in particular beginners, our study can serve as a reminder of the diverse range of situations in which children do their homework. This is the case even within a single family or group of families with relatively similar characteristics. Homework is assigned to be done in a context very different from that of the school: in spaces that are also used to prepare food, take care of babies, watch television, play; with tools that are scattered across the household; with adults who often lack the availability and sometimes the knowledge necessary to assist their children. Experts have designed many solutions for teachers and parents (Meirieu, 2004). Our observations underscore the usefulness of certain practices. Teachers could prepare a summary list of all the homework to be done for a given day/week with an estimate of the time needed, rather than leaving families to determine what is to be done from a range of notebooks, textbooks and sheets. On the same page of an assignment, they could also clearly specify the procedure to follow to complete it and, when possible, present the knowledge necessary or at least indicate where to find it, outside of the classroom.

APPENDIX I. PARTICIPANTS

Table 1. Family members and ages

Family[*]	Mother	Father	Child 1	Child 2
Cali	42	44	daughter 8	daughter 3
Cilo	38	39	daughter 13	daughter 11
Giti	34	42	daughter 8	daughter 1
Mari	47	50	daughter 13	son 8
Olmi	43	41	son 10	son 6
Pico	46	50	daughter 12	daughter 10
Quadri	44	47	son 12	daughter 10
Ripe	57	55	son 12	son 8
Total number of participants: 32				

[*] For reasons of confidentiality, we replaced the original names of individuals and families with fictional ones

Table 2. Children's school level

Participant	School level (for the children)
Sons	4 primary school; 2 lower secondary school
Daughters	4 primary school; 4 lower secondary school; 2 kindergarten
Children, total	8 primary school; 6 lower secondary school; 2 kindergarten
First-born	3 primary school; 5 lower secondary school
Second-born	5 primary school; 1 lower secondary school; 2 kindergarten

APPENDIX II. TRANSCRIPTION CONVENTIONS

[ ]	overlapping talk
=	continuous talk
(0.2)	silence in tenths of a second
(.)	micro-pause
.	final intonation
,	continuing intonation
?	rising intonation
:	prolongation of the preceding sound
speci-	cut-off
you	emphasis
°yes you	talk starts markedly soft
°yes°	softer talk
─	rise in pitch
)	fall in pitch
>yes<	talk is compressed
<because	hurried start
·h	inhalation
h	exhalation
£bye£	smiling voice
funn(h)y	laughter particle
( )	unachievable, likely or alternative hearing
(...)	talk continues but has not been transcribed

REFERENCES

Amerine, R. & Bilmes, J. (1988). Following instructions. *Human Studies*, *11*(2-3), 327-339. doi: 10.1007/BF00177308.

Arcidiacono, F. (2015). Argumentation and reflexivity. In G. Marsico, R. Andrisano-Ruggieri & S. Salvatore (Eds.), *Reflexivity and Psychology* (pp. 169-93). Charlotte, NC: Information Age Publishing.

Arcidiacono, F. & Pontecorvo, C. (2004). Più metodi per la pluridimensionalità della vita familiar [More methods for the multidimensionality of family life]. *Ricerche di Psicologia*, *27*(3), 103-118.

Breen, M. (1989). The evaluation cycle for language learning tasks. In R. K. Johnson (Ed.), *The second language curriculum* (pp. 187-206). Cambridge: Cambridge University Press. doi: 10.1017/ CBO 9781139524520.014.

Choi, J., Kim, Y. S. & Lee, D. E. (2012). Characteristics and patterns of family discourse at multicultural homes in Korea with an emphasis on mother-child interactions in homework caring situations. *Bilingual Research*, *48*, 309-342.

Cooper, H., Robinson, J. C. & Patall, E. A. (2006). Does homework improve academic achievement? A synthesis of research 1987-2003. *Review of Educational Research*, *76*(1), 1-62. doi: 10.3102/ 00346543076001001.

Corno, L. (2000). Looking at homework differently. *The Elementary School Journal*, *100*(5), 529-548.

Coughlan, P. & Duff, P. A. (1994). Same tasks, different activities. Analysis of SLA task from an Activity Theory perspective. In J. Lantolf & G. Appel (Eds.), *Vygotskian approaches to second language research* (pp. 173-193). Norwood: Ablex.

Edwards, D. & Stokoe, E. H. (2004). Discursive psychology, focus group interviews and participants' categories. *British Journal of Developmental Psychology*, *4*, 499-507. doi: 10.1348/ 0261510042 378209.

Epstein, J. L. (1992). School and family partnerships. In M. Alkin (Ed.), *Encyclopedia of educational research* (pp. 1139-1151). New York: Macmillan.

Farrell, A. & Danby, S. J. (2015). How does homework 'work' for young children? Children's accounts of homework in their everyday lives. *British Journal of Sociology of Education*, 36(2), 250-269.

Forsberg, L. (2007). Homework as serious family business. Power and subjectivity in negotiations about school assignments in Swedish families. *British Journal of Sociology of Education*, 28(2), 209-222. doi:10.1080/01425690701192695.

Foster, A. M. & Goodwin, M. H. (2006). *Correlates in parental and child behavior. Homework directives and participation structures at the family table.* Working paper, 55 UCLA. Los Angeles: Sloan Center on Everyday Lives of Families.

Hellermann, J. & Pekarek Doehler, S. (2010). On the contingent nature of language-learning tasks. *Classroom Discourse*, 1(1), 25-45. doi: 10.1080/19463011003750657.

Hoover-Dempsey, K. V., Battiato, A. C., Walker, J. M. T., Reed, R. P., DeJong, J. M. & Jones, K. P. (2001). Parental involvement in homework. *Educational Psychologist*, 36(3), 195-209. doi: 10.1207/S15326985EP3603_5.

Hoover-Dempsey, K. V. & Sandler, H. M. (1995). Parental involvement in children's education. Why does it make a difference? *Teachers College Record*, 97(2), 310-331.

Hutchison, K. (2011). Homework through the eyes of children. What does visual ethnography invite us to see? *European Educational Research Journal*, 10(4), 545-558.

Iannacconne, A. & Arcidiacono, F. (2014). Les relations école-famille: questions méthodologiques. In F. Arcidiacono (Ed.), *Hétérogénéité linguistique et culturelle dans le context scolaire* [School-family relations: methodological issues. In F. Arcidiacono (Ed.), *Linguistic and Cultural Heterogeneity in School Context*] (pp. 147-156). Bienne: Editions HEP-BEJUNE.

Jecker, D. & Weisser, M. (2015). Les devoirs à la maison comme outil de partenariat éducatif Points de vue des élèves et de leurs parents [Homework as an educational partnership tool. Views of students and their parents]. *Questions vives*, *23*, 1-15.

Jefferson, G. (2004). Glossary of transcript symbols with an introduction. In G. H. Lerner (Ed.), *Conversation analysis. Studies from the first generation* (pp. 13-31). Amsterdam: Benjamins. doi: 10.1075/ pbns.125.02jef.

Kakpo, S. (2012). *Les devoirs à la maison. Mobilisation et désorientation des familles populaires* [*Homework at home. Mobilization and disorientation of popular families*]. Paris: PUF.

Keogh, J. (1999). *The role of texts and talk in mediating relations between schools and homes.* Unpublished doctoral dissertation. Brisbane: The University of Queensland.

Lerner, G. H. (1995). Turn design and the organization of participation in instructional activities. *Discourse Processes*, *19*(1), 111-131. doi: 10.1080/ 01638539109544907.

Macbeth, D. (2011). Understanding as an instructional matter. *Journal of Pragmatics*, *43*, 438-451. doi: 0.1016/j.pragma.2008.12.006.

McDermott, R. P., Goldman, S. V. & Varenne, H. (1984). When school goes home. Some problems in the organization of homework. *Teachers College Record*, *85*(3), 391-409.

Meirieu, P. (2004). *Les devoirs à la maison. Parents, enfants, enseignants: pour en finir avec ce casse-tête* [*Homework at home. Parents, children, teachers: to end this puzzle*]. Paris: La Découverte.

Morgan, D. (1996). *Family connections. An introduction to family studies.* Cambridge: Polity.

Ochs, E., Graesch, A. P., Mittmann, A., Bradbury, T. N. & Repetti, R. (2006). Video ethnography and ethnoarchaeological tracking. In M. Pitt-Catsouphes, E. E. Kossek & S. Sweet (Eds.), *The work and family handbook. Multi-disciplinary perspectives, methods, and approaches* (pp. 387-409). Mahwah: Erlbaum.

Ochs, E. & Kremer-Sadlik, T. (Eds.) (2013). *Fast Forward Family. Home, Work, and Relationships in Middle-Class America*. Berkeley: University of California Press.

Pauletto, F., Aronsson, K. & Arcidiacono, F. (2017). Inter-generational argumentation: Children's account work during dinner conversations in Italy and Sweden. In F. Arcidiacono & A. Bova (Eds.), *Interpersonal Argumentation in Educational and Professional Contexts* (pp. 1-26). New York: Springer. doi: 10.1007/978-3-319-59084-4_1.

Petrie, P. (2005). Extending 'pedagogy'. *Journal of Education for Teaching*, *31*(4), 293-296.

Pochon-Berger, E. (2011). A participants' perspective on tasks. From task instruction, through pre-task planning, to task accomplishment. *Novitas-Royal (Research on Youth and Language)*, *5*, 71-90.

Pontecorvo, C., Liberati, V. & Monaco, C. (2013). How school enters family's everyday life. In G. Marsico, K. Komatsu & A. Iannaccone (Eds.), *Crossing Boundaries. Intercontextual Dynamics between Family and School* (pp. 3-34). Charlotte: Information Age Publishing.

Popkewitz, T. S. (2003). Governing the child and pedagogicalization of the parent. A historial excursus into the present. In B. Franklin, M. Bloch & T. Popkewitz (Eds.), *Educational partnerships and the state. The paradoxes of governing schools, children, and families* (pp. 35-61). New York: Palgrave-Macmillan.

Rayou, P. (Ed.) (2010). *Faire ses devoirs. Enjeux cognitifs et sociaux d'une pratique ordinaire* [*To do one's homework. Cognitive and social issues of ordinary practice*]. Rennes: Université de Rennes.

Sacks, H., Schegloff, E. A. & Jefferson, G. (1974). A simplest systematics for the organization of turn-taking for conversation. *Language*, *50*, 696-735. doi: 10.2307/412243.

Salvatore, S. & Valsiner, J. (2009). Idiographic science on its way: Towards making sense of psychology. In S. Salvatore, J. Valsiner, S. Strout & Joshua Clegg (Eds.), *Yearbook of Idiographic Science. Vol. 2* (pp. 9-19). Rome: Firera & Liuzzo Publishing.

Stivers, T. & Sidnell, J. (2005). Introduction: Multimodal interaction. *Semiotica*, *156*(1-4), 1-20. doi: 10.1515/semi.2005.2005.156.1.

Wingard, L. (2006). Parents' inquiries about homework. The first mention. *Text & Talk, 26*(4-5), 573-598.

Wingard, L. (2007). Constructing time and prioritizing activities in parent-child interaction. *Discourse and Society, 18*(1), 75-91. doi: 10.1177/0957926507069458.

Wingard, L. & Forsberg, L. (2009). Parent involvement in children's homework in American and Swedish dual-earner families. *Journal of Pragmatics, 41*(8), 1576-1595. doi: 10.1016/j.pragma.2007.09.010.

In: Parental Involvement
Editors: Nurit Kaplan Toren et al.
ISBN: 978-1-53616-828-0
© 2020 Nova Science Publishers, Inc.

Chapter 3

EXPLORING PARENT-TEACHER TRUST AND SCHOOL INVOLVEMENT: A FINNISH PERSPECTIVE

Viola Penttinen[*], *Eija Pakarinen*
and Marja-Kristiina Lerkkanen
University of Jyväskylä, Jyväskylä, Finland

ABSTRACT

The present study examined how parental trust in teacher predicts their school involvement during their child's primary school years and vice versa. The study is part of the longitudinal First Steps Study where parents filled in questionnaires on their trust in their child's teacher and their school involvement when the child was at primary school (grades 1-4 and 6). The results of cross-lagged path models showed that mothers' involvement in collaboration with teacher and other parents predicted their trust in teacher in the next school year whereas fathers' trust in teacher predicted their school involvement. Both mothers' and fathers' participation in parental meetings in first grade predicted their trust in teachers later. Furthermore,

---

[*] Corresponding Author's Email: viola.h.a.penttinen@jyu.fi.

the results showed that mothers trusted more in teachers than fathers did from first grade until fourth grade and had a higher school involvement during the school years. Parents of boys and girls did not differ in their trust in teacher although fathers of boys were more involved in collaboration with teacher and other parents in fourth grade than fathers of girls. Moreover, fathers of boys participated in parental meetings more in second and fourth grade than fathers of girls. The results demonstrate how parental trust and school involvement develop and change during primary school years and how trust and involvement are related to each other. In addition, teachers need to be aware of the gender differences to best support mothers and fathers in their trust and school involvement.

Keywords: parental school involvement, parental trust, teacher, primary school

PARENTAL TRUST IN TEACHER

Previous literature has shown the importance of parent-teacher interaction for a child's development of social (Serpell & Mashburn, 2011) and academic skills (Cook, Dearing, & Zachrisson, 2018) and underlines the benefits of parental involvement in school (Jeynes, 2011). The literature also notes that when parents trust in their child's teacher, they are more likely to get involved in school (Santiago, Garbacz, Beattie, & Moore, 2016). Trust can be defined as "an individual's or group's willingness to be vulnerable to another party based on the confidence that the latter party is benevolent, reliable, competent, honest, and open" (Hoy & Tschannen-Moran, 1999, p. 189). In educational context, trust can occur between individual people such as parents, teachers, and students but also between individuals and organizations such as schools or school systems (Bryk & Schneider, 2003). In the present chapter, the focus of trust is on parents' trust in their child's teacher. When a parent trusts his or her child's teacher, parent expects and believes that the teacher will act in a way that is best for the child and child's development (Adams & Christenson, 1998; Frowe, 2005). This is possible if the teacher actively invites parents to interaction and also respects their perspectives (Knopf & Swick, 2008).

In their theory of trust, Rempel, Holmes, and Zanna (1985) define three dimensions of trust: predictability, dependability, and faith. The first dimension, predictability, refers to consistent behavior, which makes it easier to predict one's actions and trust in him/her. Since teachers and parents typically meet each other on an irregular basis, trust is often built on this level based on the actions of the other person. The second dimension, dependability, is focused not on actions but on qualities and characteristics, such as reliability and honesty, that make a person trustworthy. The third and most important dimension, faith, refers to a belief that a person will act in a responsible way. Faith is necessary in addition to evidence from a person's behavior and character qualities. However, the three dimensions are not usually separated in the empirical studies concerning trust.

Several studies have demonstrated the importance of trust within schools and between schools and stakeholders (e.g., students and parents). In schools where trust between different parties is high, there is a higher desire for school improvement (Bryk & Schneider, 2003). Furthermore, in schools where teachers' trust in students and parents is high, student achievement is higher in mathematics and reading (Goddard, Tschannen-Moran, & Hoy, 2001). Parental trust in teacher is related to children's higher prosocial behavior, fewer peer problems (Santiago et al., 2016), and better reading achievement (Pennycuff, 2009). According to a study by Adams and Christenson (2000), high school students whose parents trusted in their teachers completed more courses and attended school more consistently. Moreover, in schools where parents demonstrate trust in the school and the principal, students' academic performance is higher than in schools where parents have lower trust in the school and the principal (Forsyth, Barnes, & Adams, 2006).

It seems that trust in teacher is highest when a child is in early elementary school and declines when the child moves to higher educational levels (Adams & Christenson, 2000). In the school context, trust is built between teachers, principals, students, and parents if there is mutual respect, personal regard, role competence, and integrity (Bryk & Schneider, 2003). In the parent-teacher relationship, communication is a key element in developing, maintaining, and increasing parental trust in teacher (Adams &

Christenson, 2000; Angell, Stoner, & Shelden, 2009; Chang, 2013). Parents' perception of teachers' pedagogical practices in the classroom and with their child affects their level of trust in teachers. For example, one study showed that the more child-centered a teacher's practices are, the higher a mother's trust in the teacher is during her child's first school year (Lerkkanen, Kikas, Pakarinen, Poikonen, & Nurmi, 2013). Moreover, it is important that teachers recognize children's academic, emotional, and social needs (Angell et al., 2009; Chang, 2013) and share the same values as parents (Keyes, 2002). Difficulties in building trust between parents and teachers may occur due to their role differences, power inequities, and the temporary nature of the relationship (Holtz, 2010).

Parental trust in teacher might be related to gender, either their own or their child's. So far, there is a lack of research on differences between mothers' and fathers' levels of trust, and studies have resulted in mixed findings concerning the influence of a child's gender on parental trust in teacher. Although some studies have shown no significant association between a child's gender and parental trust in his or her teacher (Adams & Christenson, 2000; Kikas, Poikonen, et al. 2011), a study by Lerkkanen and colleagues (2013) showed that in Estonia, mothers of girls trusted their child's first grade teacher more than mothers of boys did; however, the same was not true in Finland. Moreover, Powell, Son, File, and San Juan (2010) reported that parents perceived the responsiveness of their child's pre-kindergarten teacher differently depending on their child's gender. One reason behind the possible gender differences in parent-teacher trust may be that the parent-child relationship sometimes differs depending on the gender of the parent and the child (Russel & Saebel, 1997). Another reason might be the difference in gender-related expectations for girls and boys: Girls are expected to be well-behaving and better regulated (Tolman & Porche, 2000) whereas boys are expected to be strong and independent (Mahalik et al., 2003). Moreover, boys' typical lower quality of teacher-student relationship (Hughes & Kwok, 2007) might also be reflected in the parent-teacher relationship. Because of these somewhat contradictory findings concerning the role of the child's gender, together with the shortage of knowledge of the role of parents' own gender in parent-teacher trust, more research is needed on the determinants of parental trust in teacher in different cultural contexts.

PARENTAL SCHOOL INVOLVEMENT

Over the years, numerous studies have recognized the importance of parental school involvement in enhancing child development. Children whose parents show high parental involvement have better academic skills measured by school grades, math achievement and reading skills (von Otter, 2014; Pennycuff, 2009; Sebastian, Moon, & Cunningham, 2017). Moreover, they have higher school engagement (Mo & Singh, 2008), and motivation to learn (Fantuzzo, McWayne, Perry, & Childs, 2004), fewer behavior problems as well as better social skills (El Nokali, Bachman & Votruba-Drzal, 2010), and higher self-concept (Hung, 2005). Epstein (1995) has introduced six types of parental involvement: 1) parenting, 2) communicating, 3) volunteering, 4) learning at home, 5) decision making, and 6) collaborating with the community. Epstein (1995) emphasizes the importance of having school-like families and family-like schools. School-like families support children's learning and show appreciation for school, whereas family-like schools appreciate and recognize children and their families.

Based on Epstein's (1995) six types of involvement, Fantuzzo, Tighe, and Childs (2000) have divided involvement into three categories: school-based involvement, home-based involvement, and home-school conferencing. School-based involvement can mean, for example, volunteering in the classroom, going on class trips, or meeting other parents. Home-based involvement can consist of, for instance, bringing learning materials home or working on a child's math or reading skills. Home-school conferencing includes talking with the teacher about different issues related to, for example, a child's learning. Previous studies of parental involvement have shown that home-based involvement is the most common type of involvement (Kikas, Peets et al., 2011), and it predicts parents' involvement in school (Murray, McFarland-Piazza, & Harrison, 2015). Parental involvement seems to decrease over the course of a child's primary school years (Graham, 2015; Green, Walker, Hoover-Dempsey, & Sandler, 2007; Kikas, Peets, et al., 2011).

From the parents' perspective, it is the school's responsibility to provide opportunities for involvement (Baker, Wise, Kelley, & Skiba, 2016; Sormunen, Tossavainen, & Turunen, 2011). Most teachers support parental involvement via formal parent-teacher meetings and orientation activities, while some also use newsletters and social activities (Murray et al., 2015). From the parents' perspective, unclear or insufficient communication (Baker et al., 2016) as well as parents' own stress (Vera et al., 2017) can be a barrier for involvement.

Parental involvement can differ between mothers and fathers and between parents of boys and parents of girls. Several studies have reported that mothers' school involvement is higher than fathers' (Fleischmann & de Haas, 2016; Hung, 2005). Mothers are more active in ways like attending parental meetings, participating in cooperation committees, and helping their child with schoolwork (Räty, Kasanen, & Laine, 2009). Regarding the role of a child's gender in parental involvement, earlier research has yielded contradictory results. Some studies have reported that a child's gender is not related to parental involvement (Fantuzzo et al., 2004; Graham, 2015), whereas other studies have shown that parents of boys are more in contact with their preschool (McWayne, Campos, & Owsianik, 2008) or school (Mantz et al., 2004). According to Räty et al. (2009), parents of boys experience more inability to help their child in schoolwork than parents of girls. However, there might also be some cultural differences concerning genders.

TRUST AND PARENTAL INVOLVEMENT

Previous research has found several associations between trust and involvement in the school context. It is important that teachers trust different stakeholders. In schools where teachers show trust in their colleagues, the principal, students, and parents, they also collaborate more with these parties

(Tschannen-Moran, 2001). In a similar way, parental trust in teacher is important in terms of parental involvement. Studies have shown parental trust in teachers and schools to be related to their school involvement in primary (Pennycuff, 2009; Santiago et al., 2016), secondary, and high schools (Beycioglu, Ozer, & Sahin, 2013). One of the three aspects of parental involvement, home-school collaboration, seems especially to be related to trust: parents who are actively involved in home-school collaboration have higher trust in their children's teachers (Kikas, Peets, et al. 2011). Moreover, parents who feel that the teacher has invested in their child are more involved than parents who have lower trust in the teacher (Vera et al., 2017). Although previous research has shown the connection between parental trust and school involvement, there is a need to examine if parental trust predicts subsequent school involvement or vice versa to deepen the understanding of the longitudinal associations between trust and involvement.

FINNISH EDUCATIONAL SYSTEM

The present study was conducted in Finland, where compulsory formal education consists of six years in primary school (cf. elementary school in US) and three years in lower secondary school (cf. secondary school in UK and middle school and junior high school in US). Compulsory pre-primary education (cf. preschool in UK and kindergarten in US) is also provided for children the year before they begin primary school at age seven. In primary school, one classroom teacher teaches almost every subject for the students. Typically, the same teacher teaches students from grade one to grade two and from grade three to grade six. Teachers have high professional competence, and they have a master's degree in education.

Finnish parents usually have relatively high trust in their child's teacher (Lerkkanen et al., 2013). They also see collaboration with the school as important and are therefore willing to take part in it (Sormunen et al., 2011). The most common avenues for parental school involvement in Finland are participating in parental meetings and helping one's child with homework or preparation for assessments (Räty et al., 2009). Although Finland's national curriculum expects teacher-parent collaboration and parental school involvement, Finnish parents usually come to school only when they are invited and do not take part in everyday school life (Sormunen et al., 2011).

Due to the limited number of previous studies investigating the longitudinal associations between parental trust and school involvement, the present chapter aims to examine to what extent does parental trust in their child's teacher predict parental school involvement during their child's primary school years (grades 1 to 4 and 6), and vice versa. Moreover, the goal of the study was to investigate if mothers and fathers or parents of boys and girls differ in their trust in the teacher or in their school involvement.

METHOD

The present study is part of a larger, longitudinal research project called the First Steps Study (Lerkkanen et al., 2006). The First Steps Study followed approximately 2000 children from four Finnish municipalities from kindergarten through high school to investigate, for example, the development of children's academic and social skills and the quality of teacher-student interactions and teaching practices. Participants in the present study were parents of the children in the longitudinal follow-up study. A questionnaire about parental trust and school involvement was sent to these parents at five time points: in the spring of their child's first, second, third, fourth, (2008–2011) and sixth school years (2013). Number of participating mothers (who completed the questionnaire) varied between 1,469 (Grade 1) and 768 (Grade 6) and number of participating fathers between 1,003 (Grade 1) and 422 (Grade 6). The reason for the decrease in the number of participants during the primary school years was the fact that the first study period included grades 1, 2, 3 and 4, and the second phase started with new funding when the children were in grade 6. At the latter point, not all the children were participating in the study anymore; some families had moved from these locations, and some children were repeating fifth grade.

The mothers' ages ranged from 24 to 67 (M = 38.44, SD = 5.41), and the fathers' ages ranged from 27 to 69 (M = 41.02, SD = 5.82). Participants' family types and educational levels are shown in Table 1. Parents' participation in the study was voluntary, and all the parents gave written consent for their and their children's participation. Most of the families (98%) were native Finnish-speaking.

Table 1. Participants' family types and educational levels

Family type	%
Married spouses and their biological children	66.5
Unmarried spouses and their biological children	11.6
Blended family	7.6
Single parent family with children	12.2
Parents' educational level	**%**
Nine years of comprehensive school	4.2
A degree from a vocational school or high school	26.1
A bachelor's degree	36.4
A master's degree or higher	33.4

MEASURES

Parental Involvement

Family Involvement Questionnaire (Fantuzzo, Tighe, & Childs, 2000) was used to measure parental involvement in collaboration with the school. The measure originally consisted of 42 items which were translated in Finnish language, and seven of which were included in the First Steps Study questionnaire for parents, based on factor analysis (Lerkkanen et al., 2006). The present study left out two of the seven items to improve the reliability of the two constructed domains: 1) collaboration with the teacher and other parents and 2) participation in parental meetings. The first domain, *collaboration with the teacher and other parents*, consists of three items (e.g., "I talk with other parents about school meetings and events") that were originally part of the school-based involvement domain of the Family Involvement Questionnaire. This domain's reliability was good at all measurement points for both mothers (α = .66 to .71) and fathers (α = .67 to .73). The second domain, *participation in parental meetings*, includes two items (e.g., "I attend conferences with the teacher to talk about my child's learning and behavior") that are part of the home-school conferencing domain of the original inventory. The domain's reliability was good at all measurement points for both mothers (α = .69 to .73) and fathers (α = .78 to.83). Parents rated the items on a scale from one (never) to five (very often).

Parental Trust

Parental trust in their child's teacher was measured with the Trust scale that is part of the larger Family-School Relationships Survey (Adams & Christenson, 2000) which was translated in Finnish language. The Trust scale involves 19 items, of which six that were culturally meaningful in the Finnish context and had the strongest factor loadings (e.g., "Teacher is doing a good job encouraging my child's sense of self-esteem") were used in the First Steps Study (see Lerkkanen et al., 2013). Parents rated the items with a scale from one (strongly disagree) to five (strongly agree). A mean score of the six items was used in the present study as an indicator of parental trust (mothers α = .69 to.73; fathers α = .78 to .83).

DATA ANALYSIS

The data analyses were carried out in the following way. The associations between the study variables were examined with the Pearson correlation using IBM SPSS Statistics 24. As a next step, independent samples *t*-test was used to examine possible differences between mothers and fathers and between parents of boys and parents of girls in their trust in their child's teacher and in their school involvement. All participants (768–1469 mothers and 422–1003 fathers at different measurement points) were included in the *t*-test analysis. Finally, cross-lagged path models were constructed using Mplus version 7 (Muthén & Muthén, 1998–2012) to examine the extent to which parents' trust in the teacher predicts their school involvement during their child's primary school years or vice versa. Sample of 768 mothers and 422 fathers who filled in the questionnaire at every measurement point was included in the cross-lagged path models.

RESULTS

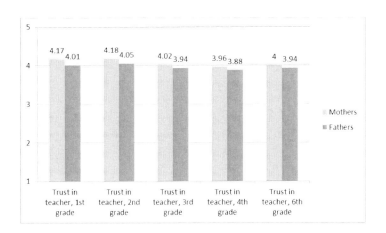

Figure 1. Mothers' and fathers' trust in their child's teacher during primary school, means.

As shown in Figures 1 and 2, parental trust in teacher was relatively high during the child's primary school years, whereas the frequency of collaboration with teacher and other parents was not as high; mothers and fathers rarely collaborated with teacher and other parents. Mothers participated in parental meetings often, and fathers sometimes (see Figure 3). Trust in teacher was correlated with collaboration with teacher and other parents (mothers: r varied between .07, $p \leq .05$ and .21, $p < .001$; fathers: r varied between .11, $p < .01$ and .28, $p < .001$) at every grade level. Parents' trust in the teacher and participation in parental meetings were positively associated at almost every grade level (mothers: r varied between .07,

$p \leq .05$ and .24, $p < .001$; fathers: r varied between .12, $p \leq .05$ and .25, $p < .001$).

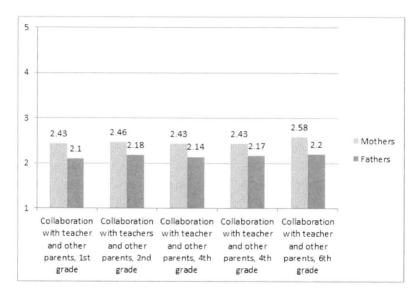

Figure 2. Mothers' and fathers' collaboration with teacher and other parents during primary school, means.

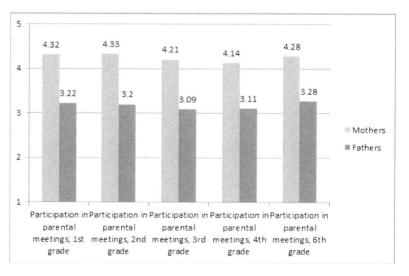

Figure 3. Mothers' and fathers' participation in parental meetings during primary school, means.

DIFFERENCES IN PARENTAL TRUST AND INVOLVEMENT

The results of the *t*-test showed that mothers trusted more in teachers than fathers did across grades 1–4 (*t* varied between 2.47, $p \leq .05$ and 5.57, $p < .001$). There were no significant differences in trust between mothers and fathers in sixth grade. Furthermore, mothers' collaboration with teacher and other parents (*t* = 7.71 – 10.66, $p < .001$) as well as participation in parental meetings (*t* varied between 17.40 and 28.33, $p < .001$) was higher than that of fathers during the primary school years. Parents of boys and parents of girls did not differ in their trust in teacher nor did mothers in their collaboration with teacher and other parents or in participation in parental meetings. However, fathers of boys were more involved in collaboration with teacher and other parents than fathers of girls in fourth grade (*t* = –2.09, $p \leq .05$) and participated in parental meetings more in second (*t* = –3.5, $p < .001$) and fourth grade (*t* = –2.25, $p \leq .05$) than fathers of girls.

CROSS-LAGGED PATHS BETWEEN TRUST AND INVOLVEMENT

Next, cross-lagged path models were specified to examine the associations between mothers' and fathers' trust in teacher and their collaboration with teacher and other parents. The results (Figure 4) showed that mothers' collaboration with teacher and other parents predicted their trust in teacher from third grade to fourth grade and from fourth grade to sixth grade. Moreover, mothers' collaboration with teacher and other parents at second grade predicted their trust in teacher at third grade, albeit marginally significantly. As shown in Figure 5, fathers' trust in their child's teacher predicted their collaboration with teacher and other parents from third grade to fourth grade and from fourth grade to sixth grade. Furthermore, fathers' collaboration with teacher and other parents in first grade predicted their trust in their child's teacher in second grade, albeit marginally significantly. Both mothers' and fathers' trust and collaboration with teacher and other parents were relatively stable during their child's primary school years. The model fit the data well (Byrne, 2012) for both mothers [χ2 (18, n = 768) = 43.637, $p < 0.01$; CFI = .988; RMSEA = .043; SRMR = .024] and fathers [χ2 (18, n = 422) = 28.596, $p = .054$; CFI = .992; RMSEA = .037; SRMR = .024].

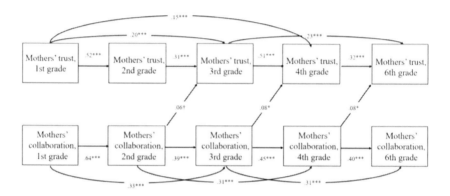

Figure 4. Cross-lagged path model: mothers' trust in their child's teacher and collaboration with the teacher and other parents during primary school. Note: Standardized estimates. Only significant associations are shown.

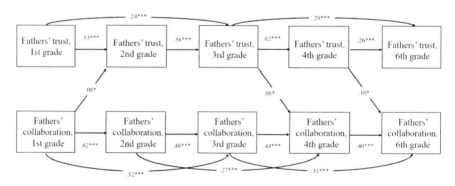

Figure 5. Cross-lagged path model: fathers' trust in their child's teacher and collaboration with the teacher and other parents during primary school. Note: Standardized estimates. Only significant associations are shown.

Second, separate cross-lagged path models were constructed to examine the associations between mothers' and fathers' trust in teacher and participation in parental meetings. As shown in Figure 6, mothers'

Exploring Parent-Teacher Trust and School Involvement 79

participation in parental meetings predicted their trust in their child's teacher from first grade to second grade and from fourth grade to sixth grade.

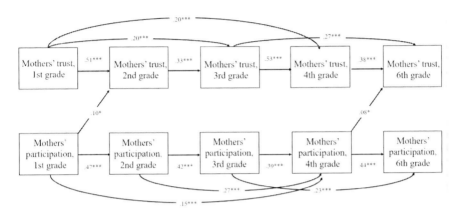

Figure 6. Cross-lagged path model: mothers' trust in their child's teacher and participation in parental meetings during primary school. Note: Standardized estimates. Only significant associations are shown.

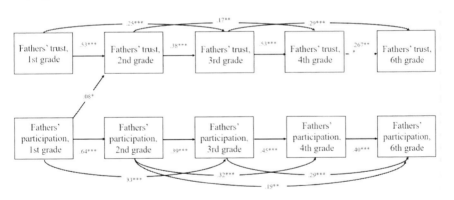

Figure 7. Cross-lagged path model: fathers' trust in their child's teacher and participation in parental meetings during primary school. Note: Standardized estimates. Only significant associations are shown.

Similarly, fathers' participation in parental meetings in first grade predicted their trust in their child's teacher in second grade (see Figure 7). As with trust and collaboration with teacher and other parents, participation in parental meetings was relatively stable for both mothers and fathers during their child's primary school years. The model fit the data well (Byrne,

2012) for both mothers [χ2 (16, n = 768) = 16.484, p = .420; CFI = 1.00; RMSEA = .006; SRMR = .016] and fathers [χ2 (17, n = 422) = 26.123, p = .072; CFI = .992; RMSEA = .036; SRMR = .023].

DISCUSSION

The aim of the present study was to examine how parents' trust in their child's teacher predicts their school involvement and vice versa during their child's primary school years. Moreover, the aim was to study differences between mothers and fathers and between parents of boys and parents of girls in their trust in teacher and school involvement. The results demonstrate how parental trust and involvement change during primary school years and how trust and involvement are related to each other differently for mothers and fathers. The results suggest that parental trust in teacher and school involvement need to be supported differently for mothers and fathers.

Results of the present study showed that in the Finnish school context parental trust in their child's teacher was high in general, even though mothers trusted their child's teacher more than fathers across grades one to four. As shown in previous research (Adams & Christenson, 2000; Kikas, Poikonen, et al., 2011) parents of boys and girls did not differ in their trust in teacher. Earlier studies have shown that parents trust more in teachers who use child-centered teaching practices (Kikas, Lerkkanen, Pakarinen, & Poikonen, 2016; Lerkkanen et al., 2013) and have high personal regard in their profession, students and students' parents (Chang, 2013). Thus, Finnish teachers' high educational level and the high respect for the teaching profession in Finnish society, as has been reported in PISA results (OECD, 2016), might at least partially explain high parent-teacher trust compared to many other countries. Moreover, Finnish teachers' emphasis on child-centered practices in the classroom (Tang et al., 2017) can strengthen parental trust.

Mothers and fathers in this sample reported rarely being in collaboration with teacher and other parents. While mothers participated in parental meetings often, fathers did so only sometimes. Mothers' involvement was higher in all grade levels in terms of both collaboration with teacher and other parents and participation in parental meetings, which indicates that fathers could perhaps benefit from both support for involvement and nontraditional ways of participating. According to Sormunen et al. (2011), discussions with teachers might be easier for mothers than for fathers, which could be one reason for their higher involvement. In Finnish schools, parents do not typically plan school activities together with teacher and for this reason, it is understandable that parents reported participating in parental meetings more than being in collaboration with teacher and other parents. Moreover, the usage of electronic communication systems in schools might have decreased parent-teacher conversations and parents' visits at school. It is important that teachers use language that is easily understandable to all parents and invite all parents to collaborate with them and to participate in parental meetings.

As in the case of trust, mothers of boys and mothers of girls did not differ in their amount of involvement. However, fathers of boys collaborated more with teacher and other parents than fathers of girls did when their child was in fourth grade and participated more in parental meetings when their child was in second and in fourth grade. Fathers may be more concerned about their sons' schooling than about their daughters', or supporting their sons' education may be more natural to fathers, as they understand boys' schooling through their own school experiences. It is also possible that in some families the parents have divided the involvement so that mothers take responsibility for daughters' schooling and fathers for their sons'. Regardless of the reason, it is important to find ways to support fathers of girls in their school involvement.

The associations between parents' trust in teacher and their collaboration with teacher and other parents were different for mothers and fathers during their child's primary school years. Mothers' collaboration with teacher and other parents predicted their subsequent trust in teacher. In contrast, fathers' trust in teacher predicted their subsequent collaboration with teacher and other parents. It is not surprising that trust and collaboration are associated, because earlier research has shown that communication is important in enhancing trust (Adams & Christenson, 2000; Angell, Stoner, & Shelden, 2009; Chang, 2013). Interestingly, the associations were different depending on the gender of the parent. Future research should focus on exploring concrete ways to support and encourage mothers in their collaboration with teacher and other parents, as it predicts their subsequent trust, whereas it would be beneficial to support fathers in their trust in teacher as it predicts their future collaboration with teacher and other parents.

For both mothers and fathers, participation in parental meetings in first grade predicted their trust in their child's teacher in second grade. The association between participation in parental meeting and trust was also statistically significant for mothers from fourth grade to sixth grade. For this reason, it is beneficial to encourage parents to participate in parental meetings, especially in first grade. According to Baker et al. (2016), parents suggest that schools could increase their involvement by providing opportunities for involvement outside working hours and by arranging childcare for siblings. Parents also desire to be welcomed at their child's school, for instance, to visit the classroom during the school day, and to have a clear role in the school.

When schools are aiming at improving parents' trust in teachers or involvement in the school, interventions can be useful. Epstein and Dauber (1991) suggest the following steps when aiming at improving parental involvement: 1) identifying a starting point for parental involvement, 2) determining the aim of parental involvement, 3) deciding the responsibilities of each party in reaching the aim, 4) assessing the results, and 5) continuing the development of parental involvement. Interventions in enhancing parental involvement are especially effective if parents and teachers together pursue to improve communication and involvement (Cox, 2005; Epstein, 1995). Moreover, interventions targeted at improving the child's academic achievement, including parent tutoring in the home, have shown promising results (Fishel & Ramirez, 2005).

This study has some limitations that need to be acknowledged. First, the dropout in the sample from study phase one (grades 1 to 4) to study phase two (grade 6) limited the number of participants included in the cross-lagged path models examining associations between parental trust and involvement during primary school. Second, there were more mothers than fathers participating in the study, which might decrease the generalization of the results. Third, although the associations between parental trust and involvement were statistically significant, the associations were not very strong. For these reasons, more longitudinal research with larger sample sizes including both mothers and fathers is needed.

The present study showed that mothers and fathers differ in their trust and school involvement. Furthermore, fathers of boys and fathers of girls differ in their school involvement. Future research should examine the reasons behind the differences and find concrete ways for teachers and policy makers to support and encourage parents and teachers in building mutual trust and parental school involvement.

CONCLUSION AND SUMMARY OF KEY POINTS

Overall, the study revealed that mothers trusted more in their child's teacher and were more active in their school involvement than fathers. Whereas mothers did not distinguish between the gender of their child when trusting the teacher, the fathers of boys were more involved than fathers of girls in collaboration with teacher and other parents in fourth grade. Moreover, fathers of boys participated in parental meetings more in second and fourth grade than fathers of girls. Furthermore, collaboration with the teacher and other parents predicted mothers' subsequent trust in teacher whereas trust in the teacher predicted fathers' subsequent collaboration. Both mothers' and fathers' participation in parental meetings in first grade predicted their trust in the teachers in later years.

Finally, the study still left us with some questions. What kind of teacher behavior can improve parental trust? How can the teacher encourage parents to collaborate with the teacher and to participate in parental meetings? How can teachers support mothers and fathers differently in their involvement? As a parent, how am I collaborating with teachers and other parents in my school? These questions (and others) open up opportunities for further research that would have a positive outcome generating greater parental involvement of parents in the schooling of their children and subsequently, in the child's academic achievement and success in life.

REFERENCES

Adams, K. S. & Christenson, S. L. (2000). Trust and the family-school relationship examination of parent-teacher differences in elementary and secondary grades. *Journal of School Psychology, 38*, 477–497. doi:10.1016/S0022-4405(00)00048-0.

Adams, K. S. & Christenson, S. L. (1998). Differences in parent and teacher trust lev-els: Implications for creating collaborative family-school relationships. *Special Services in the Schools, 14*, 1–22. https://doi.org/10.1300/J008v14n01_01.

Angell, M. E., Stoner, J. B., & Shelden, D. L. (2009). Trust in education professionals: Perspectives of mothers of children with disabilities. *Remedial and Special Education, 30*, 160–176. doi:10.1177/0741932508315648.

Baker, T. L., Wise, J., Kelley, G., & Skiba, R. J. (2016). Identifying barriers: Creating solutions to improve family engagement. *School Community Journal, 26*, 161–184. doi:10.1177/0044118X11409066.

Beycioglu, K., Ozer, N., & Sahin, S. (2013) Parental trust and parent-school relationships in Turkey. *Journal of School Public Relations, 34*, 306–329.

Bryk, A. S. & Schneider, B. (2003). Trust in schools: A core resource for school reform. *Educational Leadership, 60*, 40–44.

Byrne, B. M. (2012). *Structural equation modeling with Mplus: Basic concepts, applications, and programming.* New York: Routledge.

Chang, H. L. (2013). *Partnership as a product of trust: Parent-teacher relational trust in a low-income urban school* (Doctoral dissertation). Retrieved from ProQuest database.

Cook, K. D., Dearing, E., & Zachrisson, H. D. (2018). Is parent-teacher cooperation in the first year of school associated with children's academic skills and behavioral functioning? *International Journal of Early Childhood, 50,* 211–226. doi:10.1007/s13158-018-0222-z.

Cox, D. D. (2005). Evidence-based interventions using home-school collaboration. *School Psychology Quarterly, 20,* 473–497.

El Nokali, N., Bachman, H. & Votruba-Drzal, E. (2010). Parent involvement and children's academic and social development in elementary school. *Child Development, 81,* 988–1005. doi:10.1111/j.1467-8624.2010.01447.x.

Epstein, J. L. (1995). School/family/community partnerships. *Phi Delta Kappa, 76,* 701–712.

Epstein, J. & Dauber, S. (1991). School programs and teacher practices of parent involvement in inner-city elementary and middle schools. *The Elementary School Journal, 91,* 289–305.

Fantuzzo, J., McWayne, C., Perry, M. & Childs. S. (2004). Multiple dimensions of family involvement and their relations to behavioral and learning competencies for urban, low-income children. *School Psychology Review, 33,* 467–480.

Fantuzzo, J., Tighe, E., & Childs, S., (2000). Family involvement questionnaire: A multivariate assessment of family participation in early childhood education. *Journal of Educational Psychology, 92,* 367–376. doi:10.1037/0022-0663.92.2.367.

Fishel, M. & Ramirez, L. (2005). Evidence-based parent involvement interventions with school-aged children. *School Psychology Quarterly, 20,* 371–402.

Fleischmann, F. & de Haas, A. (2016). Explaining parents' school involvement: The role of ethnicity and gender in the Netherlands. *The Journal of Educational Research, 109,* 554–565. doi:10.1080/00220671.2014.994196.

Forsyth, P., Barnes, L. & Adams, C. (2006). Trust-effectiveness patterns in schools. *Journal of Educational Administration, 44,* 122–141.

Frowe, I. (2005). Professional trust. *British Journal of Educational Studies, 53,* 34–53. doi:10.1111/j.1467-8527.2005.00282.x.

Goddard, R. D., Tschannen-Moran, M., & Hoy, W. K. (2001). A multilevel examination of the distribution and effects of teacher trust in students and parents in urban elementary schools. *The Elementary School Journal, 102*, 3–17. https://www.jstor.org/stable/1002166.

Graham, D. (2015). Patterns of parent involvement: A longitudinal analysis of family–school partnerships in the early years of school in Australia. *Australasian Journal of Early Childhood, 40*, 119–128. doi:10.1177/183693911504000115.

Green, C., Walker, J., Hoover-Dempsey, K. & Sandler, H. (2007). Parent's motivations for involvement in children's education: An empirical test of a theoretical model of parent involvement. *Journal of Educational Psychology, 99*, 532–544. doi:10.1037/0022-0663.99.3.532.

Holtz, M. 2010. *Partnership between myth and reality: Structural asymmetries in parent-teacher relationships* (Doctoral dissertation). Retreived from ProQuest.

Hoy, W. K & Tschannen-Moran, M. (1999). Five faces of trust: An empirical confirmation in urban elementary schools. *Journal of School Leadership, 9*, 184–208.

Hughes, J., & Kwok, O. (2007). Influence of student-teacher and parent-teacher relationships on lower achieving readers' engagement and achievement in the primary grades. *Journal of Educational Psychology, 99*, 39–51.

Hung, C. (2005). Family background, parental involvement and environmental influences on Taiwanese children. *Alberta Journal of Educational Research, 51*, 261–276.

Jeynes, W. (2011). Parental involvement and academic success. New York: Routledge.

Keyes, C. R. (2002). A way of thinking about parent/teacher partnerships for teachers. *International Journal of Early Years Education, 10*, 177–191.

Kikas, E., Lerkkanen, M.-K., Pakarinen, E., & Poikonen, P.-L. (2016). Family- and classroom-related factors and mother–kindergarten teacher trust in Estonia and Finland. *Educational Psychology, 36*, 47–72. doi:10.1080/01443410.2014.895298.

Kikas, E., Peets, K., & Niilo, A. (2011). Assessing Estonian mothers' involvement in their children's education and trust in teachers. *Early*

Child Development and Care, 181, 1079–1094. doi:10.1080/03004430. 2010.513435.

Kikas, E., Poikonen, P.-L., Kontoniemi, M., Lyyra, A.-L., Lerkkanen, M.-K., & Niilo, A. (2011). Mutual trust between kindergarten teachers and mothers and its associations with family characteristics in Estonia and Finland. *Scandinavian Journal of Educational Research, 55*, 23–37. doi:10.1080/00313831.2011.539852.

Knopf, H.T. & Swick, K.J. (2008). Using our understanding of families to strengthen family involvement. *Early Childhood Education Journal, 35*, 419–427. https://doi.org/10.1007/s10643-007-0198-z.

Lerkkanen, M.-K., Kikas, E., Pakarinen, E., Poikonen, P.-L., & Nurmi, J.-E. (2013). Mothers' trust in teachers in relation to teaching practices. *Early Childhood Research Quarterly, 28*, 153–165. doi:10.1016/j.ecresq. 2012.04.005.

Lerkkanen, M.-K., Niemi, P., Poikkeus, A. -M., Poskiparta, M., Siekkinen, M., & Nurmi, J.-E. (2006). The first steps study [Alkuportaat]. Unpublished data, Consortium between the University of Jyväskylä, University of Turku, and University of Eastern Finland, Finland.

Mahalik, J. R., Locke, B. D., Ludlow, L. H., Diemer, M. A., Scott, R. P. J., Gottfried, M., & Freitas, G. (2003). Development of the Conformity to Masculine Norms Inventory. *Psychology of Men & Masculinity, 4*, 3–25. http://dx.doi.org/10.1037/1524-9220.4.1.3.

McWayne, C., Campos, R., & Owsianik, M. (2008). A multidimensional, multilevel examination of mother and father involvement among culturally diverse Head Start families. *Journal of School Psychology, 46*, 551–573. doi:10.1016/j.jsp.2004.08.002.

Mo, Y. & Singh, K. (2008) Parents' Relationships and Involvement: Effects on Students' School Engagement and Performance. *RMLE Online, 31*, 1-11, DOI: 10.1080/19404476.2008.11462053.

Murray, E., McFarland-Piazza, L. & Harrison, L. J. (2015) Changing patterns of parent-teacher communication and parent involvement from preschool to school. *Early Child Development and Care, 185*, 1031–1052. doi:10.1080/03004430.2014.975223.

Muthén, L. K., & Muthén, B. O. (1998–2012). Mplus users guide and Mplus version 7.0. Retrieved from http://www.statmodel.com/index.shtml.
OECD. (2016). PISA 2015 Results: Excellence and Equity in Education (Volume I). PISA, OECD Publishing. https://www.oecd.org/education/pisa-2015-results-volume-i-9789264266490-en.htm.
Pennycuff, L. L. (2009). *The impact of the academic component of response to intervention on collective efficacy, parents' trust in schools, referrals for special education, and student achievement* (Doctoral dissertation). Retrieved from ProQuest database.
Powell, D. R., Son, S.-H., File, N., & San Juan, R. R. (2010). Parent-school relationships and children's academic and social outcomes in public school pre-kindergarten. *Journal of School Psychology, 48,* 269–292.
Russel, A. & Saebel, J. (1997). Mother–Son, Mother–Daughter, Father–Son, and Father–Daughter: Are They Distinct Relationships? *Developmental Review, 17,* 111–147. https://doi.org/10.1006/drev.1996.0431.
Räty, H., Kasanen, K. & Laine, N. (2009). Parents' participation in their child's schooling. *Scandinavian Journal of Educational Research, 53,* 277–293. doi:10.1080/00313830902917352.
Rempel, J. K., Holmes, J. G., & Zanna, M. P. (1985). Trust in close relationships. *Journal of Personality and Social Psychology, 49,* 95–112.
Santiago, R. T., Garbacz, A., Beattie, T., & Moore, C. L. (2016). Parent-teacher relationships in elementary school: An examination of parent-teacher trust. *Psychology in the Schools, 53,* 1003–1017. doi:10.1002/pits.21971.
Sebastian, J., Moon, J.-M., & Cunningham, M. (2017). The relationship of school-based parental involvement with student achievement: A comparison of principal and parent survey reports from PISA 2012. *Educational Studies, 43,* 123–146. doi:10.1080/03055698.2016.1248900.
Serpell, Z. N. & Mashburn, A. J. (2011). Family-school connectedness and children's early social development. *Social Development, 21,* 21–46. doi:10.1111/j.1467-9507.2011.00623.x.

Sormunen, M., Tossavainen, K., & Turunen, H. (2011). Home-school collaboration in the view of fourth grade pupils, parents, teachers, and principals in the Finnish education system. *School Community Journal, 21,* 185–211.

Tang, X., Kikas, E., Pakarinen, E., Lerkkanen, M.-K., Muotka, J., & Nurmi, J.-E. (2017). Profiles of teaching practices and reading skills at the first and third grade in Finland and Estonia. *Teaching and Teacher Education, 64,* 150–161. doi:10.1016/j.tate.2017.01.020.

Tolman, D. L., & Porche, M. V. (2000). The Adolescent Femininity Ideology Scale: Development and validation of a new measure for girls. *Psychology of Women Quarterly, 24,* 365–376. http://dx.doi.org/10.1111/j.1471-6402.2000.tb00219.x.

Tschannen-Moran, M. (2001). Collaboration and the need for trust. *Journal of Educational Administration, 39,* 308–331. doi:10.1108/EUM0000000005493.

Vera, E. M., Heineke, A., Carr, A. L., Camacho, D., Israel, M. S., Goldberger, N., Clawson, A., & Hill, M. (2017). Latino parents of English learners in Catholic schools: Home vs. school based educational involvement. *Journal of Catholic Education, 20.* doi:10.15365/joce.2002012017.

Von Otter, C. (2014). Family resources and mid-life level of education: a longitudinal study of the mediating influence of childhood parental involvement. *British Educational Research Journal, 40,* 555–574. doi:10.1002/berj.3111.

In: Parental Involvement
Editors: Nurit Kaplan Toren et al.
ISBN: 978-1-53616-828-0
© 2020 Nova Science Publishers, Inc.

Chapter 4

PROCESSES AND PATHWAYS OF PARENTAL INVOLVEMENT IN EDUCATION IN ISRAEL

Nurit Kaplan Toren[*] *and Revathy Kumar*
University of Haifa, Haifa, Israel;
Oranim Academic College of Education, Tivon, Israel
and University of Toledo, Toledo, Ohio, US

ABSTRACT

Israel is a multicultural-multi-ethnic society that, for substantial periods in its history, was characterized by massive waves of immigration. Within this context, the present chapter has three goals: (a) to discuss the various attitudes regarding parental involvement in education from the points of view of parents, teachers, principals, and policymakers, (b) to describe the development and forms of parental involvement in education, and (c) to point out cultural differences in parental involvement in education. In the last 70 years, since the establishment of the State of Israel, parental involvement in education has taken on different forms and meanings, reflecting significant changes in society. This chapter sheds light on the effects of changes in the Israeli society on parent-teacher

---

[*] Corresponding Author's Email: ntoren@edu.haifa.ac.il.

relationships and on the different forms of parental involvement. Findings attest to the differences between parents' and teachers', principals' and policymakers' perceptions and point on the imperative need for clear definition of the term parental involvement and to distinguish between home-based and school-based parental involvement. Finally, differences in parental involvement based on cultural diversity were examined as reflected by Arabs' and Jews' parents' reports and adolescents' perceptions and its links to adolescents' self-evaluation as well as academic achievement.

Keywords: cultural differences, home-based and school-based, parental involvement

INTRODUCTION

In the last decades, parental involvement in the education of their children has been regarded as an important element of effective education. There is a clear gap, however, between the high estimates of parental involvement reported in the literature and in official documents, and parents' actual involvement practices. Studies have revealed a variety of factors affecting parents' involvement in education: parent and family factors (e.g., living conditions and parents' beliefs about parental involvement); child-related factors (e.g., gender, age, level of school); factors relating to the parent-teacher relationship (e.g., focusing on differing agendas, attitudes, and language used); and societal factors (e.g., historical and demographic, political, and economic issues) (Eccles & Harold, 1996; Green, Walker, Hoover-Dempsey, & Sandler, 2007; Hornby & Lafaele, 2011). Understanding of the obstacles to parental involvement is a necessary precursor to developing more effective parental involvement in education. Therefore, one of the objectives of this chapter is to shed light on the complexity of parental involvement in education in Israel, and on the challenges it presents.

DIFFERENCES IN THE ATTITUDES OF POLICYMAKERS, PRINCIPALS, TEACHERS, AND PARENTS TOWARD PARENTAL INVOLVEMENT

The first official document of the Ministry of Education in Israel discussing the importance of teacher-parent relationships published in 1996, reflects the changes experienced by Israeli society. These changes followed economic and welfare policies, and social changes that transferred more power and authority from the government to schools, parents and the communities. Moreover, many of the parents held advanced academic degrees and, having contributed financially to school activities, placed more demands on schools in return (Fisher, 2009). Nonetheless, policymakers' attitudes toward parental involvement in education in Israel is characterized by inconsistency, as reflected in recent contradictory messages conveyed by policies of the Ministry of Education. On one hand, the Ministry of Education supports and encourages parental involvement in two main ways: through workshops and instruction for parents, such as parental guidance for safe online surfing, and by inviting parents to use school websites, for example, to monitor their children's grades. On the other hand, there is an attempt by the Ministry of Education to set boundaries, and there is hesitation regarding parental involvement. Indications of setting boundaries can be found in the last Ministry of Education official document, titled "Parental representations at school and kindergarten," from September 2018 (Ministry of Education CEO, 2018). This is the sixth attempt to define the framework for cooperation between schools and parent representatives.

Two issues aroused parents' bitterness in this document: (a) the statement that the establishment of a parent representation is a privilege and not a duty of the education system, and (b) the demand that the elections for the parents' representatives be held in the presence of the school principal. In recent years, we have also seen social protests that have led to changes in the education system. For example, in 2015, in response to parents' demand to reduce the number of first-grade students in the classroom, the Minister of Education led a reform referred to as the "Sardines law," which reduced the number of students per classroom to a maximum of 34. That same year, the government decreed free public education from age three (instead of four) in kindergartens. Last year, the Minister of Education initiated a program to shorten school vacations by 10 days for children from kindergarten to third grade (TheMarker, Jun, 2017).

These inconsistent approaches toward parents' involvement in the education system is reflected also in discrepancies between the rhetoric about parental involvement and the prevalent attitudes and practices found in schools in this matter. These attitudes and practices have been reinforced by findings of two surveys supported by the Ministry of Education and conducted over the past three years. The first one was a survey conducted by Addi-Raccah and Greenstein (2016) of 492 teachers and 837 parents. Most of the parents and the teachers, both Jews and Arabs, were women from the central parts of Israel, and about 20% were from the peripheral areas. Participants were parents and teachers from elementary, junior high, and high school. Disparities between parents and teachers on three issues stood out: parent-teacher communication patterns, responsibility for the students, and the quality of parent-teacher relationships (Addi-Raccah & Greenstein, 2016). Findings show that while parents perceived themselves as those who initiate contacts with the school (43.8%), teachers perceived parents as more passive. In examining the responsibility for the students' educational and social aspects, teachers and parents agreed that parents were responsible for taking care of the children's special needs and making sure that the children arrive at school on time and with the equipment they needed. But teachers believed that they were responsible for reporting on the students' educational and social aspects, and shared responsibility with parents only with regard to the child's emotional aspects. Whereas parents considered homework to be the joint responsibility of parents and teachers, teachers thought that it was their responsibility only. Parents considered it their responsibility, more than did teachers, to report on child's social status (93% vs. 77%). Regarding the patterns of parent-teacher relationships, parents reported more positive relationships than did teachers (mean of 3.56 vs. 3.35, on a scale of 1=very low to 5=very high). Teachers focused on negative parent-teacher relationships, reflected in conflict and feelings of threat to the teaching profession, more so than did parents (mean of 2.39 vs. 2.10, on a scale from 1=very low to 5=very high). As noted above, parents perceived themselves as partners in the responsibility for the education of their children and had positive attitudes toward the parent-teacher relationship, but teachers did not perceive the parents as partners. These findings attest to the perceived differences between parents and teachers with regard to the child's academic and social-emotional development.

The second survey was conducted by Avital and Raz (2018); it included 1,043 principals, 7,715 teachers, and 1,042 parents. According to principals' reports, the primary purpose of school-parent relationship is to inform the parents about their children's situation in the school (83%), share with parents what is happening in the school (over 91%), and provide emotional support (93%), but not for parents to become involved in school-related activities, such as pedagogical decision making. In another words, principals expected a passive partnership on the part of parents. At the same time, principals' and teachers' satisfaction with their work is related to the nature of their relationship with parents. The findings of these studies revealed that when parents are more involved in school activities, and are in ongoing contact with the school, principals' and teachers' satisfaction increases. When principals believe that the parents are interfering in schoolwork (e.g., curriculum design and policy making in the school context), however, their satisfaction decreases. Parental satisfaction, on the other hand, was affected by four factors: the nature of student-teacher relationship, teaching strategies, school efforts to prevent violence, and their child's academic achievements.

In sum, principals and teachers expected passive parent-school relationships, whereas parents held more child-centred approaches, focusing on the child's wellbeing more generally. Similar studies in Finland and Estonia showed that mothers in both countries trusted teachers more if they who were characterized by higher levels of child-centred teaching practices, which were found to enhance social competence and to produce a higher level of satisfaction and more positive self-evaluation in students (Lerkkanen, Kikas, Pakarinen, Poikonen, & Nurmi, 2013). These discrepancies between the parents and the school are reflected also in the nature of the parent-teacher trust relationship, which is defined as the belief that members of the other party meet their role expectations (e.g., the role of teacher or parent) and are open, honest, benevolent, and reliable (Adams & Christenson, 2000; Adams, Forsyth, & Mitchell, 2009).

In a recent study conducted focusing on parent-teacher trust relationships in junior high school, parents (N=226) and teachers (N=39) completed a parallel form of a trust survey (Adams & Christenson, 2000). Parents and teachers rated 17 items (on 4-point Likert scale) that began with the sentence stem "I am confident that teachers…" or "I am confident that parents…" followed by different statements that reflected a variety of behaviours often performed by parents or teachers to enhance students' academic performance. Factor analysis for the trust scale revealed two factors: (a) predictability that the others (parents or teachers) perform their duties toward the child (e.g., "I am confident that teachers are doing a good job teaching my child academic subjects," or "I am confident that parents help their child resolve conflicts with peers") and (b) the others (parents or teachers) deserve respect (e.g., "I am confident that teachers are receptive to my input and suggestions," and "I am confident that parents are worthy of my respect"). The t-tests analysis for independent samples (teachers and parents) revealed significant differences. Parents scored higher than teachers on both dimensions of trust: 1) parents/teachers perform their duties toward the child [t (257)= -6.28 p<.001) with parents scoring higher (M=3.21, SD=.55) than teachers (M=2.61, SD= .48); and 2) parents/teachers deserve respect [t (257)= -2.62 p<.001) again with parents scoring higher (M=3.22, SD=.66) than teachers (M=2.88, SD= .66). The findings revealed significant differences between parents' and teachers' sense of trust in the other party with parents showing significantly higher levels of trust in teachers than vice versa (Kaplan Toren, 2017).

Trust, mutual respect, and commitment are the essential foundations for partnership between school, teachers, and parents. To nurture trust relations, however, parents and teachers need to share values and expectations about supporting the child (Christenson, 2004). The findings of the above surveys reflect the discrepancy between teachers and parents in their expectations regarding parental involvement and in their degrees of mutual trust.

Nevertheless, teacher-parent relationships depend on cultural differences. In a study exploring teacher-family relationships among diverse families (i.e., African-American, Latino and white), Nzinga-Johnson, Baker, and Aupperlee (2009) suggest that both parents' and teachers' perceived relationships affect teachers' reports of parental involvement regardless of parents' racial and socioeconomic factors. However, teachers reported that African-American and Latino parents as well as parents with low level of education were less involved in school than white parents and parents with high level of education. In Asian societies teacher-parent relationships described as a hierarchical. Asian parents are reticent to engage interactively with the school because teachers are perceived as experts and parents feel compelled to avoid criticizing teachers, or even asking for more information about their children (Van Schalkwyk, 2017).

DISTINCTION BETWEEN SCHOOL-BASED AND HOME-BASED PARENTAL INVOLVEMENT

It is difficult to find an in-depth discussion of a clear and systematic policy regarding the extent and status of parental involvement in education. To conduct such a discussion, a clear definition of parental involvement is needed. Parents' educational involvement is conceptualized as a multidimensional construct that includes parental educational aspirations, future plans for their children, educational decision making, support with school work, parental knowledge, and parental participation in the school operations (Kerr, Stattin, & Burk, 2010; Ule, Zivoder, & Du Bois-Reymond, 2015). In the literature, parental involvement practices are grouped along two dimensions. The first is home-based parental involvement, which involves practices such as listening to their children reading or supervision of homework (Hornby & Lafaele, 2011), fostering educational and occupational aspirations, discussing learning strategies with the children, preparing and planning for the future (Hill & Tyson, 2009), and emotional support (Kaplan Toren & Seginer, 2015). The second dimension refers to school-based parental involvement, which includes practices focused on parent-school communication (e.g., attending parent education workshops and parent-teacher meetings), volunteering at school, and involvement in school governance (Epstein & Sanders, 2002; Kaplan Toren, 2013). Research on parents' educational involvement in Israel has focused mainly on the relations between schools and parents, that is, school-based parental involvement (Fisher & Friedman, 2009; Rosenblatt & Peled, 2003; Shapira-Lishchinsky & Zabalbsky, 2019), and only to a lesser extent on home-based involvement, or on the differential effects of the two types of parental involvement on child's self-evaluation and academic achievement (Seginer, 1986; Seginer, 2006; Kaplan Toren, 2018).

In the last two decades, research in Israel focusing on Arab and Jewish parents and adolescents has revealed a fundamental distinction between home-based and school-based parental involvement (Kaplan Toren, 2004, 2013; Kaplan Toren & Seginer, 2015). The first three studies conducted on Jewish junior high school students and their parents revealed two correlated factors: *home-based* pertains to the parents' daily educational involvement activities at home (e.g., cognitive help, emotional and motivational support) and to parental knowledge; *school-based* pertains to communication with the school, including situations in which a problem involving the child arises, and volunteering to assist in the educational activities of the school (e.g., giving a lecture on a parent's hobby or any other topic). Parental knowledge refers to parents' awareness of their adolescents' academic and social activities and experiences in school (e.g., Kerr, Stattin & Burk 2010; Walters, 2019). During adolescence parents are dependent on adolescents' willingness to share information with them regarding their school related activities. Recently, in a confirmatory factor analysis (CFA) of Arab and Jewish adolescents' perceptions of parental involvement in education on the variance matrices for Parental Involvement Questionnaire (Seginer, 2002; Kaplan Toren, 2013) showed good measures of model fit (Figure 1). These findings underline the importance of the distinction between home-based and school-based involvement across cultures, as the first- and second-order

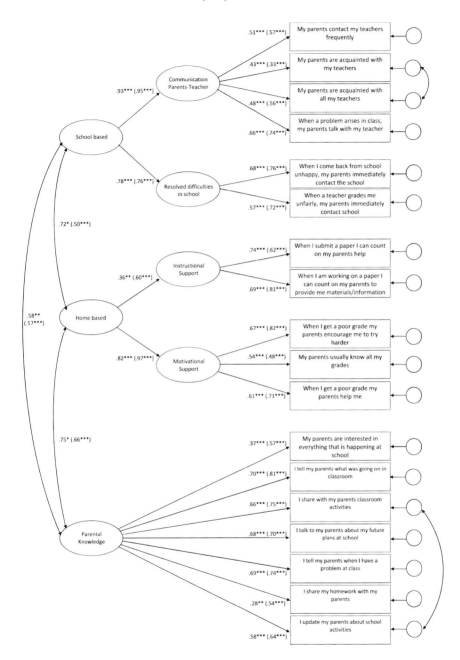

Figure 1. Arab's and Jews' Adolescents Perceptions of Parental Involvement Second order factor analysis; (Jews were marked in brackets).

factor structures do not vary across the Arab and Jewish subsamples (CFI = .90, RMSEA = .06). The three second-order parental involvement factors included school-based involvement, home-based involvement, and parental knowledge. School-based involvement included two first-order factors: parent-teacher communication (3 items) and parent involvement in resolving school-related problems (2 items). Home-based involvement also included two first-order factors: instructional support (3 items) and motivational support (2 items), and parental knowledge emerged as a first-order 7-item factor.

Similarly, in all my research of adolescent boys and girls in Israel, home-based parental involvement was positively related to the adolescents' self-evaluation, which in turn, was linked to academic achievement. Both Israeli and US findings distinguish between home-based and school-based parental involvement and report positive links between home-based parental involvement and adolescents' functioning in school. Education policymakers, educators, teachers, and parents should pay attention to the different contributions of each dimension of parental involvement and strive to improve home-based parental involvement practices.

CULTURAL DIFFERENCES IN ISRAEL: ARAB AND JEWISH PARENTAL INVOLVEMENT

Israel is a multicultural-multi-ethnic society. Its young population of school age youth consists of 70.5% Jews (religious and secular), 23.4% Muslims, 1.6% Christians, 1.7% Druze, and 2.8% others (Berman, 2014). In Israel, Arabs and Jews learn in different school systems, with 75% of all children enrolled in Jewish schools and 25% (i.e., Muslims, Christians, Druze, and Bedouins) in Arab schools.

The segregated schools reflect different cultural traditions and provide instruction in their respective languages, Arabic in Arab schools and Hebrew in Jewish schools. Culturally, Arabs—both Christians and Muslims—follow more collectivistic practices, whereas Jews adhere to more individualistic practices (Flum & Cinamon, 2006). Arab parents, especially males are more authoritarian (Dwairy, Achoui, Abouserie, Farah, Sakhleh, & Khan, 2006) while Jewish parents are more authoritative (Mayseless & Salomon, 2003) in their parenting practices.

The educational values and socioeconomic status of the two groups also deserve consideration (Kaplan Toren, 2017). Although the overall educational level of Jewish parents is higher than that of Arab parents, in the past decades the educational level of Arabs in Israel has increased dramatically (Al-Haj, 2003). Israeli-Arabs value education highly and seek to avail themselves of educational opportunities to enhance their socioeconomic status (Seginer & Vermulst, 2002). Because cultural, demographic, and economic issues determine the type of parental involvement (Eccles & Harold, 1996; Lee & Bowen, 2006; Green, Walker, Hoover-Dempsey, & Sandler, 2007), we therefore should account for the different group membership of Arabs and Jews when studying parental involvement in Israel. In both school systems, Arab and Jewish parents are equally committed to being involved in their adolescents' education (Lavenda, 2011).

Harel-Fisch, Walsh, Steinmetz, Lubel, Reis, Tessler, and Habib (2014) found that both Arab and Jewish parents showed willingness to help resolve their children's school-related problems, help with homework, and visit their children's school, if required. But the nature of involvement is likely to differ in the two cultural groups (Lopez, Scribner, & Mahitivanichcha, 2001). For example, research suggests that Jewish parents participated voluntarily and actively in school-based activities, whereas Arab parents generally waited to be invited by school personnel to participate in school-based activities (Lavenda, 2011). Avital and Raz (2018) found that Arab parents reported a higher level of teacher-parent consultation about ways to promote student learning than did Jewish parents (79% vs. 50%), whereas Jewish parents reported a higher level of feeling that they have someone to talk to at school than did Arab parents (97% vs. 83%).

Consistent with these findings, we looked at the different variables of parental educational involvement in the Arab and Jewish groups (Kaplan Toren & Kumar, 2015). The research questions were: (a) What are the differences between Arabs and Jews concerning parental involvement? and (b) What matter more: home-based, school-based, or parental knowledge? In other words, which of the three dimensions of parents' educational involvement is a better predictor of adolescents' functioning in school among Arabs and Jews?

The Arab sample was derived from three schools located in a large city in northern Israel, where Arabs constitute 10% of the population (Israeli Central Bureau of Statistics). The Jewish sample was derived from 5 urban schools located in central and northern Israel. Cross-sectional data were collected from 604 8th-grade adolescents (Arabs = 125; Jewish =479; female = 47%). The sample included 257 parents (Arabs = 62; Jews =195; mothers = 70%). Both adolescents and their parents completed parallel Parents Involvement questionnaires (Seginer, 2002; Kaplan Toren, 2013), and adolescents completed also the Perceived Competence Scale for Adolescents (Harter, 1982). This measure included two 6-item subscales: Global self-worth and scholastic competence.

In response to the first question about the differences between Arabs and Jews concerning parental involvement, we conducted comparative t-test analysis between Arab and Jewish groups of measures concerning parental involvement. The tests revealed that Arab parents reported being more involved in school than were Jewish parents [t (257)= -3.87 p<.001), Arabs parents scored higher (M=4.02, SD=.98) than Jewish parents (M=3.63, SD= .88), and were perceived as such by their adolescent children[t (604)= -5.60 p<.001), Arabs adolescents perceived their parents higher in school-based parental involvement (M=3.70, SD=.87) than Jewish adolescents perceived their parents (M=3.27, SD= .85); by contrast, Jewish parents reported being more involved educationally at home than were Arab parents [t (257)= 3.52 p<.001), Jewish parents scored higher (M=4.14, SD=.77) than Arabs parents (M=3.82, SD= .85), and were perceived as such by their adolescent children [t (604)= 11.03 p<.001), Jewish adolescents perceived their parents home-based parental involvement higher (M=3.81, SD=1.13) than Arabs adolescents (M=2.67, SD= 1.30). Explanations for this difference may be based partially on the structure of schools in Israel. As noted above, Arab and Jewish adolescents in Israel study in two different systems, each system reflecting its own community values and culture. Therefore, Arabs parents' high level of school-based involvement reflects their positive perception of the invitation for involvement they receive from school (Lavenda, 2011). Another likely explanation is that these findings reflect cultural differences in valued parenting styles.

In Arab society, there is an expectation from children to obey their parents and fulfil their expectations. This may lead to a distance between the generations, which explains why Arabs parents feel less welcomed by their adolescents to become involved in their school life at home. By contrast, in Jewish society, relationships between parents and adolescents are more democratic, therefore, Jewish adolescents may be more willing to involve their parents in their activities at home and at school.

In response to the second question, about the type of knowledge (home-based, school-based, or parental knowledge) that matters most, we conducted a cluster analysis. Our objective was to examine the relationships between adolescents' perceptions of different types of parents' educational involvement and their self-evaluation (global self-worth, scholastic competence).

Cluster analysis for Arab and Jewish adolescents revealed three clusters based on the adolescents' perception of home- and school-based educational involvement and parental knowledge: high (35%), medium, (43%), and low (22%). To examine the relationships between adolescents' perceptions of different types of parents' educational involvement and their self-evaluation (global self-worth, scholastic competence) two MANOVAs (cluster membership × gender) were conducted for Arabs and Jews separately.

The MANOVA analysis for the Arab sample revealed a significant main effect for cluster membership ($F(6, 236) = 2.15$, $p<.05$) and a significant gender × cluster-membership interaction ($F(6, 236) = 2.60$, $p=.02$) for Arab adolescents' scholastic competence and global self-worth. Follow-up Bonferroni post hoc analyses revealed that, on average, cluster 1 members were significantly more scholastically competent than cluster 3 members (Table 1). Cluster 1 members also had significantly higher average global

Table 1. ANOVA main and interactive effects of parents' educational involvement clusters, group membership, and gender on adolescents' scholastic competence, self-esteem, and academic achievement (GPA)

Students' function	Cluster 1 Girls $n=25$	Cluster 1 Boys $n=18$	Cluster 2 Girls $n=32$	Cluster 2 Boys $n=23$	Cluster 3 Girls $n=13$	Cluster 3 Boys $n=14$	Girls (all) $n=70$	Boys (all) $n=55$	Cluster 1 (all) $n=43$	Cluster 2 (all) $n=55$	Cluster 3 (all) $n=27$	F Gender	F Cluster	F Interact
Arab sample (n = 125)														
Scholastic competence	3.23 (.45)	3.10 (.60)	3.03 (.49)	2.86 (.61)	2.46 (.50)	3.03 (.68)	2.91 (.07)	3.00 (.07)	3.16 (.08)	2.94 (.07)	2.74 (.10)	.76	4.96**	4.62**
Global self-worth	3.35 (.56)	3.03 (.57)	2.98 (.53)	2.91 (.60)	2.68 (.91)	3.07 (.46)	2.97 (.07)	3.01 (.08)	3.21 (.09)	2.90 (.08)	2.87 (.11)	.12	3.80*	2.60
Academic achievement	73.32 (16.86)	71.88 (16.56)	69.45 (17.54)	68.92 (14.94)	69.69 (17.04)	63.14 (14.98)	70.82 (2.11)	67.98 (2.26)	72.60 (2.54)	69.19 (2.25)	66.41 (3.17)	.83	1.20	.31
Jewish sample (n = 479)	$n=112$	$n=61$	$n=81$	$n=117$	$n=38$	$n=70$	$n=231$	$n=248$	$n=173$	$n=198$	$n=108$			
Scholastic competence	2.95 (.61)	3.09 (.59)	2.83 (.50)	2.91 (.53)	2.52 (.62)	2.84 (.55)	2.76 (.04)	2.93 (.037)	3.02 (.04)	2.87 (.04)	2.68 (.05)	11.01***	10.63***	1.47
Global self-worth	3.16 (.55)	3.21 (.45)	3.02 (.49)	3.15 (.49)	2.59 (.63)	3.03 (.48)	2.92 (.03)	3.13 (.03)	3.19 (.04)	3.09 (.03)	2.81 (.05)	17.32***	16.53***	4.67**
Academic achievement	78.53 (10.67)	74.30 (12.70)	78.98 (9.14)	74.54 (11.00)	76.90 (12.03)	74.88 (10.45)	78.14 (.79)	74.58 (.71)	76.42 (.86)	76.76 (.78)	75.89 (1.09)	11.12***	.21	.44

*p < .05, **p < .01, ***p < .00.

Note: Cluster 1 = high level of parents' educational involvement; Cluster 2 = medium level of parents' educational involvement; Cluster 3 = low level of parents' educational involvement.

self-worth than did cluster 2 members. Regarding the interaction effect, the average scholastic competence for cluster 3 Arab girls was significantly lower than that of Arab girls in clusters 1 and 2. Similar MANOVA analysis for the Jewish sample revealed significant main effects for cluster membership (F(6, 944) =6.73, p<.001) and gender (F (3, 471) =13.65, p<.001). Similarly to the Arab sample, follow-up Bonferroni post hoc analysis revealed that Jewish adolescents in cluster 1 were overall significantly more scholastically competent than their counterparts in cluster 3. Unlike the Arab sample, in the Jewish sample, both cluster 1 and cluster 2 members had significantly higher average global self-worth than did cluster 3 members. Regarding the main effects of gender on Jewish adolescents' outcomes, boys were, on average, significantly higher on scholastic competence and global self-worth than were girls, although girls had higher average academic achievement. There was also an interaction effect between the cluster membership and gender for the Jewish sample (F(6, 940) =3.23, p=.02). Although cluster membership did not make a significant difference on any of the outcomes for boys, global self-worth of cluster 3 Jewish girls was significantly lower, on average, than it was for cluster 1 Jewish girls.

Finally, based on cluster analysis results, it was found that in both cultural groups, a high level of parental educational involvement has a beneficial effect on adolescents' scholastic competence and their global self-worth. The results demonstrate that cultural differences in Arab and Jewish parents emphasise involvement at home and at school notwithstanding higher levels of involvement both at home and in school, and adolescents sharing information regarding school and schoolwork (parental knowledge) are important for adolescents' academic and psychological wellbeing. All parents, regardless of group membership, need to become involved in all aspects of their children's education, and just as important, pay closer attention to how their behaviours are perceived by their adolescent children.

CONCLUSION

This chapter opens a window to the processes taking place in Israel among Arabs and Jews regarding parental involvement in the education of their children. It also provides an opportunity for stakeholders (principals, teachers, parents, and students) to voice their opinions about the role and importance of parental involvement. There is broad consensus about the important influence of the school-parent relationship for students and for the school at large (Epstein, 2001). However, there is still lack of clarity of the term "parental involvement," as well as the different definitions of parental responsibility and parent-teacher relationship by various stakeholders. The findings underline three main insights. The first one concerns the gap between the stakeholders' perceptions. According to the data presented in this chapter, parents wish to be proactive in initiating contact with the school and share the responsibility for their children, but teachers perceived parents as passive in teacher-parent relationships, and not as proper or relevant partners in the educational process. Overall, parents showed a higher level of trust in teachers than teachers showed in parents.

Furthermore, studies confirmed that there is a discrepancy in parents', principals', teachers', and adolescents' perceptions of responsibility and parental involvement. For example, in a study that explores the language of the three key stakeholders (parents, teachers, and students) with respect to responsibility for student success and failure, teachers and parents focused mostly on the importance of the student-teacher relationships, whereas students (13-15 years old) placed the responsibility primarily on themselves and on their own effort (Peterson, Rubie-Davies, Elley-Brown, Widdowson, Dixon, & Irving, 2011). Recently, a study conducted in Israel found negative correlations between principals' and teachers' perceptions of school-based parental involvement and students' perceptions of their parents' involvement (Zabalbsky & Shapira-Lishchinsky, 2019).

Given the disparity between parents' and teachers' attitudes regarding parental involvement, schools should nurture a positive environment, conducive to parental involvement (Bailey, 2017). Schools and teachers play an important role in inviting parents to be more involved in their children's education (Green, Walker, Hoover-Dempsey, & Sandler, 2007). Therefore, schools are expected to reshape the school-community relationship by empowering both parents and teachers (Addi-Raccah & Ainhoren, 2009). To this end, four steps are recommended:

1) Knowledge and awareness. Teachers need to deepen their knowledge about parental involvement and the contributions parents could make to students, teachers, and schools. That will help educators to view the family as partner with the school in children's education and development (Epstein, 2010). Moreover, teachers and principals need to modify their attitudes toward parents and learn how to work with them in efficient ways.
2) Communication. Schools and teachers should improve and broaden communication channels for developing parent-teacher dialogue.
3) Empowering. Teacher-parent dialogue should be conducted in an equitable way. Both teachers and parents need to feel that they can contribute to the school and express their opinions (Addi-Raccah & Ainhoren, 2009). Therefore, parents should be encouraged to learn how to take action and play a constructive part in school and at home in their child's education.
4) Congruence of expectations. Agreement in the expectations of various groups has important implications for teacher-parent partnership and parental involvement. Yet, the present chapter revealed a mismatch between teachers' and parents' expectations, therefore teachers and parents should discuss the expectation and priorities of both partners (Epstein, 2010). This will make it possible for them to understand the other side and will raise their awareness of the differences and similarities between them. Willingness to conduct a dialogue and awareness of the other's point of view are the key to reducing the gaps between parents and teachers. Teachers and parents should ask themselves how they can work together to promote the educational experiences and the performance of students (Christenson, 2004).

Preparing teachers to work with parents, teacher training should provide tools for communicating with parents and strategies for engaging parents and strengthening parental involvement. It should offer hands-on training opportunities, such as simulated parent-teacher conferences (Walker & Dotger, 2012), using parent stories (Broomhead, 2013), role-playing (Mehling & Shumow, 2013), or experiential learning (Kaplan Toren & Buchholz Holland, in press) designed to address the challenges of parent-teacher relationships.

The second insight concerns the need for a clear definition of parental involvement. There are different ways of conceptualizing parental involvement. The findings of the present study support the distinction between home-based and school-based parental involvement and its links to adolescents' academic and social-emotional functioning. Epstein (2008) outlined various ways in which parents can participate in school activities (e.g., establishing a home environment that supports teaching and learning, and enhancing effective communication between school and home). Schools, teachers, and parents can choose the form that is most appropriate for them, but the definition should be accepted by all partners. Generally, schools experience various challenges relating to the involvement of parents in school (Addi-Raccah & Ainhoren, 2009). There are two good reasons for nurturing and empowering home-based parental involvement: (a) it is adequate for adolescents' developmental needs (Seginer, 2006; Sy, Gottfried, & Gottfried, 2013), and (b) some teachers perceive school-based parental involvement as a disadvantage, because the relationship with parents requires investment of time and other resources (Friedman & Fisher, 2003). In such cases, schools can assist families in establishing a home environment that supports the child's functioning in school (Hirano & Rowe, 2016).

The third insight is that according to adolescents' perceptions, parental involvement is essential for the adolescents' self-evaluation, irrespective of cultural differences. Parental involvement may change its form and extent as students enter adolescence (Seginer, 2006; Kaplan Toren, 2013), However, the findings of the present study show the importance of parental involvement for the adolescents' scholastic competence and general self-worth. These findings are consistent with other study showing that adolescents valued their parents' involvement and expected their parents to be involved in supporting and encouraging their learning (Peterson et al, 2011).

The importance of connection between home and school for the child's optimal functioning is clear. The quality of family-school connections significantly associates with parents' motivational beliefs which in turn affects children's adaptive functioning in school (Moorman Kim, Sheridan, Kwon, & Koziol, 2013). However, parental involvement includes wide range of parental behaviours in two foci: home-based and school-based. Given that parental involvement differs based on cultural/multi-ethnic diversity we must account for the different groups' characteristics and needs in order to promote and nurture parental engagements.

REFERENCES

Adams, C. M., Forsyth, P. B., & Mitchell, R. M. (2009). The formation of parent-school trust. *Educational Administration Quarterly, 45,* 4-33. doi: 10.1177/0013161X08327550.

Adams, K. S., & Christenson, S. L. (2000). Trust and the Family–School Relationship Examination of Parent–Teacher Differences in Elementary and Secondary Grades. *Journal of School Psychology, 38* (5), 477–49. doi: 10.1016/S0022-4405(00)00048-0.

Addi-Raccah, A. & Ainhoren, R. (2009). School governance and teachers' attitudes to parents' involvement in schools. *Teaching and Teacher Education, 25,* 805-813. doi: 10.1016/j.tate.2009.01.006.

Addi-Raccah, A., & Greenstein, Y. (2016). *Parent-Teacher Relations in School: Types of Capital as a Framework for Examining Parental School Involvement.* Research report submitted to the Chief Scientist, Ministry of Education. (in Hebrew).

Al-Haj, M. (2003). Higher education among the Arabs in Israel: Formal policy between empowerment and control, *Higher Education Policy, 16,* 351-368. doi: 10.1057/palgrave.hep.8300025.

Avital, D., & Raz, T. (2018). *Parental partnership in school activity in the eyes of principals, teachers and parents.* National Authority for Measurement and Evaluation, Ministry of Education. (in Hebrew).

Berman, Z. (Eds.) (2014). *Children in Israel Yearbook.* Jerusalem: The Israel National Council for the child. (pp. 9, 40).

Broomhead, K. E. (2013). 'You cannot learn this from a book'; pre-service teachers developing empathy towards parents of children with Special Educational Needs (SEN) via parent stories. *European Journal of Special Needs Education, 28,* 173-186. doi: 10.1080/08856257.2013.778109.

Christenson, S. (2004). The family-school partnership: An opportunity to promote the learning competence of all students. *School Psychology Review, 33,* 83-104. doi: 10.1521/scpq.18.4.454.26995.

Dwairy, M., Achoui, M., Abouserie, R., Farah, A., Sakhleh, A.A. & Khan, H. K. (2006). Parenting style in Arab societies a first cross-regional research study. *Journal of Cross-Cultural Psychology, 37,* 230-247. doi: 10.1177/0022022106286922.

Eccles, J. S., & Harold, R. D. (1996). Family involvement in children's and adolescent's schooling. In A. Booth & F. J. Dunn (Eds.), *Family–school links: How do they affect educational outcome?* (pp. 3–33). Hillsdale, NJ: Erlbaum.

Epstein, J. L. (2001). *School, family and community partnership.* Colorado/Oxford: Westview Press.

Epstein, J. L. (2008). Improving family and community involvement in secondary schools. *The Education Digest, 73,* 9-12.

Epstein, J. L. (2010). School family community partnerships: Caring for the children we share. *Phi Deltta Kappa, 92,* 81-96.

Epstein, J. L., & Sanders, M. G. (2002). Family, school and community partnerships, In M. H. Bornstein (ed.) *Handbook of parenting volume 5 Practical Issues in Parenting.* Lawrence Erlbaum Associations; New Jersey (pp. 407-438).

Fisher, Y. (2009). Defining parental involvement: The Israeli case. *US-China Education Review, 6,* 33-45.

Fisher, Y., & Friedman, Y. (2009). Parents and School: Interaction and Involvement, *Dapim, 47,* 11-40. (in Hebrew).

Flum, H. & Cinamon, R. G. (2006). Linking the levels: Network and relational perspectives for community psychology, *Journal of Educational and Vocational Guidance, 6,* 123-140. doi: 10.1007/s10464-014-9654-2.

Green, C. L., Walker, J. M. T., Hoover-Dempsey, K. V., & Sandler, H. M. (2007). Parents' motivations for involvement in children's education: An empirical test of a theoretical model of parental involvement. *Journal of Education Psychology, 99,* 532–544. doi: 10.1037/0022-0663.99.3.532.

Harel-fisch, Y., Walsh, Y., Steinmetz, N., Lubel, S., Reis, Y., Tessler, R., & Habib, G. (2014). *Health behavior in school-age children (HBSC) A world health organization cross-national study,* Department of Education, Bar Ilan University, Ramat Gan.

Harter, S. (1982). The perceived competence scale for children. *Child Development, 53,* 87–97.

Hirano, K. A. & Rowe, D. A. (2016). A conceptual model for parent involvement in secondary special education, *Journal of Disability Policy Studies, 27,*43-53. doi: 10.1177/1044207315583901.

Hornby, G., & Lafaele, R. (2011). Barriers to parental involvement in education: An explanatory model, *Educational Review, 63,* 37-52. doi: 10.1080/00131911.2010.488049.

Kaplan Toren, N. & Buchholz Holland, C. (in press) Preparing pre-service teachers to work with parents. *International Journal of School Based Family Counseling,*

Kaplan Toren, N. & Kumar, R. (2015). Arabs' and Jews' students' similarity and differences perceptions of parents' educational involvement and its effect on students functioning in school, *International conference "Not in My Back Yard,"* Oranim, Israel.

Kaplan Toren, N. & Seginer R. (2015). Classroom climate, parental educational involvement, and school functioning in early adolescence: A longitudinal study. *Social Psychology of Education.18,* 811-827. doi: 10.1007/s11218-015-9316-8.

Kaplan Toren, N. (2004). *Parental involvement: Links to young adolescents' self-evaluation and academic achievement*, Doctoral dissertation, University of Haifa, Israel. (in Hebrew).
Kaplan Toren, N. (2013). The multiple dimensions of parental involvement and its links to young adolescent self-evaluation and academic achievement. *Psychology in the Schools, 50,* 634–649. doi: 10.1002/pits.21698.
Kaplan Toren, N. (2017). Israeli's unique socializing context affecting youth behavior, Comment on Huesmann et al. *Development and psychopathology, 29,* 51-52.
Kaplan Toren, N. (August, 2017). *What makes parents trust their child's teachers? Parents' educational active involvement as a predictor of Parents' teachers trust*. Presented at Oxford symposium in school-based family counselling, Venice, Italy.
Kaplan Toren, N. (2018). Links between two close context, home and school, and their effect on adolescents' school functioning in Israel. *Dapim, 67,* 131-160. (in Hebrew).
Kerr, M., Stattin, H., & Burk, W. J. (2010). A reinterpretation of parental monitoring in longitudinal perspective. *Journal of Research on Adolescence, 20,* 39-64. doi: 10.1111/j.1532-7795.2009.00623.x.
Lavenda, O. (2011). Parental involvement in school: A test of Hoover-Dempsey and Sandler's model among Jewish and Arab parents in Israel. *Children and Youth Services Review, 33,* 927-935. doi: 10.1016/j.childyouth.2010.12.016.
Lee J. S., & Bowen, N. K. (2006). Parental involvement, cultural capital and the achievement gap among elementary school children. *American Educational Research Journal, 43,* 193-218. doi: 10.3102/00028312043002193.
Lerkkanen, M.K., Kikas, E., Pakarinen, E., Poikonen, P.L., & Nurmi, J.E. (2013). Mother's trust toward teachers in relation to teaching practices, *Early Childhood Research Quarterly, 28,* 153-165. doi: 10.1016/j.ecresq.2012.04.005.
Lopez, G. R., Scribner, J. D., & Mahitivanichcha, K. (2001). Redefining Parental Involvement: Lessons from high-performing migrant-impacted

schools, *American Educational Research Journal, 38,* 253-288. doi: 10.3102/00028312038002253.

Mayseless & Salomon, (2003). Dialectic contradictions in the experiences of Israeli Jewish adolescents. In F. Pajares & T. Urdan (Eds.), International Perspectives on Adolescence. USA: Information Age Publishing Inc. (pp. 151-173).

Mehling, L. M. & Shumow, L. (2013). How is my child doing? : Preparing pre-service teachers to engage parents through assessment. Teaching Education, 24, 181-194. doi: 10.1080/10476210.2013.786892.

Ministry of Education CEO Procedures (September, 2018). Retrieved from: https://apps.education.gov.il/Mankal/Horaa.aspx?siduri=175.

Moorman Kim, E., Sheridan, S. M., Kwon, K., & Koziol, N. (2013). Parent beliefs and children's social-behavioral functioning: The mediating role of parent-teacher relationships. *Journal of School Psychology, 51,* 175-185. doi: 10.1016/j.jsp.2013.01.003.

Nzinga-Johnson, S., Baker, J. A. & Aupperlee, J. (2009). Teacher-parent relationships and school involvement among racially and educationally diverse parents of kindergarteners, *The Elementary School Journal, 110,* 81-91.

Peterson, E. R., Rubie-Davies, C. M., Elley-Brown, M. J., Widdowson, D. A., Dixon, R. S., & Irving, S. E. (2011). Who is to blame? Students, teachers and parents view on who is responsible for student achievement, *Research in Education, 86,* 1-12. doi: 10.7227/RIE.86.1.

Rosenblatt, Z., & Peled, D. (2003). Ethic climate and parents involvement in schools. *Studies in Education Administration and Organization, 27,* 177-204. (in Hebrew).

Seginer R. (1986). Mothers' behavior and sons' performance: An initial test of an academic achievement path model. *Merrill-Palmer Quarterly, 32,* 153-166.

Seginer, R. & Vermulst, A. (2002). Family environment, educational aspirations and academic achievement in two cultural settings. *Journal of Cross-Cultural Psychology, 33,* 540-558. doi: 10.1177/0022002210 2238268.

Seginer, R. (2006). Parents' educational involvement: A developmental ecology perceptive. *Parenting: Science and Practice, 6,* 1–48.doi: 10.1207/s15327922par0601_1.

Sy, S.R., Gottfried, A. M., & Gottfried, A. E.,(2013). A Transactional model of parental involvement and children's achievement from early childhood through adolescence. Parenting: Science and practice, 13, 133-152. doi: 10.1080/15295192.2012.709155.

TheMarker (Jun, 2017). The plan: 10 days less vacation. Retrieved from: https://www.themarker.com/news/education/1.4210928.

Ule, M., Zivoder, A. & Du Bois-Reymond, M. (2015). "Simply the best for my children": patterns of parental involvement in education. International Journal of Qualitative Studies in Education, 28, 329-348. doi: 10.1080/09518398.2014.987852.

Van Schalkwyk, G. J. (2017). Socio-cultural barriers to entry for school-based family counseling. *International Journal for School-Based Family Counseling, 7,* 1-9.

Walker, J. M. T. & Dotger, B. H. (2012). Because wisdom can't be told: Using comparison of simulated parent-teacher conferences to assess teacher candidates' readiness for family-school partnership. *Journal of Teacher Education, 63,* 62-75. doi: 10.1177/0022487111419300.

Walters, G. D. (2019). Mothers and fathers, sons and daughters: Parental knowledge and quality of the parent-child relationship as predictors of delinquency in same-and cross-sex parent-child dyads. *Journal of Child and Family Studies, 28,* 1850-1861. doi: 10.1007/s10826-019-01409-5.

Zabalbsky, E., & Shapira-Lishchinsky, O. (2019). Perceptions of principals, teachers and students about the involvement of parents in their children's education and the links to achievements in mathematics according to international exams (TIMSS). *Dapim, 68,* 79-109. (in Hebrew).

In: Parental Involvement
Editors: Nurit Kaplan Toren et al.
ISBN: 978-1-53616-828-0
© 2020 Nova Science Publishers, Inc.

Chapter 5

THE DETERMINANTS OF PATERNAL AND MATERNAL INVOLVEMENT IN CHILDCARE

Mariana Pinho[*] *and Ruth Gaunt*
University of Lincoln, Lincoln, United Kingdom

ABSTRACT

This study tests the hypotheses derived from three theoretical approaches to the determinants of parents' involvement in childcare: economic and structural models, gender ideologies, and family systems theory. Two hundred and thirty-seven Israeli couples with three 40-month-old infants completed self-report questionnaires that measured the father's and the mother's socio-demographic and employment characteristics, gender ideologies, relationship quality and various forms of involvement in childcare. The findings provided evidence for a structural model, showing that fathers' childcare hours were negatively related to the degree of overlap between the parents' work hours. Partial support was also found for the gender ideology model, as the mother's gender attitudes correlated with her hours of care and the distribution of childcare tasks. Weak support was found for the family systems theory. The findings highlight the importance of distinguishing different forms of involvement in childcare as each is affected by a different set of determinants.

---

[*] Corresponding Author's E-mail: mpinho@lincoln.ac.uk.

Keywords: economic, structural models, gender ideologies, family systems theory, childcare, parental involvement

INTRODUCTION

The benefits of paternal involvement in childcare have been demonstrated in numerous studies. Research shows that increased paternal involvement in child-rearing has a positive effect on the child's development as well as on the fathers' and mothers' wellbeing. In particular, increased father's involvement facilitates the cognitive and social development of the child (Bronte-Tinkew, Carrano, Horowitz, & Kinukawa, 2008; Lamb, 2010) and improves children's educational attainment (Goldman, 2005; Lamb, 2010). For example, children whose fathers are more involved in their upbringing develop greater self-confidence and self-esteem (Flouri, 2005). Shared literacy activities have the potential to strengthen the bond between fathers and their children (Clark, Osborne & Dugdale, 2009) and fathers are among the most inspirational figures to influence children and young people to read (Clark et al., 2009). Children and adolescents with involved fathers have higher academic motivation; express more positive attitudes towards school and education; and are less likely to fail a grade, have poor attendance or exhibit behavioral problems at school (Alfaro, Umana-Taylor, & Bamaca, 2006; Mosley & Thompson, 1995). On the contrary, the lack of involved male role models in literacy related activities has been proposed as one of the causes for declining school achievement for boys (Wragg, Wragg, Haynes & Chamberlain, 1998). Involved fathers also report a greater sense of closeness to their children (Solomon, 2014), enjoy increased self-confidence, self-esteem and experience greater satisfaction from their role as a parent (Ferketich & Mercer, 1994; Hudson, Elek & Fleck, 2001). Moreover, greater paternal involvement in childcare contributes to mothers' and fathers' marital satisfaction and well-being (Pleck, 2010; Schindler, 2010).

Despite the many findings accumulated on effects of paternal involvement on the wellbeing of all family members and factors that determine levels of paternal involvement in childcare (Deutsch, Lussier & Servis, 1993; Fox & Bruce, 2001), many argue that the available evidence regarding the determinants of paternal involvement in childcare is only partial and often contradictory or inconsistent (e.g., Marsiglio, Amato, Day & Lamb, 2000). As a result, the picture that emerges from the research is still vague, and there is a need for greater clarity, depth and exploration of maternal characteristics and involvement. The research reported in this chapter is devoted to exploring parental involvement in childcare drawing on three theoretical perspectives: economic and structural approaches; family systems theory and gender ideology model. It has the advantage of focusing on both paternal and maternal involvement, enabling the investigation of dyadic mutual influences and the effect of each partner's characteristics on the other partner's involvement. Furthermore, it distinguishes between different operationalization of involvement in childcare: performance of childcare tasks and the number of hours in which each parent is the sole care provider for the child. This is done in an attempt to examine whether certain factors differentially affect different dimensions of involvement in childcare. Therefore, the focus of research presented in this chapter is on heterosexual married or cohabiting couples who have at least one child together and are currently employed. Other family structures were not included as they either do not account for cohabitating dynamics of division of family labor or do not have a history of inequality in domestic labor (e.g., same-sex couples).

THEORETICAL APPROACHES TO THE DETERMINANTS OF PARENTS INVOLVEMENT IN CHILDCARE

Several approaches from an economic perspective have been proposed to account for parental participation in housework and childcare. The principal approaches in this category are: (1) Human Capital Theory, which assumes that the distribution of labor is based on considerations of efficiency, so that the task is allocated to the partner who can perform the chore better with smaller time investment (Becker, 1981; Bergen, 1991); (2) the Relative Resources Model (Brines, 1994), which focuses on the balance of power and external resources (e.g., income, education) between the partners and suggests that the partner who has more power will perform less undesirable tasks; and (3) the Structural Model, which centers on the relationship between the extent to which the male's participation is demanded and his ability to respond to this demand (e.g., Hook, 2012). A number of predictions were generated based on these approaches regarding the significance of the father's and the mother's respective earnings, working patterns, their education, and the number and age of the children.

Consistent with both Human Capital Theory and the Relative Resources Model, several studies have found that the greater the income and education of the father, the less his involvement in childcare (e.g., Aldous, Mulligan & Bjarnason, 1998; Caspar & O'Connell, 1998; Glass, 1998). Less is known about the effect of the mother's earnings on the father's involvement. Some studies found that the higher the mother's earnings and education, the greater the involvement of the father (Glass, 1998; Raley, Bianchi & Wang, 2012; Sullivan & Gershuny, 2016), but other studies yielded the opposite conclusion (Greenstein, 2000; Killewald & Gough, 2010).

Many studies have found that paternal involvement increases in proportion to the work hours of the mother and decreases as father's work hours increase (e.g., Aassve, Fuochi & Mencarini, 2014; Gaunt & Scott, 2014). Nevertheless, several other studies do not find such associations (Deutsch et al., 1993; Marsiglio, 1991; Yeung, Sandberg, Davis-Kean & Hofferth, 2001). It has also been found that the smaller the overlap between the respective work hours of the father and mother, the more children they have (Cabrera et al., 2000; Glass, 1998), and the younger their children's ages (Glass, 1998), the greater the father's involvement. These findings support the theory that paternal involvement is determined by the father's accessibility when needed (Caspar & O'Connell, 1998; Glass, 1998).

Although these theories explain some patterns and identify determinants in the division of family labor, in particular the number of parental work hours, the picture that they provide is incomplete. It should be noted that these approaches are based on the assumption that domestic labor, including childcare, involves unpleasant tasks whose reward is solely extrinsic, ignoring the possibility that a person might derive intrinsic enjoyment from performing them (e.g., cooking). As a result, they do not account for other social-psychological and interpersonal factors. Furthermore, their emphasis on economic factors assume mechanisms that are independent of gender. Some theorists argue that the division of family labor cannot be fully explained without recognizing the impact of family structures, cultural and institutional contexts (Hohmann-Marriott, 2011; Sullivan, Gershuny & Robinson, 2018). Family systems theory and gender ideology model complement the economic and structural models by addressing gender, psychological and interpersonal factors and provide a complementary explanation for contradictory results.

FAMILY SYSTEMS THEORY

Family systems theory proposes that the subsystems within the family are interrelated, such that dynamics in the spousal subsystem have a significant impact on the parent-child subsystem (Aldous, 1996; Belsky, Youngblade, Rovine, & Volling, 1991). According to this theory, the emotional interactions with the partner have an impact on the overall feelings of the parent and on the extent to which he or she feels a desire to be involved in the family system. When the interaction between the couple is favorable, their responses to their children follow suit (Lee & Doherty, 2007). Conversely, negative marital interaction is associated with dysfunctional parenting (Cummings & Davis, 1994). In general, men are less able than women to separate the feelings generated by the spousal relationship from their own relationship with their children (Belsky et al., 1991); consequently, the quality of the relationship between the couple is expected to have a strong impact on the fathers' involvement in child-rearing.

Research also demonstrates that parenting practices are related to parents' marital satisfaction (Linville et al., 2010). The resultant hypothesis with respect to paternal involvement and marital satisfaction postulates that fathers who are not satisfied with their marriages will be less involved in raising their children. Several studies in fact support this hypothesis and indicate that marital satisfaction prior to the birth of the child is a predictor of the extent of paternal involvement following the birth (e.g., Volling & Belsky, 1991). Nonetheless, other studies do not find such an association (e.g., Deutsch et al., 1993).

GENDER IDEOLOGY

The gender ideology approach assumes that gender norms influence a couple's beliefs about the tasks that are appropriate for men and women and determine the division of labor within the couple (Deutsch et al., 1993). Thus, this approach suggests that women and men with traditional attitudes regarding gender will allocate chores along traditional lines such that the father takes on the role of breadwinner while the mother is responsible for childcare. By contrast, couples with egalitarian, non-traditional attitudes will allocate the chores more equally, leading to greater paternal involvement in childcare.

Several studies have in fact found an association between non-traditional attitudes on the part of the father and greater involvement in child-rearing (e.g., Aldous et al., 1998; Gaunt, 2018), but there are also studies that have not arrived at such findings (e.g., Marsiglio, 1991). Additionally, gender ideologies and attitudes are also influenced by other factors such as cultural norms, education and income level. Highly educated fathers and higher-income families are less prone to endorse traditional gender attitudes (Doucet, 2013; Karre, 2015). Deutsch and colleagues (1993), found that the gender ideology of the father prior to the birth of the child is a good predictor of his involvement following the birth, even more so than the attitudes of the mother. Findings also show that egalitarian men value the benefits of maternal employment (Kaufman & White, 2016).

OVERVIEW AND HYPOTHESES

The research literature offers three different theoretical approaches explaining parental involvement in childcare. Studies conducted so far have provided partial support for each approach, but their findings are inconsistent. Therefore, it is important to test the different approaches in one research design, which will enable us to examine the relative contribution of each theory explaining paternal and maternal involvement in childcare. The present study, therefore, tests hypotheses derived from the three economic/structural approaches, the family systems theory and the gender ideology model. In particular, the human capital theory predicts that the higher the father's earnings, and the more hours he works, the lower will be his involvement in childcare. The relative resources model predicts that the higher one partner's earnings, education and professional status compared to the other partner, the less involved this second partner will be in childcare. The structural model predicts that the father involvement in childcare will increase the longer the mother's work hours, the fewer and more flexible the father's work hours, the more children they have and the younger the children are. According to family systems theory, the greater marital satisfaction, the more involved parents will be in childcare. Finally, gender ideology model predicts that father's involvement in childcare will increase among couples who endorse egalitarian gender ideologies.

These hypotheses were tested in a sample of Israeli couples. In Israel, as in other Western-oriented countries, there has been a massive entry of women into the labor force over the last few decades (Lavee & Katz, 2003). As a result, the dual-earner family pattern has become the most frequent one, and over 80% of Jewish Israeli mothers are in the labor force (Israel Central Bureau of Statistics, 2018). In a cross-cultural comparison of attitudes toward maternal employment, only 10% of Israeli women (compared to an average of 45% in several English-speaking countries) agreed that mothers should not be employed when they have a pre-school child (Charles & Cech, 2010). In spite of these liberal views and high employment rates, Israeli women continue to bear primary responsibility for housework and childcare

(Lavee & Katz, 2003) to a similar extent as women in other Western countries (Knudsen & Waerness, 2007).

METHOD

The current study tests three different approaches in one survey design using self-report questionnaires, and which will enable us to examine the relative contribution of each of them to explain paternal and maternal involvement in childcare.

PARTICIPANTS AND PROCEDURE

Participants in the study were a convenience sample of 237 Jewish Israeli couples recruited by research assistants in both central and peripheral areas of Israel. Criteria for inclusion in the study were the following: the couples were married, both spouses were the target child's biological parents, and they had at least one child aged three months to three and a half years (parents with more than one child within this age range were asked to report on the older one). This age range was chosen for several reasons: (1) Infants are more dependent and demand more intensive care than older children, and providing care for them may be especially challenging; (2) Compared with engagement in activities with older children, providing care for infants is strongly perceived as a "woman's job", and participation of fathers is less frequent; (3) Limiting the sample to a relatively homogeneous age group enabled the use of highly detailed measures of involvement in childcare, which assumingly increased the validity of parents' reports. The decision to limit the sample to children above the age of three months was based on the assumption that assignment of family roles becomes more stable at this age, when many women return to work outside the home. The mean age of the target children in this study was 19 months.

The fathers' ages ranged from 22 to 54 (M = 33); the mothers' ages ranged from 20 to 45 (M = 30). The couples represented a broad range of socioeconomic levels. Sixty-six percent of the fathers and 77% of the mothers in the study had a college-level education, and approximately 5% of the participants had not finished high school. Ninety-one percent of the fathers and 52% of the mothers worked full-time outside the home. Presented with the average monthly income in Israel at the time of the survey (7,000 ILS), 11% of the fathers and 18% of the mothers reported that they had an average income; the income of 21% of the fathers and 53% of the mothers was below average, and the income of 68% of the fathers and 29% of the mothers was above average. Forty-nine percent of the families had one child, 27% had two children, 17% had three children, and 7% had four or more children.

PROCEDURES AND MEASURES

An initial telephone screening was conducted to ensure that families met the inclusion criteria. Upon agreeing to participate, the families were scheduled for a home visit by a research assistant. During that visit, the fathers and mothers completed comprehensive self-report questionnaires. The questionnaires included questions on their values, their routine work schedules, and their involvement in care giving activities, as well as numerous background questions, personality and attitudes measures extending beyond the scope of this particular study. The questionnaires took approximately one hour to complete.

Involvement in Childcare

There were several measures of parental involvement. First, to assess the amount of time (hours per week) that fathers spend with their infants, both the mothers and the fathers indicated the amount of time during which the fathers were the sole care provider while the mother (or any other care provider) was away from home. Second, to assess the amount of time (hours per week) that mothers spend with their infants, both the mothers and the fathers indicated the amount of time that the mothers were the sole care provider while the father (or any other care provider) was away from home. Pearson correlations between the fathers' and the mothers' assessments of weekly hours of care were .77 for hours of care by the mother and .65 for hours of care by the father, suggesting a high level of convergent validity. The final measures of hours of care were obtained by averaging the assessments given by the father and the mother.

Childcare Tasks

Another measure asked: "Who does what?" in terms of 36 specific childcare tasks. The 36 tasks were selected to reflect those types of involvement typical of both fathers (e.g., playing, talking) and mothers (e.g., preparing food, packing child's bag). Some tasks were designed to tap physical care activities (e.g., feeding, changing diapers), some were designed to reflect responsibility for the child (e.g., choosing day care, deciding whether to take the child to the doctor), and some were selected to reflect companion (e.g., who does the child turns to when gets hurt?). Fathers and mothers were asked: "In the division of labour between you and your spouse, which of you performs each of the following tasks?" A rating of 1 indicated "almost always my spouse", a rating of 2 "more often my spouse", a rating of 3 "both of us equally", a rating of 4 "more often myself", and a rating of 5 "almost always myself." For the mothers, the scale was converse so that higher ratings indicated more participation by the father. Respondents were also given the opportunity to rate 8 "(no longer or not yet) applicable to my child" and 9 "usually performed by another person (day-care provider, grandmother, nanny)." For the purpose of further analyses, these two ratings were regarded as missing cases. The average Pearson correlation between the mothers' and the fathers' ratings for each of the 36 tasks was .53 (range .84 to .23), suggesting an acceptable level of convergent validity. The mean score for each task was obtained by averaging the ratings given by the father and the mother for that task. An average of the 36 task ratings was calculated to create a measure of total involvement in childcare tasks. Cronbach's alpha for this measure was .93.

In order to empirically distinguish major forms of involvement in childcare tasks, a principal-components factor analysis (with varimax rotation) was completed on the 36 items. Only those items that loaded on a component at a level greater than .45 were retained. This analysis yielded a three-factor solution. The first factor relates to physical care for the infant's daily needs (e.g., feeding, changing diapers). This factor also relates to the ongoing responsibility for the performance of these daily tasks (e.g., deciding when the child should be fed). Cronbach's alpha for this factor was .92. The second factor focuses on the higher-order, indirect responsibility for the infant (e.g., choosing day care, taking the child to the doctor). Cronbach's alpha for this factor was .75. Finally, the third factor concerns the parents' relationship with the infant, including companionship (e.g., play) as well as emotional care and support (who does child turn to when upset). Cronbach's alpha for this factor was .90. This classification is closely related to two forms of parental involvement suggested by Lamb (1987) and Pleck, Lamb & Levine (1986).

The intercorrelations among involvement measures are presented in Table 1. These correlations were moderate, suggesting that the measures are relatively independent indices of involvement. It is interesting to note, that the number of weekly hours of care by the father was not related to the number of weekly hours of care by the mother. This is inconsistent with the notion that couples use fathers as care providers in order to compensate for the mother's absence due to employment.

Parents' Socio-Demographic Characteristics

The parents were asked detailed information about their work hours and work schedules, including the time invested in travelling/commuting and the time devoted to work at home. They also reported their age, religiosity, educational level, and income. The age of the focal child and the number of children in the household were recorded.

Gender Ideologies

Both parents responded to a five-item scale designed to measure traditional and non-traditional gender ideologies (e.g., "It is best for everyone if the man earns a living and the woman takes care of the home and children, "Men and women should share housework when both are employed"). A rating of 1 indicated "strongly disagree" and a rating of 5 "strongly agree." Responses were recoded so that a high score reflected more egalitarian attitudes toward gender. The average score for the five items was computed in order to measure the respondent's gender ideology. Cronbach's alphas for this measure were .69 for the fathers and .68 for the mothers.

Marital Satisfaction

Participants' marital satisfaction was measured via the short version of Enriching Relationship Issues, Communication, and Happiness (ENRICH; Fowers & Olson, 1993). This is a 10-item Likert-type scale that assesses the respondent's perceived quality of marriage across 10 dimensions of the relationship (spouse's personal traits, communication, conflict resolution, financial management, leisure activities, sexuality, child rearing, relationship with the extended family, division of labor, and trust). Responses are indicated on a 7-point scale, ranging from 1 = fully disagree to 7 = fully agree. An additional item asked the participants to indicate their overall satisfaction with their marital relationship, on a 7-point scale that range from 1 = dissatisfied to 7 = extremely satisfied. An average of the 11 items was calculated to create a measure of overall marital satisfaction. Cronbach's alpha for this measure was .78.

RESULTS

Intercorrelations among Involvement Dimensions

The intercorrelations among the different forms of involvement in childcare are presented in Table 1. Seven dimensions were examined: the father's and mother's relative share of physical care, companion and overall responsibility for childcare, their total share of childcare tasks, the number of weekly hours in which each of the parents is the sole care provider for the child, and the number of weekly hours of non-parental care.

Table 1. Intercorrelations among Parental Involvement Measures

	1	2	3	4	5	6	7
Involvement in childcare tasks							
1. Physical care	--						
2. Companion	.61***	--					
3. Responsibility	.56***	.48***	--				
4. Total involvement	90***	79***	74***	--			
Hours of care							
5. Hours of father care	.38***	.27***	.35***	38***	--		
6. Hours of mother care	-.41***	-.43***	-.31***	-.44***	-.05	--	
7. Hours of other care	.31***	.36***	.18***	.34***	-.05	-.70***	--
M	2.22	2.52	2.06	2.24	7.24	25.30	31.13
SD	.61	.49	.53	.45	5.90	16.42	16.64

Note. Tests of significance were two-tailed.
*** $p < .001$.

Among the correlations presented in Table 1, the negative correlation between the mother's hour of care and the number of non-parental hours of care is particularly strong. Also important is the lack of correlation between the father's hours of care and the mother's and non-parental hours. This pattern of correlations suggests that the provision of childcare is the responsibility of the mother. For the most part, when the mother is not available for this role, she is replaced by non-parental carer rather than by the father. In this way, the care of the child is split mainly between the mother and the non-parental carer while the father remains out of the picture.

Involvement in Childcare and the Determinants Derived from Three Theoretical Approaches

Table 2 presents the correlations between the socio-demographic characteristics of the father and mother, their satisfaction with marriage, their attitudes towards gender roles, and their involvement in childcare.

The two most important factors are the mother's work hours and the number of hours in which she does not work for pay while the father is at work. Consistent with the structural model, the more hours the mother worked, the less time she spent at home alone with the children and the less she was involved in childcare tasks. Results presented in Table 2 also indicate that the more the mother worked, the greater amount of time the father spent alone at home with the child and the more involved the father was in all childcare tasks. On the other hand, the higher the number of hours in which the mother was home alone while the father was at work, the more time she spent caring for the children and the less involved in all childcare tasks was the father. Father's work hours were also related to his relative involvement and time dedicated to childcare. The more hours the father worked, the less involved in childcare tasks he was, the smaller was the number of hours he spent providing care and the more hours mothers spent alone at home.

Other important determinants are the mother's income and education level and the number of hours in which the father does not work for pay while the mother is at work. The higher education and income the mother had the less time she spent caring for the children and the more educated she was the higher was the father's relative involvement in childcare tasks. These findings are consistent with the relative resources model, and have not been frequently found before (Glass, 1998). The fathers' income and education were only related to the father's involvement in responsibility. Thus, consistent with human capital and relative resources models, the higher the father's income, the lower was his involvement in responsibility for childcare and the less hours he spent caring for his child (Caspar & O'Connell, 1998). However, the higher the father's education level, the

Table 2. Pearson Correlations between Parents' Socio-demographic Characteristics, Marital Satisfaction, Gender Ideologies and Involvement in Childcare

	7	8	9	10	11	12	13	14	15	16	17	18	19	20
1. Total involvement	-.19**	-.10	.09	.25***	.40***	.24***	.18*	-.38***	.22***	-.01	-.02	.12	.32***	.39***
2. Physical care	-.18**	-.03	.10	.21**	.34***	.25***	.17**	-.38***	.24***	.05	-.08	.06	.31***	.36***
3. Companion	-.16*	-.12	-.01	.19**	.38***	.14*	.07	-.27**	.13*	-.04	.02	.14*	.24***	.33***
4. Responsibility	-.15*	-.14*	.19**	.23**	.29***	.19**	.20***	-.23**	.08	-.08	.03	.16*	.30***	.29***
5. Hours mother of care	.12	-.01	.04	-.08	-.59***	-.34***	-.16*	-.51***	-.34***	.01	.06	.06	-.23***	-.38***
6. Hours of father care	-.17**	-.14*	-.04	.53***	.12	.09	.05	.06	.06	.04	.01	.02	.08	.11
7. Father's work hours	--	.14*	.01	.19**	.33***	.39***	.44***							
8. Father's income	.14*	--	.33***											
9. Father's education	.01	.14*	--											
10. Hours father at home while mother works	-.39***	-.08	-.08	--										
11. Mother's work hours	.04	.01	-.04	.19**	--									
12. Mother's income	.01	.20**	-.03	.17*	.46***	--								
13. Mother's education	-.06	.08	.56***	.12	.09	.10	--							
14. Hours mother at home while father works	.33***	.10	.02	.11	-.58***	-.35***	-.14	--						
15. Focal child's age	.02	.10	-.10	-.05	.25***	.21***	-.03	-.15*	--					
16. Number of children	.04	.20**	-.10	-.05	-.03	.08	-.02	.11	.10	--				
17. Father's marital satisfaction	.06	.04	.16*	-.08	-.01	.01	.09	.02	-.18**	.05	--			
18. Mother's marital satisfaction	-.01	.01	.08	.02	-.08	.01	.11	.08	-.21**	.09	.49***	--		
19. Father's gender ideology	-.03	.15*	.08	.03	.23***	.28***	.09	-.14*	.04	-.08	.16*	.09	--	
20. Mother's gender ideology	-.01	.17***	-.03	.15*	.39***	.32***	.14*	-.29***	.14*	-.09	-.05	.04	.45***	--
M	54.50	3.67	4.39	7.03	33.55	2.51	4.56	26.78	19.52	1.80	5.78	5.82	3.78	4.00
SD	16.37	1.29	.91	10.73	19.70	1.42	.81	18.21	10.86	.97	.76	.71	.72	.66

Note. Tests of significance were two-tailed.
* $p < .05$. ** $p < .01$. *** $p < .001$.

greater was his involvement in responsibility (Yeung et al., 2001). In general, the mothers' characteristics were more influential than the fathers' in determining parental involvement levels. The focal child's age was related to the mother's working hours, the number of hours mother spent at home alone and the mother's childcare time. The older the child was the more the mother worked, the less time she spent at home alone while the father was at work and the less time she spent on childcare. On the other hand, the older the child was the more involved the father was in nearly all childcare tasks, which is contrary to the structural model. This inconsistency can be partially explained by the average age of the focal child in our study and the importance attributed to maternal care and breastfeeding during the first years.

As shown in Table 2, marital satisfaction of each parent was related to each other, indicating that the more one partner was satisfied with their relationship, the higher the other partner's relationship satisfaction was as well. However, inconsistent with the family systems theory, the findings presented in Table 2 do not support the hypothesis regarding the associations between partners' marital satisfaction and their involvement in childcare. The only exception is the associations found between the mother's marital satisfaction and the father's involvement in companionship and responsibility. Therefore, the findings do not provide support for the family systems theory.

Furthermore, Table 2 shows that the findings are in line with the predictions derived from the gender ideology model. In particular, the more egalitarian mother's and father's gender ideologies were, the greater was father's share of childcare tasks relative to the mother's, the lower number of hours mothers spent caring for the child and less time mothers spent at home alone. However, there were no associations between the parents' gender ideologies and the father's hours of care. Additionally, mother's and father's gender ideologies were related to mother's working hours, indicating that the more mother's and father's hold egalitarian attitudes the greater number of hours mothers spent working. Finally, the more educated the mother was the greater egalitarian ideologies she expressed.

Predicting Involvement in Childcare from the Three Theoretical Perspectives

In order to determine the relative contribution of each of the three approaches to explaining various forms of parental involvement more specifically, we ran a set of multiple regression analyses. In each analysis, a variable pertaining to one form of involvement was regressed on the set of predictors derived from the three theories. The results are presented in Table 3.

To examine the contribution of the economic and structural models to explaining involvement in childcare, each of the six forms of involvement was regressed on the set of father's and mother's socioeconomic characteristics. As can be seen in Table 3, the regression equations were significant overall and accounted for 19% - 42% of the variance in parental involvement in childcare. Two of the factors—the hours in which each parent is at home while the other is at work—were significant predictors in all six equations. This means that the smaller the overlap between the father's and the mother's work hours, the greater was the father's share of childcare compared to the mother.

Additionally, father's education was a significant predictor in his involvement in two types of childcare tasks (see Table 3). The more educated the father was the more involved he was in physical care and responsibility. The child's age was also a significant predictor of father's involvement overall and particularly in tasks related to physical care and the number of caring hours by mothers. The older the child was the more the father was involved in childcare, in tasks related to physical care and the less time the mother spent caring for the child.

Family systems theory's contribution to explaining involvement in childcare was examined by regressing each of the six forms of involvement on father's and mother's marital satisfaction. As it can be observed in Table 3, only one regression equation was significant and indicated that mother's marital satisfaction was a significant predictor of fathers' involvement in responsibility and accounted for 3% of the variance. The more satisfied the mother was with the relationship the more responsibility tasks the father was involved in. Father's marital satisfaction did not predict any form of parental involvement in childcare. However, mother's marital satisfaction was a significant predictor of father's overall involvement in childcare and his involvement in companion tasks in particular.

Table 3. Hierarchical Regression Analyses Predicting Parental Involvement in Childcare Tasks from Three Theoretical Perspectives

	Total Involvement	Physical Care	Companion	Responsibility	Hours of mother care	Hours of father care
Economic and Structural Models						
Father						
Work hours	.10	.08	-.01	.17	-.04	.08
Income	-.01	.01	.01	-.08	-.19*	-.05
Education	.15	.18*	-.03	.23*	.04	-.03
Hours father at home while mother works	.32***	.30***	.22*	.29**	-.17*	.51***
Mother						
Work hours	-.01	-.07	.14	-.12	-.02	.10
Income	-.02	-.01	-.12	.09	.03	.01
Education	.11	.06	.09	.01	-.01	.07
Hours mother at home while father works	-.53***	-.52***	-.28*	-.40**	.61***	.11
Child's age	.23**	.22**	.13	.08	-.20**	.02
Number of children	-.05	.04	-.07	-.11	.07	.03
F (10, 210)	8.31***	6.64***	3.24***	3.69***	9.92***	.33***
R^2	.38	.33	.19	.21	.42	.32
Family Systems Theory						
Father's marital satisfaction	-.10	-.13	-.05	-.05	.04	.01
Mother's marital satisfaction	.17*	.12	.16*	.18*	.03	.01
F (10, 210)	2.56	1.83	2.45	3.08*	.51	.05
R^2	.02	.01	.02	.03	.01	.01
Gender Ideology Model						
Father's gender ideology	.18**	.17*	.11	.22**	-.08	.03
Mother's gender ideology	.32***	.29***	.30***	.20**	-.35***	.10
F (10, 210)	27.94***	22.23***	18.55***	16.73***	22.06***	1.65
R^2	.19	.16	.14	.13	.16	.01

Note. Standardized beta coefficients are reported.
*$p < .05$. **$p < .01$. ***$p < .001$.

Finally, a regression was conducted in order to assess the contribution of gender ideology model to involvement in childcare, with each of the six forms of involvement being regressed on father's and mother's gender ideologies. Table 3 shows the majority of the equations were significant and accounted for 13% - 19% of the variance in parental involvement in childcare. Parents' egalitarian gender ideologies significantly predicted father's overall involvement in childcare and specifically in tasks related to physical care and responsibility. The more egalitarian ideologies were endorsed by parents the more the father was involved in childcare tasks and in particular physical care and responsibility tasks. Furthermore, mother's gender ideologies, predicted father's higher involvement in responsibility and a lower number of hours that mothers spent providing childcare. Table 3 indicates that the more mother's held egalitarian ideologies the more the father was involved in responsibility related tasks and the less time she dedicated to childcare. Nonetheless, neither father's nor mother's gender ideologies predicted hours of father care.

DISCUSSION

The study examined the contribution of three theoretical approaches to explaining the involvement of fathers and mothers in caring for their children. In general, the findings indicate the great importance of the degree of overlap, or lack of overlap, in the couple's work hours for parental involvement in the care of their children, thus providing strong support for the structural model. In addition, the mother's attitudes contribute to explaining the father's involvement and provide strong support for the gender ideologies model. The family systems theory received little support from the findings.

Little support was found in the present study of the family systems theory consistent with studies that do not find a link between marital satisfaction and parental involvement (Deutsch et al., 1993). However, the lack of support for the family systems theory contradicts findings from earlier studies that showed that the father's satisfaction with marriage predicts his involvement in the care of his children (Volling & Belsky, 1991). The conflicting findings may be due to differences in the operationalization of the family systems approach in this study using only one measure, namely marital satisfaction. The examination of other aspects of relationship in the marital system, such as the existence of conflicts or stress, may have yielded other findings.

The findings from this study point to the importance of the distinction between different dimensions of involvement. The findings show that the factors that influence involvement in the performance of tasks differ from the factors that influence the hours of mother and father care. In particular, the hours of the father's supervision are related only to the lack of overlap in the couple's work hours, while the couple's involvement in the tasks and hours of mother care are also influenced by the child's age, the mother's attitudes, and father's income and education. It is therefore important to apply this distinction to future research as well.

Conclusion

Overall, the findings shed light on the importance of including multiple factors when investigating parental involvement in childcare. They allow us to understand how structural factors such as paid work hours interact with gender ideologies to shape parents' involvement in childcare. These findings provide evidence for addressing couples' ideologies as well as developing workplace policies to support a more balanced division of family labor and greater gender equality in the family.

The weakness of this study lies in its cross-sectional design, which does not provide certainty in the causal direction of the relationships between the variables. In order to overcome this weakness, future research should adopt a longitudinal design in which the predictive factors will be measured during the first pregnancy of the woman, and the involvement in childcare will be measured a few months after birth. Such a design will ensure the temporal order and will enable us to conclude more confidently about the direction of causality. Another limitation of the study is its sample being characterized by an over-representation of highly educated couples. The findings should, therefore, be considered with caution, as less-educated couples from a lower socioeconomic background may be more restricted in terms of their choices of childcare and employment. In particular, families where two incomes are absolutely necessary can have a restricted range of choices despite their beliefs or preferences. Furthermore, all the measures relied on self-report recall measures that could be subject to social-desirability concerns and reduced reliability. Previously research exposed that partners tend to overestimate their own contribution to household labour or underestimate each other's contribution (Lee & Waite, 2005). Future research would benefit from including time diaries and direct observations in the home setting.

Overall, the findings from this study strengthen the accumulating evidence of the important role played by structural constraints alongside with couples' gender ideologies in their involvement in childcare (Deutsch et al., 1993; Gaunt, 2018). Results suggest that equality at home and higher involvement in childcare by the father, might be related to the lack of overlap in the couple's work hours and the extent to which they hold egalitarian ideologies, believing that both parenting roles are more similar than different.

Considering the results from the current study, policymakers should attempt to increase paid benefits and financial incentives that would encourage fathers to take parental leave. Consequently, by taking parental leave alone, fathers are more likely to develop egalitarian parenting beliefs and develop parenting skills (Wall, 2014) while allowing mothers to be active in the labour market. Educators and practitioners developing parenting programs should generate awareness of structural constraints and the importance of paternal involvement in childcare as well as addressing parents' gender ideologies. By understanding the barriers and facilitators that can increase parental involvement, parents can be informed of the possible changes and adaptions they can make to face the greater demands of the labor market. It is also essential that educators highlight the impact of parents' involvement in their child's life and emphasize the valuable impacts of father's involvement in children's development (e.g., Lamb, 2010).

Moreover, educational courses targeting parents would benefit from demonstrating how parents' well-being can benefit from father's involvement in childcare (Pleck, 2010; Schindler, 2010).

REFERENCES

Aassve, A., Fuochi, G. & Mencarini, L. (2014). Desperate housework, relative resources, time availability, economic dependency, and gender ideology across Europe. *Journal of Family Issues*, 35(8), 1000-1022. doi:10.1177/0192513X14522248.

Aldous, J. (1996). *Family Careers: Rethinking the Developmental Perspective*. Thousand Oaks, CA: Sage. doi: 10.4135/9781483327310.

Aldous, J., Mulligan, G. M. & Bjarnason, T. (1998). Fathering over time: What makes the difference? *Journal of Marriage and the Family*, 60, 809-820.doi: 10.2307/353626.

Alfaro, E. C., Umana-Taylor, A. J. & Bamaca, M. Y. (2006). The influence of academic support on Latino adolescents' academic motivation. *Family Relations*, 55(3), 279-291. doi:10.1111/j.1741-3729.2006.00402.x.

Becker, G. (1981). *A treatise on the family*. Cambridge, MA: Harvard University Press.

Belsky, J., Youngblade, L., Rovine, M. & Volling, B. (1991). Patterns of marital change and parent–child interaction. *Journal of Marriage and the Family*, 53(2), 487-498. doi:10.2307/352914.

Bergen, E. (1991). The economic context of labor allocation: Implications for gender stratification. *Journal of Family Issues*, 12, 140-157. doi:10.1177/019251391012002001.

Brines, J. (1994). Economic dependency, gender, and the division of labor at home. *American Journal of Sociology*, 100, 652-688. doi: 10.1086/230577.

Bronte-Tinkew, J., Carrano, J., Horowitz, A. & Kinukawa, A. (2008). Involvement among resident fathers and links to infant cognitive outcomes. *Journal of Family Issues, 29*(9), 1211-1244. doi:10.1177/ 0192513X08318145.

Cabrera, N. J., Tamis-LeMonda, C. S., Bradley, R. H., Hofferth, S. & Lamb, M. E. (2000). Fatherhood in the twenty-first century. *Child Development, 71*, 127–136. doi:10.1111/1467-8624.00126.

Caspar, L. M. & O'Connell, M. (1998). Work, income, the economy, and married fathers as childcare providers. *Demography, 35*, 243-250. DOI: 10.2307/3004055.

Charles, M. & Cech, E. (2010). Beliefs about maternal employment. In J. Treas & S. Drobnič (Eds.), *Dividing the domestic: Men, women, and household work in cross-national perspective*, (pp. 147-174). Palo Alto, CA: Stanford University Press.

Clark, C., Osborne, S. & Dugdale, G. (2009). *Reaching out with role models*. London: National Literacy Trust.

Coltrane, S. (2000). Research on household labor: Modeling and measuring the social embeddedness of routine family work. *Journal of Marriage and the Family, 62*, 1208-1233. doi:10.1111/j.1741-3737.2000.01208.x.

Cummings, E. M. & Davies, P. T. (1994). Maternal depression and child development. *Journal of Child Psychology and Psychiatry, 35*, 73-112. doi:10.1111/j.1469-7610.1994.tb01133.x.

Deutsch, F. M., Lussier, J. B. & Servis, L. J. (1993). Husbands at home: Predictors of paternal participation in childcare and housework. *Journal of Personality and Social Psychology, 65*, 1154-1166. doi: 10.1037/0022-3514.65.6.1154.

Doucet, A. (2013). Gender roles and fathering. In N.J. Cabrera & C.S. Tamis-LeMonda (Eds.), *Handbook of father involvement: Multidisciplinary perspectives* (2nd ed.), (pp. 297-319). New York, NY: Routledge.

Ferketich, S. & Mercer, R. (1994). Predictors of parental role competence by risk status. *Nursing Research, 43*, 80–85.

Flouri, E. (2005). *Fathering and child outcomes*. London: Wiley.

Fox, G. L. & Bruce, C. (2001). Conditional fatherhood: Identity theory and parental investment theory as alternative sources of explanation of fathering. *Journal of Marriage and the Family*, *63*, 394-403. doi:10.1111/j.1741-3737.2001.00394.x.

Fowers, B. J. & Olson, D. H. (1993). ENRICH Marital Satisfaction Scale: A brief research and clinical tool. *Journal of Family Psychology*, *7*(2), 176-185. doi:10.1037/0893-3200.7.2.176.

Gaunt, R. (2018). Social psychological predictors of involvement in childcare: the mediating role of changes in women's work patterns after childbirth. *Community, Work and Family*, *22*(2), 183-202. doi: 10.1080/13668803.2018.1428170.

Gaunt, R. & Scott, J. (2014). Parents' involvement in childcare: Do parental and work identities matter? *Psychology of Women Quarterly*, *38*(4), 475-489. doi:10.1177/0361684314533484.

Glass, J. (1998). Gender liberation, economic squeeze, or fear of strangers: Why fathers provide infant care in dual-earner families. *Journal of Marriage and the Family*, *60*, 821-834. doi:10.2307/353627.

Goldman, R. (2005). *Fathers' involvement in their children's education*. London: National Family and Parenting Institute.

Greenstein T. N. (2000). Economic dependence, gender, and the division of labor in the home: A replication and extension. *Journal of Marriage and Family*, *62*(2) 322–335. doi:10.1111/j.1741-3737.2000.00322.x.

Hohmann-Marriott, B. (2011). Co-parenting and father involvement in married and unmarried co-resident couples. *Journal of Marriage and Family*, *73*, 269–309. doi:10.1111/j.1741-3737.2010.00805.x.

Hook, J. L. (2012). Working on weekend: Fathers' time with family in the UK. *Journal of Marriage and Family*, *74*, 631-642. doi: 10.1111/j.1741-3737.2012.00986.x.

Hudson, D., Elek, S. & Fleck, M. (2001). First-time mothers' and fathers' transition to parenthood: infant care self-efficacy, parenting satisfaction, and infant sex. *Issues in Comprehensive Pediatric Nursing*, *24*(1), 31-43. doi:10.1080/014608601300035580.

Israel Central Bureau of Statistics. (2018). *Women and Men 2016*. Retrieved from: https://www.cbs.gov.il/he/Statistical/statist166_h.pdf.

Karre, J. (2015). Gender-based attitudes and father involvement: Amount, assessment, and desires for more. *Fathering, 13*(3), 231-244. doi:10.3149/fth.1303.231.

Kaufman, G. & White, D. (2016). 'For the good of our family': Men's attitudes toward their wives' employment. *Journal of Family Issues, 37*(11), 1585–1610. doi:10.1177/0192513X14546719.

Killewald, A. & Gough, M. (2010). Money isn't everything: Wives' earnings and housework time. *Social Science Research, 39*(6), 987–1003.doi:10.1016/j.ssresearch.2010.08.005.

Knudsen, K. & Waerness, K. (2007). National context and spouses' housework in 34 countries. *European Sociological Review, 24*, 97–113. doi: 10.1093/esr/jem037.

Lamb, M. E. (1987). *The father's role: Cross-cultural perspectives.* Hillsdale, NJ: Erlbaum.

Lamb, M. E. (2010). *The role of the father in child development* (5th ed.). Hoboken, NJ: John Wiley & Sons.

Lavee, Y. & Katz, R. (2003). The Family in Israel: Between Tradition and Modernity. *Marriage and Family Review, 35*(1-2), 193-217. doi:10.1300/J002v35n01_11.

Lee, C. S. & Doherty, W. J. (2007). Marital satisfaction and father involvement. *Fathering, 5*, 75-96. doi: 10.3149/fth.0502.75.

Lee, Y. S. & Waite, L. J. (2005). Husbands' and wives' time spent on housework: A comparison of measures. *Journal of Marriage and Family, 67*(2), 328–336. doi:10.1111/j.0022-2445.2005.00119.x.

Linville, D., Chronister, K., Dishion, T., Todahl, J., Miller, J., Shaw, D. & Wilson, M. (2010). A longitudinal analysis of parenting practices, couple satisfaction, and child behavior problems. *Journal of Marital & Family Therapy, 36*(2), 244-255. doi:10.1111/j.1752-0606.2009. 00168.x.

Marsiglio, W. (1991). Paternal engagement activities with minor children. *Journal of Marriage and the Family, 53*, 973-986. doi:10.2307/ 353001.

Marsiglio, W., Amato, P., Day, R. D. & Lamb, M. E. (2000). Scholarship on fatherhood in the 1990s and beyond. *Journal of Marriage and the Family, 62*, 1173-1191. doi:10.1111/j.1741-3737.2000.01173.x.

Mosley, J. & Thompson, E. (1995). Fathering Behavior and Child Outcomes: The role of race and poverty. In W. Marsiglio, (Ed.), *Fatherhood: Contemporary theory, research, and social policy*, (pp. 148-165). Thousand Oaks, CA: Sage.

Pleck, J. H. (2010). Fatherhood and masculinity. In M. E. Lamb (Ed.), *The role of the father in child development*, (5th ed., pp. 32-66). New York, NY: Wiley.

Pleck, J. H., Lamb, M. E. & Levine, J. A. (1986). Epilog: Facilitating future change in men's family roles. In R. A Lewis & M. Sussman (Eds.), *Men's changing roles in the family*, (pp. 11-16). New York: Haworth.

Raley, S., Bianchi, S. M. & Wang, W. (2012). When do fathers care? Mothers' economic contribution and fathers' involvement in child care. *American Journal of Sociology*, *117*, 1422–1459. doi:10.1086/663354.

Schindler, H. S. (2010). The importance of parenting and financial contributions in promoting fathers' psychological health. *Journal of Marriage and Family*, *72*, 318-332. doi:10.1111/j.1741-3737.2010.00702.x.

Solomon, C. (2014). "I feel like a rock star": Fatherhood for stay-at-home fathers. *Fathering*, *12*(1), 52-70. doi: 10.3149/fth.1201.52.

Sullivan, O. & Gershuny, J. (2016). Change in spousal human capital and housework: A longitudinal analysis. *European Sociological Review*, *32*(6), 864–880. doi:10.1093/esr/jcw043.

Sullivan, O., Gershuny, J. & Robinson, J. P. (2018). Stalled or uneven gender revolution? A long-term processual framework for understanding why change is slow. *Journal of Family Theory and Review*, *10*, 263-279. doi:10.1111/jftr.12248.

Volling, B. L. & Belsky, J. (1991). Multiple determinants of father involvement during infancy in dual-earner and single-earner families. *Journal of Marriage and the Family*, *53*, 461-474. doi:10.2307/ 352912.

Wall, K. (2014). Fathers on leave alone: does it make a difference to their lives? *Fathering*, *12*(2), 196–210.

Wragg, E. C., Wragg, C. M., Haynes, G. S. & Chamberlain, R. P. (1998). *Improving literacy in the primary school*. London: Routledge.

Yeung, J. W., Sandberg, J. F., Davis-Kean, P. E. & Hofferth, S. L. (2001). Children's time with fathers in intact families. *Journal of Marriage and the Family, 63*, 136-154. doi:10.1111/j.1741-3737.2001.00136.x.

In: Parental Involvement
Editors: Nurit Kaplan Toren et al.
ISBN: 978-1-53616-828-0
© 2020 Nova Science Publishers, Inc.

Chapter 6

TEACHERS' PERSPECTIVES OF THE PARENT INVOLVEMENT HEXIS IN UNDER-RESOURCED URBAN SCHOOLS

Nyna Amin[*], *PhD*
School of Education, University of KwaZulu-Natal
Durban, KwaZulu-Natal, South Africa

ABSTRACT

This chapter explores the notion of parent involvement in three secondary schools situated in the province of KwaZulu-Natal in South Africa. The schools are under-resourced, multi-cultural, multi-lingual, and multi-racial in nature and are characterised by large enrollments of students from low socio-economic backgrounds. The data is drawn from a teacher work project, which explored the nature of teachers' work. Semi-structured interviews with nine teachers were analysed. Five tropes emerged from the data that ranged from keeping parents out of school to no parent involvement from child-headed households. The findings indicate that distrust, stereotyping and 'us and them' rhetoric complicate parent involvement in situations of poverty and under-resource. Based on the

---
[*] Corresponding Author's Email: amin@ukzn.ac.za.

findings, getting parents involved in multi-cultural, multi-racial, multilingual, impoverished schools is a complex endeavour that will require 'a temperament of receptivity' and shifts of perspective. Recommendations include sensitivity training and skills development for in-service teachers, complemented with the incorporation of topics on parent involvement in the curriculum for pre-service teachers.

Keywords: ethnography, parent involvement, semi-structured interviews, teacher perspectives, under-resourced school, urban school

INTRODUCTION

The value attributed to parent involvement in school is prolific in the literature, especially as it pertains to learning success (see e.g., DePlanty, Coulter-Kern & Duchane, 2007; Dotterer & Wehrspann, 2016; Heystek, 1999; Patrikakou, 2005; Swap, 1993; Topor, Keane, Shelton, & Calkins, 2012). The studies infer that the more parents are involved, the more the likelihood of student academic success. To that end, a number of endeavours to increase the participation of parents in schools were pursued as evident in a number of studies (e.g., Belenardo, 2001; Flynn, 2007; Jeynes, 2007; Okeke, 2014; Reece, Staudt & Ogle, 2013).

In contrast, some studies suggest that the reactive thesis explains the involvement of parents of low performers (Catsambis, 1998; Epstein, 1988). In others words, parents are more likely to be involved when student performance is low. However, in 2012, McNeal tested this hypothesis by sampling 7,983 students, to which he concluded that empirical evidence did not support the reactive thesis. Instead, he suggested that poor achievement and truancy were likely to inhibit parents' involvement in schools. Furthermore, McNeal's comprehensive survey of the literature highlighted three key findings. First, the relationship between academic performance and parent involvement is neither linear nor predictable; second, parent involvement may be necessary for behavioural outcomes instead of school achievement; finally, McNeal shows that the parent school relationship can be either positive or negative. In other words, parent involvement is complicated, unpredictable and contradictory with constant clarification needed. For instance, Deslandes and Bertrand (2005) caution that parent involvement needs to be distinguished in terms of place, like home or school, with teachers ideally desiring participation in both of these spaces.

Much has also been written about the absence of parents in schools with varied explanations. A number of studies impute these to minority group perceptions and attitudes (Levine-Rasky, 2009; Snell, Miguel & East, 2009), immigrant experiences (Theodorou, 2008), and low parent engagement in multi-cultural and multi-racial settings (Denessen, Bakker & Grieved, 2007; Van den Berg & Van Reekum, 2011; Gordon & Nocon 2008; LaRocque, 2013). Studies have also found that parent involvement can increase the divide between middle-class and minority student performance (Theodorou, 2008; Gordon & Nocon, 2008). Additionally, a number of scholars provide recommendations to attract and improve parent involvement by encouraging positive teacher perceptions of parent involvement (Deslandes & Bertrand, 2005), partnering with parents as 'promotara' (lay) inquirers in participatory action research (Snell, Miguel & East, 2009), creating parent-friendly school environments (Lemmer & Van Wyk, 2004b), and communicating with parents with sensitivity (LaRocque, 2013).

Although there exists an abundance of information on parent involvement, the literature is both complex and unclear in terms of its impact. For instance, articles that question the role of race, class, gender, wealth, and privilege are few (Hill & Craft, 2003; Tosolt, 2010; Vellymalay, 2012). Moreover, these studies pay less attention to the influence of the combination of historical, political and contextual dimensions on the relationship between schools and parents, between living conditions and education objectives, and between the values of the school and the living realities of poor families.

The imperative, therefore, is to provide a description of the interlocking adversities in context that work against parent involvement. The description should not be interpreted as an oppositional or antagonistic stance. Instead, it provides a basis for a critique of teachers' perspectives, and for offering nuanced explanations that take into account the background, history, class relations, economics, and politics that are rendered invisible by a narrow focus on pedagogical benefits for students.

A second imperative is a critique of the analytical foci of much of the literature on parent involvement. The concepts and models are largely derived from research in schools where parent involvement evolved over decades. In contrast, for most schools in South Africa, especially in the three schools in this study, parent involvement became a practice because it was mandated by law (DoE, 1996). In the years since the promulgation of the policy which prescribes parent involvement in school governance, reports suggest that it has not been well received by schools (see e.g., Graaff, 2017; Ramadikela, 2012).

Policy, Lemmer (2007) argues, undermines the informal relationships which may be more important for successful learning than formal measures to enhance school governance. Furthermore, few studies focus on the under-resourced character of schools; instead the focus is on the race profile of schools (Heystek, 1999; Msila, 2012; Singh, Mbokodi & Msila, 2004; Van Wyk, 1996). Thus the selection of teacher participants from under-resourced schools to explore their perspectives of parent involvement provides opportunities to bridge existing gaps and omissions, especially as they relate to a setting in the South. That is not to say that there is an absence of scholarly work on parent involvement in the South (see e.g., Lemmer, 2007; 2009; Lemmer & Van Wyk, 2004a; 2004b; Makgopa & Mokhele, 2013; Mbokodi & Singh, 2011; Mestry & Grobler, 2007; Mmotlane, Winnaar & Wa Kivilu, 2009; Nojaja, 2009; Olatoye & Ogunkola, 2008; Smit & Liebenberg, 2003).

However, the concern is the obedience paid to the values ascribed to parent involvement in scholarly works where schooling arrangements, school community ecologies, and the broader impact of the "intercausal triad of state, market and family" (Esping-Andersen, 1999, p. 35) is absent or dealt with in isolation. I begin with a brief description of inequality in South Africa which serves as a lens to explain the data.

PARENT INVOLVEMENT IN THE CONTEXT OF INEQUALITIES AND SOCIO-ECONOMIC STRATIFICATION

Schools in South Africa are complex spaces, reflecting a vast array of inequalities, diversities, adversities, and opportunities (see e.g., Amin & Ramrathan, 2009; Engelbrecht, Nel, Nel & Tlale, 2015; Isseri, Muthukrishna & Philpott, 2018). Although a quarter of a century has passed since apartheid was displaced, many schools continue to reflect disparities inherited from the fractious political arrangements of the past. At present, a funding model designed to nullify the toxic effects of the past, classifies schools according to five quintiles based on the wealth of the community in which the school is located. Quintile 1 schools are, arguably, the most deprived, while quintile 5 schools are the least deprived. Funding is proportionately highest for the former and least for the latter quintile. Higher levels of funding do not necessarily ameliorate the deprivation of quintile 1 schools as the challenges faced are formidable and may be described by Peters (2017) as "wicked challenges" which are characterized by poor problem definition, inability to provide clear solutions, and exhibiting symptoms which are linked to other problems (for the full explanation, see p. 388). To complicate matters, the quintile classification is contentious, as the criteria appear to be fuzzy and arbitrary:

> When we focus on Q2-Q4, we find that while the quintile system may be able to identify schools at the absolute ends of the spectrum, the schools in the middle often look similar and may appear better or worse in unexpected ways. Schools from Q1-Q4 are barely distinguishable in relation to mean proportion of disadvantaged learners in the school. With respect to average proportion of affluent learners, schools in Q1 are actually better off than schools in Q2 (Chutgar & Kanjee, 2009, online).

For a broad-based understanding and deep examination of the complexities that complicate parent involvement in schools, it is necessary to highlight the poverty profile of South Africa in general, and KwaZulu-Natal in particular. I turn to Statistics South Africa's (2017) poverty trends report to substantiate the assertion that "inequality has remained stubbornly constant over time and at alarmingly high levels" (p. 23). According to the report, unemployment rates in the country stand at 26.7% (StatsSA, 2017, p. 44), and in 2015, 12 million children received state grants (p. 52). Furthermore, nationally, 30.4 million (55.5%) people of the population live in poverty, of which 13.8 million people live in absolute poverty (p. 14), while 38.8% live in urban areas (p. 68). Poverty is closely tied to parent involvement as reported by Graaff (2017, p. 5):

> Parents in poorer communities, if employed, make considerable sacrifices in time and money when they participate in their children's school. If not employed, the dynamic is more complicated.

In terms of the provincial landscape of poverty, KwaZulu-Natal is the smallest and one of the poorest in the country with 68.1% identified as poor (StatsSA, 2017, p. 65). The province also has the largest share of poverty at 24.4% (p. 68). Furthermore, 79.2% of poor adults have no formal education. Poor households spend 30% of their income on food whilst non-poor households spend 0.5% (StatsSA, 2017, p. 100). More importantly, they often do not possess the cultural capital for successful navigation of a structure like education (Bourdieu, 1973, 2006; Bourdieu & Passeron, 1977). In contrast, Everett Reimer makes the following assertion:

> [teachers represent, present, and] distribute values of all kinds among all the peoples of the world, largely replacing the family, church and the institution of private property in this capacity. In capitalist countries it may be more accurate to say that schools confirm rather than replace the value-distribution functions of these older institutions (1973, p. 26).

Reimer makes clear the distinctions between the teachers and the community that sends their children to school: the teachers possess the cultural capital about schools and education. Furthermore, the teacher participants are literate, educated, and are employed, widening the gap between the school personnel and the parents whose involvement they (the school) desire.

METHOD

Teachers' perspectives of parent involvement were explored ethnographically. Ethnographic approaches are culture and context orientated and are sensitive to interpersonal relationships and communication modes (Atkinson, Coffey & Delamont, 2007). The approach is consistent with research in natural milieus, especially from "the native's points of view" (Geertz, 1974); in other words, to get insiders' (teachers) account of their work (Hammersley & Atkinson, 2007). The focus was not on parent involvement per se, and the questions were not directed thereto. Instead, the intention was to identify the work teachers do across all quintiles and to analyse the nature of teachers' work as part of a project funded by the National Research Foundation, namely 'Teachers' work and working teachers: Working in times of uncertainty'. Multiple methodologies, both qualitative and quantitative, were deployed (survey, interviews, focus group interviews, artefacts, transect walks, work diaries, and observations). Three teachers per school from 75 schools were interviewed once.

Table 1. Semi-structured interview questions

Is there work that you have to do that is not related to teaching? Explain.
How much time is spent on home visits?
Are there aspects of work that teachers do but should not be doing?
What support (if any) does the school receive from external sources?
What aspects of teaching work do you experience as complicated?
Is pastoral care a core duty of teachers' work? Explain.

During interviews with teachers, who work in secondary schools in KwaZulu-Natal, direct references were made to parent involvement by nine participants in the funded project. Coincidentally, the nine participants came from three urban schools with common features. All three are classified as quintile 4, and under-resourced with a majority enrolment of students from impoverished backgrounds. The data on teachers' perspectives of parent involvement emerged in these interviews, with particular reference to the questions in Table 1.

Participation in the study was voluntary. Full disclosure about the project, aims, methods, and outputs were furnished and confidentiality and anonymity were assured. Because of the assurances given, no names of the schools or the participants were appended to data; instead, codes were used. To prevent accidental identification of the schools and teachers in the project, a system of unique symbols comprising an alphanumeric code was utilised (e.g., TIS37 signifies Teacher, Indian, Secondary). For reading convenience, pseudonyms for the teachers and the schools have been used to replace the alphanumeric codes in this chapter (see Table 2).

Table 2. Snapshot profile of participants and their place of employment

School	Teacher	Sex	Years of experience
Emerald Secondary. No of teachers 24 Est. 1980. Enrolment: 847	Esther	Female	24
	Evelyn	Female	23
	Elvis	Male	32
Pearl Secondary. No of teachers 22 Est. 1981. Enrolment: 888	Paul	Male	16
	Patricia	Female	19
	Prudence	Female	35
Topaz Secondary: 25 Est. 1981. Enrolment: 891	Terry	Male	21
	Tommy	Male	5
	Tina	Female	34

THE RESEARCH CONTEXTS

The participants teach in three secondary schools with similar characteristics, demographics, student and teacher numbers, and history. The schools were built in the early 1980s for Indian communities. In all three schools, only Indian teachers are in employment, whilst more than 90% of the students are African. The race transformation and under-funding of the school has complicated the relationships between schools and the communities they serve and has led to the exodus of many middle-class students and the entry of students from poor backgrounds. The unchanged teacher profile has contributed to the alienation felt by African parents (Chindanya, 2011; Amin, 2010). However, the situation should not be interpreted as resistance to change by institutions and teachers because in South Africa, it is the state, not the teacher, that makes decisions regarding employment placement. A change of school can occur when an application for promotion to a senior level in another school is successful, and when an incumbent is in access of the requirements of a school the state transfers the teacher to another school where a vacancy exists. Consequently, employment and placement policies hamper the opportunity to transform the teaching body of an institution.

Furthermore, the schools are severely under-resourced, challenging effective teaching and management of the school. For example, there are shortages of textbooks, printing paper, library books, art supplies, computers, digital media, chalk and chalkboard cleaners. The furniture is inadequate for the number of students and infrastructure is aging and in need of refurbishment. Each school is characterised by poor infrastructure, a high teacher–student ratio and problematic socio-economic conditions in the surrounding communities, which comprise impoverished families living in informal, make-shift homes without proper access to services like electricity, piped-water, and sanitation. Violence, drug use, teenage pregnancy, high absenteeism, and bullying amongst students is endemic to all three settings. Educational psychologists, counsellors, and social workers do serve the schools intermittently, described by a participant teacher in this way, "If we're lucky, one measly visit every few years."

NORMATIVE AND DISRUPTIVE PERSPECTIVES ON PARENT INVOLVEMENT

Following Manning and Kunkel (2014), folk terms are used to classify the data. Folk terms "are those introduced by the social scene, whereas analytic terms are those derived and labelled by the researcher" (Manning & Kunkel, 2014, p. 103). Participant-generated tropes are aligned to ethnographic approaches. A constellation of five tropes were identified for the purpose of analysing and crystallising the data, namely "keep out," "when you want them ... they won't come," "we can work together," "parents are involved," and "no parents, no involvement." Each trope is discussed based on the actual transcripts from interviews. The discussion is faithful to the data and connections to literature follow in the section thereafter.

Keep Out

> Keep out! Yes, if I was the principal, I will put up that sign. Let the professionals do their work. What do these parents know about education? How things have changed. Many have no education. I work hard but no-one is appreciative. They are not our bosses. They're supposed to support us. But, the parents want to be bosses. Here I have so many bosses, the department, the principal, HoDs [heads of department], parents. Parents are not welcome here. They should take care of their children at home. (Evelyn)
> What I say is: why do they want to interfere in my work? They know nothing about education. The department [of Education] is to blame for the mess here. Look at the state of the school. They say we are quintile 4, but the children come from quintile 1 backgrounds. ... What's their understanding? They waste our time. No support. Why do we need parents? Because the Department says so. They cannot even provide their children with lunch. You won't see me going to my daughter's school and telling her teachers what to do. I trust the school. They should help their children with homework. With 42 learners in my class, I cannot supervise them on my own. (Terry)

Two teachers (Evelyn and Terry) from two different schools hold a deficit perspective of parents. There is a clear distinction between 'us' and 'them'. They are suspicious of parents' motives for involvement, assuming it to be a quest for power and authority. The frustration of having to report to employers (the Department of Education), school head (principal) and academic leaders (HoDs), she fears, will be compounded by parents' involvement. Terry also believes it is a form of interference.

It is ironic though that the teachers expect parents who "know nothing about education" to support the school and to supervise homework. From teachers' points of view, parents do not seem to add value to school effectiveness or to teachers' roles. Indeed, parents seem to be the targets of teacher anger, which should be directed at the Department of Education as parents do not determine the quintile classification of a school, and parents are not the makers of policy that require their (the parents') representation on school governing bodies or exemption from school fee payment. From the participants' perspectives, poor parents are to blame for enrolling their children at Emerald and Topaz Secondary School. Indeed, for the additional responsibilities they carry in situations of adversity, it is the Department of Education that should appreciate and reward teachers. In a sense, the teachers' expectations of support from parents is misguided. Rather, it is evident that parents are stereotyped as unknowing, incompetent interlopers who should be kept out of school. Poverty in the parent community and their lack of school knowledge, consistent with Bourdieu's (1973) notion of cultural capital, serve to justify Terry's perspective to reject parent involvement.

When You Want Them ... They Won't Come

> We have seasonal parents. Good season and bad season parents. Since the good kids left our school, everything is different. These parents come for good things like awards, choir performance and our concert. But, I tell you, when you want them to know about bad behaviour they won't come but will fight with us when their child fails. That's why the work of teachers is so hard. (Terry)
>
> The parents here are ...what you call it ... ummm ... ungrateful and yes, irresponsible. I see them wearing shoes that cost lots of money but fees ... they don't pay fees. One child in my class is so naughty. I dread coming to school because this child is a bully and violent, does not do homework, steals and bunks classes. When I called the parent to school, she came with lots of excuses, ummm, lies, why she can't come here. So how can I help if the parent does not want to be involved? (Patricia)

Terry and Patricia have a pejorative view of parent involvement. It appears that they are irked by the strategic choices that parents can exercise regarding participation, payment of fees, and student behaviour. On the other hand, teachers have no choice regarding where to teach or who to teach. There is also generalisation in the way all parents are judged as negligent or disinterested, and students who left for other schools are deemed to be 'good' students. Furthermore, because of their sartorial choices, parents are adjudged negatively. Evidently, there is some glossing over of the value of parents who are involved, perhaps due to the disproportionately small ratio of such parents, or because of teachers' excessive workloads concomitant with the lack of institutional and structural support from professionals who should be servicing the school like school counsellors, education psychologists, and social workers. Furthermore, the teachers note that parents only seem to attend activities that are celebratory and pleasurable, such as award functions, where they form part of a crowd. The converse is thus plausible: parents avoid being summoned for their children's offences because it requires meeting with teachers individually, giving credence to McNeal's (2012) rejection of the reactive hypothesis. Alternatively, as revealed in interviews with parents, Finders and Lewis (1994) found that parents do not want to hear about their child's academic inabilities or ill-discipline and, like teachers, parents too are frustrated by teachers' attitudes and prejudices.

We Can Work Together

> If only they were interested in their child's future, we can work together. I can do my thing here and they do their bit at home. At least they can monitor homework. Yes, we can cooperate. In white schools, parents help a lot but not in Indian schools. In white schools, black parents are interested; here they show no interest. (Tommy)
>
> Parents' involvement is needed. They must show interest in their children's learning. With the old community there were no problems but now it is different. Now there are such big problems and the community should work with us. There is so much poverty and gangsters, hijackers, drugsters [sic] and things like that. All that is happening in front of parents. Together, we can do something. Yes, they must work with the school. (Tina)

Tina and Tommy realise the importance of parent involvement. Nevertheless, their perspectives are stereotypical responses that centre on race and selective reminisces of a past portrayed as problem- and crime-free. The result is disengagement by teachers rather than by parents. Teacher disengagement counters the arguments in the literature which suggest that parents keep away because of negligence and lack of interest in student achievement. It transpires that 'us and them' is a common trope and refrain. Comparisons to parent-school co-operation in white schools provide additional insights.

While it is true that most white schools are classified as quintile 5, and are able to set fees at levels that enable them to employ teachers over and above state norms and teacher-student ratios that schools like Emerald, Topaz and Pearl have to comply with, the race discourse can be seen as the use of a convenient excuse (Farred, 2006, p. 55) by teachers to explain parent non-involvement in their school. The issue raised by Tommy about parent involvement at white schools distracts from adopting initiatives that need to be taken to attract parent involvement. The race discourse, in this instance, entrenches and intensifies the 'us and them' divide between teachers and parents and serves to neutralise harmony which underpins desirable school community relations.

Contrary to literature which suggest that schools should initiate school-parent relations (see e.g., Belenardo, 2001; Denessen, et al., 2007; Levine-Rasky, 2009), Tina and Tommy expect parents to make overtures to be involved, as they envisage that working together with parents could improve student achievement and student discipline problems. The latter issue relates to the emerging perspective that parents endorse wrongdoing. Additional complexities relate to significant differences between parents and teachers. Parenting is not a profession but teaching is.

As professionals, the teachers in the study are trained to manage students. However, they (the teachers) are not adequately prepared for the challenges that surface in multi-racial, multi-cultural, multi-lingual, and over-crowded classrooms. The classroom situations at Topaz, Emerald and Pearl reveal the predicaments and frustrations faced by teachers in school contexts that are absent in teacher education curricula, resulting in the blame games that impinge on school community relations and potential parent involvement.

Parents Are Involved

> The parents who come want their children to succeed. They show their love. They get involved in their child, the school and our functions. We have a mother who always helps out in the lower grades when a teacher is absent. Another parent helps with the choir. Parents are involved. (Esther)
> Without parent support, we would not have extra teachers and the workload would be so high. We are lucky because they help a lot with fund-raising and things like that. (Prudence)

The perspectives of Esther and Prudence provide insights into the kinds of involvement that teachers appreciate, viz. attending school functions, substituting for absent teachers and paying for and or supporting the employment of additional teachers. The teachers of Emerald and Pearl assume that there is a correlation between parent engagement and school success and that it is an overt demonstration of being caring and loving parents and by implication, that parents who are not involved are uncaring and unloving. In fact studies have shown that the assumption that parents do not care is a myth (Epstein 2001; Van Wyk & Lemmer 2009). The impediment for the realisation of these expectations are the complex challenges associated with poverty and cultural capital. From a realistic perspective, the overwhelming majority of parents are not in a position to improve or contribute to the school's finances, which explains why so few parents provide support.

The personal and situational needs of the majority of parents supercede the needs of schools. It is evident too, that a myopic perspective is at play. In under-resourced schools like Emerald and Pearl, there is a greater tendency to stereotype parents as teachers are overwhelmed by high workloads and their immediate concern is reduction of workload. The need for parent involvement blinds them to the realities of the communities around the school—high rates of unemployment, poor parents, elderly grandparents who have to care for orphans or abandoned children, and households headed by children. Indeed, seeking amelioration of the pressures of work from parents is unrealistic and as noted in the data, sustains teacher prejudice and contributes to 'us and them' rhetoric.

No Parents, No Involvement

> It is sad for us that we have children with no parents. They live by themselves. No parents, no involvement. So we have to work with no support whatsoever. (Tina)
>
> We have many children living with grannies. The grannies are illiterate or sick. Some cannot afford transport to come if there's problems. They cannot help with homework. It is difficult to be a teacher here. (Tommy)
>
> Has the department even considered child-headed families? It's a joke to expect parent engagement when the head of the family is a learner. (Terry)

All three participants teach in the same school and they hold a realistic perspective of the misery of the students' lives. In stark contrast to Prudence, Paul and Esther, Tina, Tommy and Terry are aware of the hardships faced by child-headed households, orphans and abandoned or migrant children living with grandparents. It is clear then, that the harsh realities of students' situations is better known at Topaz than at Emerald or Pearl, perhaps because Topaz has a larger number of children without parents than the other two schools. The above excerpt also indicates that teachers are emotionally affected by the children's unfortunate circumstances and it impacts on their role as teachers. Undoubtedly, emotional labour and teacher impotence complicates and intensifies their work as teachers and the absence of parents of some students means fewer parents who can be involved. There is some anger too, directed at the Department of Education's policy that imposes parent involvement in school governance without due consideration of peculiar contextual adversities or circumstances.

DISCUSSION OF THE FINDINGS

Teachers perspectives range from total exclusion (keep out) to not possible (no parent, no involvement) on a continuum of five categories with various possibilities in-between. The various categories that emerged from the data do not provide sufficient insight about a way forward; nevertheless, under-resourced schools bring out in stark relief the complexities of parent involvement in education. The needs of the schools seem to influence teacher perspectives of parent involvement and teacher prejudice and stereotyping of the poor. A number of issues that together constitute a conundrum have been identified. These include interconnected discourses on teachers' work conditions, parents' living conditions, socio-economic factors and class differences. Whilst the discourses are similar to those found in the literature, one insight that emerges is that there is a cohort of students without parents or guardians and who do not reside in orphanages or children's homes. These students have no family member who can be involved in school. The situation of orphans seems to anger teachers and to be a source of frustration.

Changes in teachers' work conditions are not conducive for harmonious relationships with the parent community, setting up the conditions for hostility. Predictably, the course of the political history of the country and changes associated therewith has complicated the workspace for this profession (Morrow, 2007). It transpires that teachers in poor communities have more non-teaching responsibilities (care work, counselling work, social work, parenting) than their counterparts in wealthier environments. For example, a study carried out by Maharaj (2019) in a school resembling the work conditions at Emerald, Pearl and Topaz, found that the work teachers do is emotionally intensive and more demanding. The work conditions frustrate and anger teachers which is then aimed at parents.

An underlying source of frustration and anger expressed for parents' lack of involvement is the limitations placed on teacher mobility by the state. While student movement is flexible, the same does not apply to teachers, making it impossible to escape the changes in working conditions since 1994. The years of professional experience of eight of the nine participants (16-34 years) suggest that when they were young, this cohort probably attended schools that were culturally homogeneous. In other words, these teachers probably learnt to teach in higher education institutions and garnered their early experiences in similar schools. While they continue to work in the same schools, the characteristics, dynamics and work conditions have changed, such as the scarcity of resources and the increased teacher-student ratios resulting in more anger, frustration and discomfit targeted at parents.

It seems that professional experience has not prepared teachers for changes to their comfort zones—especially in the pluralised character of their classrooms: multi-lingual, multi-racial and multi-cultural. Limited contact during the crucial period of the formative years of professionalisation and limited social interaction, has resulted in pejorative views of parents from poor socio-economic backgrounds, regarding them with suspicion and distrust, and a tendency to resort to stereotyping. It may be prudent to note that while teachers exist in familiar spaces, these spaces have morphed into unfamiliar ones, making them strangers in their workplaces. Whilst the literature indicates that parents are alienated in multicultural settings, in this instance, teachers too feel alienated in their schools. Whilst the idea of understanding cultures from within—by making the familiar strange and *vice versa*—is welcomed and actively pursued by anthropologists (Myers, 2011), it is certainly counter-productive when imposed in some school settings.

Institutional change adds another dimension to the complexity regarding parent involvement. For instance, change at the schools is incomplete because it has only taken place at student level while the teacher complement has remained wholly mono-racial resulting in racial, cultural and linguistic divisions between the teachers and the parents. The divide is not necessarily antagonistic, but it does highlight a lack of social cohesion between school and community. Race, language and culture differences also imply worldview and class differences. Whilst the teachers (educated and employed) are economically better off since the fall of apartheid, the disadvantages for the parents (unemployed) has worsened (StatsSA, 2017), increasing the gap between the 'haves' and 'have-nots' at these three sites. It follows that the priorities and aspirations of the middle-class and the poorer classes would differ too as evident in low parent involvement and high teacher desire for parent involvement. Undoubtedly, parent involvement is an option that will not be exercised in school contexts like Emerald, Pearl and Topaz because of the underlying discourses of prejudice and stereotyping and dissatisfaction with work conditions embedded in teachers' perspectives.

Though invisible in literature, in settings like the three schools in this study, parent involvement takes on a complexity that demands a different politics of understanding. We can infer that poverty, albeit of different kinds, is distributed to both the community in which parents live and in the schools where the teachers work. In both settings, displacements have intensified hardships. The incoming community live in situations of poverty, vulnerability and deprivation, and the remainders—that is the teachers— have to work in untenable, under-resourced conditions for which they lack preparedness. Furthermore, the teachers' familiarity of school space has been displaced by a zone of strangeness and insufficient resources and funding in line with the respective schools quintile categorisations. With the study reported here, we gained some clarity of the problem of parent involvement in schools like Emerald, Topaz and Pearl: structural conditions like rampant poverty, high unemployment lack of basic services and teacher work conditions that need to be attended to by the state and teachers prejudice which can be dealt with at school level.

These conditions destabilise normative sensibilities about parent involvement in education. Though lauded in recent literature (e.g., Dotterer & Wehrspann, 2016; Okeke, 2014; Reece, et al., 2013; Topor, et al., 2012), it may just be untenable in the way it is theorised currently for secondary schools like Emerald, Topaz and Pearl. Even when research indicates that there are problematic aspects, recommendations still settle on a model, intervention or practice to draw in parents. The pursuit and desire to engage parents is not surprising when one factors in the enormous benefits for parents, children, school, and community. Correspondingly, resistance by parents and lack of desire by teachers for collaboration may set up the situation for antagonism or resentment based on group stereotyping, differences in class values and socio-economic challenges faced by both parents and schools with regard to everyday survival and curriculum delivery, respectively. Undoubtedly, schools that are not adequately prepared for transformation, that are inadequately financed by the state, lack professional support services, and are surrounded by an impoverished, highly unemployed and precarious community, may see parent involvement as an additional burden. Under these conditions, should the idea of parent involvement be abandoned? Obviously not. Conversely, it may necessitate rethinking the starting point and factoring in the cautions about the nature of wicked problems:

> The nature of wicked, and/or complex, problems is that there will be no magic bullet to solve the problems, but a better understanding of the problems and how they may be processed, can only help to facilitate what may be only limited answers (Peters, 2017, p. 395).

CONCLUSION: SHIFTING PERSPECTIVES

Researching parent involvement in under-resourced schools in a low socio-economic environment does provide insights that are well worth considering. On the one hand, when teachers are consumed by anger and frustration with work conditions they are more likely to reject parent involvement and to harbour prejudices that are uninviting for good school community relations. The teachers are aware but disregard the realities that poor communities face. On the other hand, poor communities live in unsafe homes, without food security, stripped of dignity and bruised by the constant struggle to survive each day. In such situations how can parent involvement be embraced by teachers and parents? Perhaps shifting perspectives may be useful.

First, teacher prejudice needs to be replaced by tolerance and open-mindedness. Seminars that educate teachers about the rich benefits of teaching in multicultural, multilingual and multi-racial classrooms should be conducted. More importantly, the seminars must reduce teacher anger and frustration by providing them with appropriate pedagogies and classroom management skills for the diversity in their classrooms.

Second, sensitivity training for school personnel may have to go beyond effective communication modes as suggested by LaRocque (2013). Drawing on and appropriating Wilde's (1969/1891) contemplation on art for a different purpose, "a temperament of receptivity" should be encouraged (p. 17). In other words, a spirit of generosity may be crucial to counteract the reproduction of inequalities and the distribution of poverty that engulf schools and communities. Although schools are burdened with the impact of poverty in the execution of work and by the additional demands of providing emotional care to poor children (Morrow, 2007), they may need to re-invent their institutions so that its ethos is inviting. An inviting ethos may draw parents to schools for the value it adds to their unfortunate lives, e.g., allowing them access to computers or providing assistance with drawing up a curriculum vitae or completing applications for employment, social and pension grants. These overtures may foster trust, build connections and repair fragile relations created by 'us and them' perceptions. An offshoot of such endeavours may improve relations and set-up the foundations for parent involvement. Parent involvement, in this instance, is an outcome, not the intention. While it is true that this suggestion shifts the obligations of the state from caring for its citizens to its employees in schools, not doing so may complicate an already precarious situation. The rewards, though, may be worth the effort.

Finally, a shift from a narrow perspective to a broader one is imperative. In other words, the focus should not only be on in-service teachers, it must also focus on pre-service teachers. The latter will need an education about the dynamic landscape of education, the inequalities and challenges of survival in under-resourced schools and in situations of growing poverty, rising unemployment rates and scarce resources. For pre-service teachers, Flynn (2007) suggests a curriculum that stresses the importance and benefits of parent involvement, arranging fieldwork experiences like observing teacher parent conferences, and preparing a toolkit for communicating with parents. Future teachers, we can assume, who are prepared for parent involvement are more likely to be receptive and to embrace school community partnerships.

REFERENCES

Amin, N. (2010). *A paradox of knowing: Teacher knowing about students*. Saarbrucken: Lambert Academic Publishers.

Amin, N., & Ramrathan, P. (2009). Preparing students to teach in and for diverse contexts: A learning to teach approach. *Perspectives in Education,* 27(1), 69-77.

Atkinson, P., Coffey, A., & Delamont, S. (Eds.). (2007). *Handbook of ethnography.* London, Thousand Oaks and New Delhi: Sage Publications.

Belenardo, S. (2001). Practices and conditions that lead to a sense of community in middle schools. *NASSP Bulletin,* 85, 33–45. doi: 10.1177%2F019263650108562704.

Bourdieu, P. (1973). Cultural reproduction and social reproduction. In, R. Brown (Ed.). *Knowledge, education and cultural advantage.* London: Tavistock.

Bourdieu, P. (2006). The form of capital. In H. Lauder, P. Brown, J. Dillabrough & A. Halsey (Eds.). *Education, globalization and social change.* Oxford: Oxford University Press.

Bourdieu, P., & Passeron, J. (1977). *Reproduction in education, society and culture.* Trans. R. Nice. London: Sage.

Catsambis, S. (1998). *Expanding knowledge of parent involvement in secondary education: Effects on high school academic success.* (Report 27). Retrieved from http://www.csos.jhu.edu/crespar/techReports/Report27.pdf.

Chindanya, A. (2011). *Parental involvement in primary schools: A case study of the Zaka District of Zimbabwe.* Unpublished doctoral thesis. Pretoria: University Of South Africa.

Chutgar, A., & Kanjee, A. (2009). School money funding flaws. *HSRC Review,* November. Available at http://www.hsrc.ac.za/en/review/november-2009/school-money.

Denessen, E., Bakker, J., & Grieved, M. (2007). Multi-ethnic schools' parental involvement policies and practices. *School Community Journal,* 17(2), 27-43.

DePlanty, J., Coulter-Kern, R., & Duchane, K. A. (2007). Perceptions of parent involvement in academic achievement. *The Journal of Educational Research,* 100(6), 361-368. doi: 10.3200/JOER.100.6. 361-368.

Deslandes, R., & Bertrand, R. (2005). Motivation of parent involvement in secondary-level schooling. *The Journal of Educational Research*, 98(3), 164-175. doi: 10.3200/JOER.98.3.164-175.

DoE. (1996). *South African Schools Act 84 of 1996*. Department of Education, Pretoria: Government Printer.

Dotterer, A. M., & Wehrspann, E. (2016). Parent involvement and academic outcomes among urban adolescents: Examining the role of school engagement. *Educational Psychology*, 36(4), 812-830. doi: 10.1080/01443410.2015.1099617.

Engelbrecht, P., Nel, M., Nel, N., & Tlale, D. (2015). Enacting understanding of inclusion in complex contexts: classroom practices of South African teachers. *South African Journal of Education*, 35(3), 1-10. doi: 10.15700/saje.v35n3a1074.

Epstein, J. (1988). *Homework practices, achievements, and behaviors of elementary school students.* (Report No. 26). Baltimore, MD: Johns Hopkins University, Center for Research on Elementary and Middle Schools.

Epstein, J. L. (2001). *School, family and community partnerships: Preparing educators and improving schools.* Boulder, Colorado: Westview Press.

Esping-Andersen, G. (1999). *Social foundations of postindustrial economies.* Oxford: Oxford University Press.

Farred, G. (2006). "Shooting the white girl first": Race in post-apartheid South Africa. In, *Globalization and race: Transformations in the cultural production of blackness.* K.M. Clarke & D.A. Thomas (Eds.). Durham, NC: Duke University Press.

Finders, M., & Lewis, C. (1994). Why some parents don't come to school. *EducationalLeadership*, 51(8), 50-54.

Flynn, G. (2007). Increasing parental involvement in our schools: The need to overcome obstacles, promote critical behaviors, and provide teacher training. *Journal of College Teaching & Learning*, 4(2), 23-30.

Geertz, C. (1974, Oct). "From the Native's Point of View": On the nature of anthropological understanding. *Bulletin of the American Academy of Arts and Sciences*, 28(1), 26-45.

Gordon, V., & Nocon, H. (2008). Reproducing segregation: Parent involvement, diversity, and school governance. *Journal of Latinos and Education*, 7(4), 320-339. doi: 10.1080/15348430802143634.

Graaff, J. (2017). Governance in the poorer public schools in South Africa from the perspective of the parent governor. Working Papers: 08/16. A working paper of the Research on Socioeconomic Policy Group (RESEP) at the University of Stellenbosch.

Hammersley, M., & Atkinson, P. (2007). *Ethnography principles in practice. Third edition*. London and New York: Routledge.

Heystek, J. (1999). Parents as partners in black schools: So important but why so unreliable? *Koers*, 64(1), 97-112.

Hill, N. E., & Craft, S. A. (2003). Parent-school involvement and school performance: Mediated pathways among socioeconomically comparable African American and Euro-American families. *Journal of Educational Psychology*, 95, 74-8. Retrieved from doi: 10.1037/0022-0663.95.1.74.

Isseri, S., Muthukrishna, N., & Philpott, S. C. (2018). Immigrant children's geographies of schooling experiences in South Africa. *Educational Research for Social Change*, 7(2), 39-56.

Jeynes, W. H. (2011). Parental involvement research: Moving to the next level. *School Community Journal*, 21(1), 9-18.

LaRocque, M. (2013). Addressing cultural and linguistic dissonance between parents and schools, preventing school failure. *Alternative Education for Children and Youth*, 57(2), 111-117. doi: 10.1080/1045988X.2012.677961.

Lemmer, E. M. (2007). Parent involvement in teacher education in South Africa. *International Journal about Parents in Education*, 1, 218-229.

Lemmer, E. M. (2009). Teachers' experiences of parental involvement with diverse family types. *Tydskrif vir Christelike Wetenskap*, 45, 87–105.

Lemmer, E., & Van Wyk, N. (2004a). Home-school communication in South African primary schools. *South African Journal of Education*, 24(3), 183-188.

Lemmer, E., & Van Wyk, N. (2004b). Schools reaching out: Comprehensive parent involvement in South African primary schools. *Africa Education Review*, 1(2), 259-278. doi: 10.1080/18146620408566284.

Levine-Rasky, C. (2009). Dynamics of parent involvement at a multicultural school. *British Journal of Sociology of Education*, 30(3), 331-344. doi: 10.1080/01425690902812604.

Maharaj, N. (2019). *Teachers' work in a context of diversity*. Unpublished doctoral thesis. Durban, South Africa: University of KwaZulu-Natal.

Makgopa, M., & Mokhele, M. (2013). Teachers' perceptions on parental involvement: A case study of two South African schools. *Journal of Educational and Social Research*, 3(3), 219-225. doi: 10.5901/jesr.2013.v3n3p219.

Manning, J., & Kunkel, A. (2014). *Researching interpersonal relationships: Qualitative methods, studies and analysis*. Los Angeles, London and New Delhi: Sage.

Mbokodi, S. M., & Singh, P. (2011). Parental partnerships in the governance of schools in the Black townships of Port Elizabeth. *Perspectives in Education*, 29(4), 38-48.

McNeal Jr, R. B. (2012). Checking In or checking out? Investigating the parent involvement reactive hypothesis. *The Journal of Educational Research*, 105(2), 79-89. doi: 10.1080/00220671.2010.519410.

Mestry, R., & Grobler, B. (2007). Collaboration and communication as effective strategies for parent involvement in public schools. *Educational Research and Review*, 2(7), 176-185.

Mmotlane, R., Winnaar, L., & Wa Kivilu, M. (2009). Personal characteristics that predict South Africans' participation in activities of their children's schools. *South African Journal of Education*, 29, 527-540.

Morrow, W. (2007). What is teachers' work? *Journal of Education*, (41)1, 3-20. doi:10.1111/j.1939-3466.2011.00007.

Msila, V. (2012). Black parent involvement in South African rural schools: Will parents ever help in advancing effective school management. *Journal of Education and Social Research, (2)2*, 203-213.

Myers, R. (2011). The familiar strange and the strange familiar in Anthropology and beyond. *General Anthropology,* 18(2), 1-4. doi: 10.1111/j.1939-3466.2011.00007.
Nojaja, J. M. (2009). *A model for parental involvement in disadvantaged South African schools.* Unpublished doctoral thesis. Vanderbijlpark, SA: North-West University.
Okeke, C. I. (2014). Effective home-school partnership: Some strategies to help strengthen parental involvement. *South African Journal of Education,* 34 (3), 1-9.
Olatoye, R. A., & Ogunkola, B. J. (2008). Parental involvement, interest in schooling and science achievement of junior secondary school students in Ogun State, Nigeria. *College Teaching Methods & Styles Journal,* 4(8), 33-40. doi:10.19030/ctms.v4i8.5563.
Patrikakou, E. (2005). *School-family partnerships for children's success.* New York, NY: Teachers College Press.
Peters, B. G. (2017). What is so wicked about wicked problems? A conceptual analysis and a research program. *Policy and Society,* 36(3), 385-396. doi: 10.1080/14494035.2017.1361633.
Reece, C., Staudt, M., & Ogle, A. (2013). Lessons learned from a neighborhood-based collaboration to increase parent engagement. *School Community Journal,* 23(2), 207-226.
Ramadikela, P. M. (2012). The management of parent involvement in historically disadvantaged secondary schools secondary in Tshwane West District, Gauteng. Unpublished Master of Education dissertation. Pretoria: University of South Africa.
Reimer, E. (1973). *School is dead.* Hammondsworth, Middlesex, England: Penguin Books.
Singh, P., Mbokodi, S. M., & Msila, V. T. (2004). Black parental involvement in education. *South African Journal of Education,* 24(4), 301-307.
Smit, A. G., & Liebenberg, L. (2003). Understanding the dynamics of parent involvement in schooling within the poverty context. *South African Journal of Education,* 23(1), 1-5.

Snell, P., Miguel, N., & East, J. (2009). Changing directions: Participatory action research as a parent involvement strategy. *Educational Action Research*, 17(2), 239-258. doi: 10.1080/09650790902914225.

StatsSA. (2017). *Poverty trends in South Africa: An examination of absolute poverty between 2006 and 2015*. Report No 03-10-06. Pretoria: Statistics South Africa. Retrieved from https://www.statssa.gov.za/publications/Report-03-10-06/Report-03-10-062015.pdf.

Swap, S. M. (1993). *Developing home-school partnerships: From concepts to practice*. New York: Teachers College Press.

Theodorou, E. (2008). Just how involved is 'involved'? Re-thinking parental involvement through exploring teachers' perceptions of immigrant families' school involvement in Cyprus. *Ethnography and Education*, 3(3), 253-269. doi: 10.1080/17457820802305493.

Topor, D. R., Keane, S. P., Shelton, T. L., & Calkins, S. D. (2012). Parent involvement and student academic performance: A multiple mediational analysis. *Journal of Prevention & Intervention in the Community*, 38(3), 183-197. doi: 10.1080/10852352.2010.486297.

Tosolt, B. (2010). Gender and race differences in middle school students' perceptions of caring teacher behaviors. *Multicultural Perspectives*, 12, 145–151. doi: 10.1080/15210960.2010.504484.

Van den Berg, M., & Van Reekum, R. (2011). Parent involvement as professionalization: Professionals' struggle for power in Dutch urban deprived areas. *Journal of Education Policy*, 26(3), 415–430. doi: 10.1080/02680939.2010.543155.

Van Wyk, J. N. (1996). *Parent involvement in black urban communities in Gauteng*. Unpublished doctoral thesis. Pretoria, South Africa: University of South Africa. Retrieved from https://pdfs.semanticscholar.org/395e/84c6f35c05ea2f814dae1521ced2472c3b83.pdf.

Van Wyk, N., & Lemmer, E. (2009). *Organising parent involvement in South African Schools*. Cape Town: Juta.

Vellymalay, S. N. (2012). Parental involvement at home: Analyzing the influence of parents' socioeconomic status. *Studies in Sociology of Science*, 3(1), 1-6. doi:10.3968/j.sss.1923018420120301.204.

Wilde, O. (1969/1891). *The artist as critic: Critical writings of Oscar Wilde.* R. Ellmann (Ed.). New York: Random House.

In: Parental Involvement
Editors: Nurit Kaplan Toren et al.
ISBN: 978-1-53616-828-0
© 2020 Nova Science Publishers, Inc.

Chapter 7

PRIMARY SCHOOL TEACHERS' EXPERIENCES OF PARENTAL INVOLVEMENT IN A TOWNSHIP SCHOOL: A SOUTH AFRICAN CASE STUDY

Mantsose Jane Sethusha[*]
University of South Africa, Pretoria, South Africa

ABSTRACT

Parental involvement has become a major challenge in schools in South Africa. It affects learners, teachers and the entire school community. Research conducted in the area of parental involvement has documented its influence on performance, attendance, behavior and children's positive attitudes towards school. These attributes contribute towards children's appreciation of the importance of education and provides a support network for them in curricula and extra-curricular activities, as well as in their social lives. Consequently, learners whose parents participate in their school lives are more likely to have higher self-esteem and be motivated, are better disciplined, and perform better in class regardless of their ethnic,

[*] Corresponding Author's E-mail: sethumj@unisa.ac.za.

social or racial backgrounds. In this chapter, we explore parental involvement practices in one school in a township in South Africa focusing on the identification of the challenges and provision of improvement and intervention strategies. A qualitative design and a case study approach were employed with semi-structured interviews used to collect data from participants. Participants were Foundation Phase (Grades R and 1-3) teachers from a primary school located in a township in one of the nine provinces in South Africa. Thematic analysis was used to analyse and to make sense of the teachers' narratives. All narratives provided a more robust understanding of the engagements, relations and communication necessary in a school-family relationship. It is envisaged that this study will provide workable strategies towards parental involvement in primary schools and also offer insightful accounts that may assist other parents and teachers.

Keywords: performance, teachers' experiences, improvement strategies, parental involvement, teaching and learning, classroom practices, learners, parents

INTRODUCTION

The education system in South Africa recognizes the important role that parents play in the schooling of their children. This is documented in the governance policy of the Department of Education in South Africa (The South African Schools Act No 84; 1996) and facilitated through the election of School Governing Bodies (SGBs) that represent the parent community on the school board. Through the existence of SGBs, parents and teachers are required to focus on creation of positive relationships that support holistic development of children. Parents can be involved in a variety of programs, in core and extra curricula activities, and in school governance and management. In this way, the parent community takes ownership of the vision and mission of the school and work together with teachers and School Management Teams (SMTs) to establish academic excellence and instill social goals in enhancing the schools' comprehensive plans. This in no way suggests that parents are managers of schools, prescribe how SMTs should be managing schools or how teachers should teach, but allows them (the parents) to take full accountability of governing matters and to ensure that the interests of their children are not compromised.

Parental involvement refers to the participation and involvement of parents and key caregivers in their children's school activities both at home and in the school environment (Guo & Kilderry, 2018). This participation enhances and contributes towards academic performance. Schools require parents to contribute their various skills, insights and knowledge, thereby strengthening relations between the school and its community. Bailey (2017) argues that schools and teachers must create positive and conducive environments for parental involvement initiatives to be successful. These initiatives need to be part of a contextually focused school improvement process. Bailey also points out that activities taking place in non-conducive school settings are more likely to lead to negative outcomes, such as poor academic performance of learners.

Despite the powers given to parents regarding the governance of schools, schools generally experience various challenges related to the involvement of parents (Addi-Raccah and Ainhoren, 2009). Several studies have explored parental involvement in schools with special emphasis on previously disadvantaged areas, high schools, urban settings and racially diverse schools (Charamba, 2016; Salwiesz, 2015; Page, 2016). The task of the school, in these cases, is to equip parents with knowledge and skills related to a range of programs in the school and to empower parents with the ability to execute the various tasks and activities allocated to them. In so doing, successful parental involvement is enhanced (Maluleke, 2014). Orientation programs for parents are important, as some parents come from previously disadvantaged backgrounds and might need continuous guidance and support. In certain instances, parents face barriers to effectively participate in their children's schooling because they themselves (the parents) had minimal education. They might not know where and how to begin and even may encounter language barriers given that South African is a multi-lingual country. Various scholars (O'Donoghue, 2014; Murray, Finigan-Carr, Jones, Copeland-Linder, Haynie, Cheng, 2014) highlighted lack of time, teacher attitudes, parental attitudes, cultural or socio-economic differences to be associated with lack of parental involvement in schools.

In this chapter, the focus is on teacher's perceptions of parental involvement in a township school in one of South Africa's nine provinces. The majority of learners in this township school are from an informal settlement (i.e., a township) with a demographic dominated by poverty and low educational background of the parents. The aim was to explore parental involvement in this particular school setting and provide ways in which teachers could deal with challenges posed by parental involvement or the lack thereof.

LITERATURE REVIEW AND THEORETICAL FRAMEWORK

Research regarding parents' participation in their children's schooling activities has shown benefits such as an improvement of learner achievement, a reduction of the dropout rate as well as delinquency, and generally fostering a more positive attitude towards school (Obayopo, 2017; Mwirichia, 2013). Such involvement often requires parents to use their own resources and time to support school activities. Epstein (2008) outlines various forms in which parents can participate in school activities. These are (a) establishment of home environments that support teaching and learning, (b) enhancing effective communication between school and home, (c) getting involved in school programs and supporting learners, (d) studying and learning at home, (e) being involved in school decision-making processes, and (f) collaborating with various stakeholders to support the school. Often, these parental involvement activities are classified into two broad categories, namely home-based parent involvement and school-based parent involvement (El Nokali, Bachman, & Votruba-Drzal, 2010; Epstein, 2008). Home-based parental involvement entails activities taking place at home, where parents take the lead and assist their children towards achieving academic success. These activities refer to schoolwork activities, such as helping children with homework, projects, discussions, performance and other academic related activities. Similarly, Maluleke (2014) argues that parental involvement goes beyond parents contacting the school and includes participating in general activities of the school, communicating with teachers and other stakeholders, participating in school events, and providing services to the school community.

Parental involvement activities also include parents' positive attitudes about education and their communication of expectations concerning academic performance of their children. Thuba, Kathuri and Mariene (2017) identified academic socialization as a form of parent involvement that promotes quality of education in schools. According to this approach, parenting practices such as communication of expectations about educational achievements, instilling academic and career aspirations, linking schoolwork and other current events form a key part of home-school partnerships. Epstein (2008) further emphasizes that home-school relations are extremely important, particularly in previously disadvantaged communities indicating that school and family should act in partnership in the best interest of the learners.

This relationship contributes towards young children success in schooling activities and in later life. According to Hirano and Rowe (2016) parental involvement in schooling activities include activities where schools assist families to establish home environments that support children's learning and assessment. Communication between the school and home is required to contribute towards school programs and learner progress. Parents are encouraged to volunteer and assist in organising events, recruiting, and organizing parental help and support. Parental involvement is also observable in activities where children study and learn at home (Guo & Kilderry, 2018; Yoder & Lopez, 2013), implying that schools need to provide parents with the necessary information and skills on how to assist learners at home with homework and other curriculum-related activities.

One of the major roles that parents are expected to play in schools is that of decision-making. In the South African context, parents are involved in this role of school-based decisions through SGB parent leaders and representatives. Collaborating with the parent community is often emphasized by schools and this entails identifying and integrating resources and services from the community to strengthen school programs, family practices, and student learning and development (Epstein, 2008).

However, the school faces numerous challenges getting parents involved in schooling activities, particularly in disadvantaged communities. Parents also face some barriers in as far as being involved in schooling activities is concerned. Some of these barriers often arise due to physical limitations and lack of opportunities for involvement. Other barriers include lack of time due to parents' work commitments, lack of academic knowledge and the required guidelines needed in order to assist their children in schooling activities.

Parents from low socioeconomic status often feel left out in schooling activities (Maluleke, 2014). In South Africa, people from low socio-economic status often live in townships that are underdeveloped and racially divided, semi-urban areas close to major cities. Informal settlements, on the other hand, evolved even further afield and are not ordinarily identified for residential purposes. Houses in informal settlements are shacks and makeshift structures providing "home" to people from extremely low socio-economic status. Due to their disadvantaged backgrounds, parents in townships and informal settlements often feel that they are inferior to the better-educated teachers and school administrators. These parents also do not have the required resources, knowledge and skills to allow them to effectively engage in collaborative relationships with schools (Maluleke, 2014; Page, 2016).

In the study reported in this chapter, the theoretical framework as outlined by Eccles and Harold (1996) was utilised to highlight five areas of parent involvement, namely monitoring, volunteering, involvement, contact about progress, and contact about how children can be supported. This framework is relevant to the study as it emphasizes parent's commitment to assisting their children with school work, participating in school activities, belonging to school committees and providing full support to all activities in the school. The limitations of this framework could be that it does not provide clear examples of how parents can be motivated to participate in schooling activities and how they can be equipped with skills to monitor such activities and to participate fully in academic programmes.

METHODS

The aim of this chapter is to explore primary school teachers' experiences of parental involvement in a township school in South Africa. The study used a case study approach and qualitative interpretive paradigm as guided by Creswell (2007). This paradigm outlines that the research rests within a methodological and philosophical frame, which aims at understanding social reality. The following questions guided the research:

- How do teachers perceive and experience parental involvement in a township primary school?
- How do these experiences influence teaching and learning?

Participants

Four teachers from a primary school were invited to participate in the study. These teachers taught in the Foundation Phase of schooling catering for learners from the Reception year class (Grade R) and Grades One, Two and Three. The ages of learners in the Foundation Phase range from six and nine years of age. One teacher from each grade level volunteered and participated in the study, which implied convenience sampling in a community that might otherwise be difficult to access.

The participating teachers were all from the same public primary school located in a township area and accommodating learners from surrounding villages as well as informal settlements. The school accommodated all primary school levels from Grade R to Grade 7 (as per the South African education system). The total learner enrolment across all eight years of schooling comprises 1,800 with a teacher: student ratio of about 1:42-45 per class. In Foundation Phase alone, there are eight classes (i.e., two classes per grade level) and the teachers of these classes work closely together, and share resources and materials for teaching and learning.

Data Collection

Semi-structured interviews were collected with four volunteer teachers allowing them to share their perceptions and experiences working with parents at the school. The researcher provided participants with orientation pertaining to the study and sought their consent in recording their responses. The central question was: "How do teachers create opportunities for parental involvement in your school?" and further prompts were used to gain an understanding of how the teachers worked with parents at the level where they were teaching. For example, the teachers were asked how they involved parents in schooling activities, how they encouraged parents to participate, which intervention strategies they used to ensure maximum parental involvement, how they created opportunities for parental involvement and which programmes or activities they exposed the parents to. Interview questions were asked and responded to in English since all teachers could speak and were confident speaking English. The interviews were audio-recorded in order to capture the teachers' responses. The researcher also made notes and recorded nuances, in order to capture key ideas that the teachers shared.

The teachers' narratives were transcribed in order to provide a written account for analytic purposes. The transcripts ensured authenticity of the responses to the interview questions and allowed the researcher to interpret the responses in line with the framework proposed by Eccles and Harold (1996).

The teachers shared their stories and experiences based on personal interactions with parents, as well as their own perspectives on parental involvement in the schooling of their children. Content analysis was used to identify and organise patterns in the teachers' responses (Neuendorf, 2002), and to gain an understanding of how parental involvement evolved in the township school where the study was conducted. Since this is a qualitative study, the researcher adopted a reflexive stance bracketing preconceived ideas and staying close to the transcribed textual data with the objective of understanding the participating teachers' perceptions and experiences of parental involvement in their respective classes. This reflexivity allowed the researcher to conduct the coding, analysis and synthesis of the meanings presented by the participants. Discussion with colleagues and other researchers enabled the author to maintain a high degree of credibility and trustworthiness interpreting the textual data. In the next section, I present the teachers' responses as direct quotes and in their own voices and discuss the findings in terms of the theoretical framework, concluding with some recommendations for how teachers could possibly engage with parents in poor communities.

FINDINGS AND DISCUSSION

The following section presents the narratives of the four volunteer teachers with the purpose of exploring their respective experiences of parental involvement. The teachers revealed how they tried to cope with the challenges relating to parental involvement and how the lack of parental involvement influenced effective teaching and learning in their classrooms. Each teacher's responses are presented after first presenting a brief biographical description of the teacher's experience as a teacher and concluding each case with an initial discussion of the theme evident from the interview.

The section concludes with a synthesis drawn from the major themes elaborating further on the challenges affecting teachers' attempts to involve parents in the schooling of their children. The findings of this research revealed that parental involvement is a concern for teachers in this particular township primary school and that its absence negatively influenced effective teaching and learning. Pseudonyms are used throughout and all other identifying information have been removed to ensure protection of the participants' privacy.

THE GRADE R TEACHER: MRS MOSIMA: PARENTAL CARE AT HOME IS IMPORTANT

Mrs Mosima is an energetic young teacher. In the interview, she indicated that she was in her fourth year as a reception year teacher. Despite holding a Certificate in Grade R teaching, Mrs Mosima was underqualified according to the South African credentialing system and therefore not recognized as a permanent member of staff at the school. However, she was in the second year of studying for the Bachelor of Education degree with the aim of acquiring such credentialing as a school teacher. Mrs Mosima highlighted challenges that she faced on a daily basis in relation to parental involvement, expressing her frustration as follows;

> *My class comprises of five to six-year olds. These are small children who still need care and nurturing from home. One of the challenges I face is health related, specifically on the side of cleanliness. I have learners who are not well cared for and have been trying to call their parents to discuss this. Unfortunately, these parents do not show up and this influences teaching and learning.*

The above quote reflects just one of the challenges that Mrs Mosima faces daily. Health education forms part of the curriculum for the foundation phase in the Life Skills subject as per the Curriculum and Assessment Policy Statement (Department of Education, 2015). The Life Skills curriculum covers aspects such as healthy habits and good hygiene practices, cleanliness, diseases, safety and nutrition. Effective teaching and learning of all these concepts require some form of collaboration between the home and school, and certainty that knowledge gained in the classroom is applied in practice at home. This includes parents preparing and presenting their children to schools in a responsible manner. Parental involvement includes parental care and hygiene of their children and provision of the neccessities needed at school. Children who lack parental care and early learning of basic life skills may be exposed to all kinds of neglect and potential exploitation and abuse, and a home environment that has inadequate care can negatively influence children's holistic development, and leave them extremely vulnerable.

Mrs Mosima also reflected on how she manages to cope with the challenge she presented. She mentioned the following;

> *I do not despair, I keep on calling parents of learners who are affected. In one instance, I requested the chairperson of the SBG to intervene. She visited the parents and I later observed changes with the appearance of the learner.*

According to the South African Schools Act (Department of Education; 1996), parents and representatives of parents (e.g., grandparents or other caregivers) must see to it that learners are properly cared for at home. The school is tasked with ensuring such care is taken at home and teachers should communicate good practice to parents. In the absence of parent-teacher cooperation, other community members could be called in to assist with communicating good practice to parents. In Mrs Mosima's quote above, it is clear that she understands the roles of SGB and that she acknowledges the importance of their intervention to gain parental involvement in the care of the children in her class. It also seems that the SGB at this township primary school took responsibility executing their roles on behalf of the teacher, bringing about the necessary changes in parental care at home with the subsequent improvement for the children.

As reflected in the quote above, the family is the first support structure to the child's success in school and in life (El Nokali et al., 2010). Early childhood education requires that children are cared for, nurtured and supported as it represents a critical period in their lives, having an effect on success in school and in later life. Caño, Cape, Cardosa, Miot, Pitogo, Quinio, and Merin (2016) posit that active collaboration between teachers and parents through parental involvement has been proven to benefit learners and contribute towards good learner performance. As Caño et al. (2016) posit, responsive parenting, which provides a strong foundation for optimal development in the early years, supports learners' holistic development.

GRADE 1 TEACHER: MS SMITH: HOW PARENTAL INVOLVEMENT CAN BE ENHANCED

Ms Smith had been teaching at the school for seven years and at the time of this study was in her second year of teaching Grade 1. She holds a Bachelor of Education degree, having specialized in the foundation phase of schooling, and was in the process of registering for a master's degree with specialization in Inclusive Education. When asked about her experiences of parental involvement, Ms Smith highlighted the following:

> *I honestly do not find any joy with parental involvement in my class. I have tried to attract parents by sending out notes in the learners' books, but this has only worked for a few parents. I can safely say that parental involvement in my class is minimal. Our school is basically overcrowded, I have forty-two learners in my class and the absence of their parents' involvement in school activities makes it difficult for me to teach effectively. Another contributory factor is that some of the parents in this community are young and still in school, others work in towns and are therefore not able to attend to school activities when required. This leaves parenting to grandparents who are then not educated and who feel they cannot contribute anything towards school activities.*

The school where this research was conducted is a township school that also accommodated learners from a nearby informal settlement. I did observe that the school was overcrowded, as all foundation phase classes had an enrolment of over forty learners. This posed serious challenges in as far as classroom management and control is concerned. It is evident from the quote above that Ms Smith introduced some intervention processes (i.e., sending notes) to involve parents of learners in her class. However, Ms Smith also attributed the lack of parental involvement to the fact that most parents were young and sought employment in nearby towns and as such were not available during the week—some of them not even at home to care for their children. Most learners, as she highlighted, were under the care of grandparents who appeared disinterested in school activities. Ms Smith also added;

> In our school, parents are required to collect their children's quarterly reports and this responsibility is often not properly attended to. There are some reports that were not collected from the previous quarter. This simply means that these parents are not aware of the achievements and progress of their children and as such would not be able to support their children as expected.

Despite any other involvement, parents need to collect children's report cards in person so as to keep track with their children's academic performance. Collecting learners' reports from school is a general practice in most South African schools. It is an opportunity where parents and teachers meet and talk about the learner's performance. Like in most schools, teachers at the school where the study took place used these parent-teacher report meetings as a strategy to enhance parental involvement in their school.

O'Donoghue (2014), Page (2016) and others argue that parental involvement enhances envisaged outcomes expected of schools, particularly if parents motivate their children for improving their performance. Attending at least some school activities such as collecting the child's report card, healthy relations between parents and the school are encouraged, and this contributes to parental involvement and parents serving as advocates for the school. If, however, parents do not become involved even in the teacher-parent meetings and collecting the report cards, there is little chance of motivating the child towards greater achievement in the school setting. With no meaningful interaction between teachers and parents, learning activities at home also suffer. Nonetheless, it seems that Ms Smith is aware of some of the challenges parents face engaging with the school such as time constraints, language barriers and apparent varying expectations by the parents themselves. It seems that the demographic of the school where the present study took place—that is, the township and informal settlement area—posed a major barrier gaining accountability from parents, a key stakeholder in the successful progress of the children attending the school.

GRADE 2 TEACHER: MS PILLAY: COMMUNICATION IS KEY

Ms Pillay had been teaching at the school for ten years and was the head of the department (HoD) for the foundation phase. Her responsibilities included managing and supporting the whole foundation phase, over and above taking care of her Grade 2 class. The responses she provided, therefore, were from the perspective of both a class teacher and the HoD. She supported the foundation phase with curriculum related activities pertaining to learning areas. During the interview, Ms Pillay mentioned that she encouraged teachers in the foundation phase to keep on contacting parents and encouraging them to participate in school activities. She shared her support as follows:

> *I always request teachers to keep records of all communication that they send to parents. You know.... Some parents have a tendency of saying they were not aware of announcements or communication sent to them. Some parents do not participate in positive aspects of the school, they only wait for something negative to happen ...that is the only time we see them at school*

Mrs Pillay's response above shows that teachers at this school keep evidence of attempts to communicate with parents, to avoid later being accused of failing to contact parents or to involve them in school activities. The teachers seemed concerned about their reputation to protect themselves in cases where disputes could arise, relating to lack of communication from the side of the school. On the other hand, communication is therefore crucial in enhancing the quality of teaching and learning and is therefore a means to enhance parental involvement (Peterson, Rubie-Davis, Elley-Brown, Widdowson, Dixon, & Irving; 2011). Nevertheless, in spite of keeping record of their communications with parents there is still a lack of parental involvement most likely due to parents' inability to grasp these communications due to lacking literacy skills.

Mrs Pillay also highlighted her concern that she does not give homework because the learners in her class do not do it. She reflected as follows:

> *I used to give learners homework every day, asked learners to do some reading at home or do some research or collect artefacts. Only a few learners will bring evidence that this was done, but most just indicate that they do not have resources and no one to help them at home. One learner in my class told me that her parents said they do not know how to help her at home.*

It is evident from the quote above that some families probably experience predicaments that prevent them from providing the necessary resources to assist learners at home (Epstein, 2008; Murray et al., 2014). Learners are encouraged to read at home and this activity requires having books or magazines to read, and parental involvement in early literacy development when parents read to the child. Bailey (2017) also posits that learning at home is one way of enhancing parental involvement. However, when the parents themselves are challenged with limited literacy skills due to their own lack of education, such home-based involvement is not possible and, as in the extract above, homework activities suffer.

GRADE 3 TEACHER: MRS TATE: SUPPORT FOR PARENTS IS ESSENTIAL

Mrs Tate had been teaching for seven years at the school. She started as a temporary teacher, but later obtained a Teachers Diploma in Education. At the time of this research, she was in her second year for the Bachelor of Education degree specialising in the foundation phase. She was a full-time teacher and was in her third year of teaching Grade 3. She mentioned that over the years her experiences with parental involvement were mostly on the negative side as reflected in the following extract:

> *I honestly think parents in our community do not understand their role with respect to supporting the school. I heard other teachers saying that parents here do not care, but I believe this goes beyond that. I feel that sometimes parents do not understand how to support their children in school activities. The sad part is that when we call them to parent information sessions, very few parents come, and it is these few parents who then take decisions on behalf of all the parents.*

As indicated in the above extract, parents in the community served by this particular school need to be guided and oriented towards school programs and how they can be involved (O'Donoghue, 2014). However, parents need to attend these orientations and information sessions offered by the school; if they do not attend, such guidances cannot be given. Possible reasons why parents are unwilling to attend orientation sessions could be lack of literacy levels of parents, and their unwillingness to share the knowledge they do have in fear of being judged as incompetent (Van Schalkwyk, 2017). Another reason could be the timing of school events and meetings schedules. Early communication of meeting times could encourage parents to attend. However, with many parents in the township community working long hours and far away from home, teachers might have to adjust the meeting times to accommodate parents availability, which is not always possible (for the teachers). Schools therefore need to be accommodative of parents' circumstances and maintain open lines of communication between parents and teachers.

SYNTHESIS

The findings of this study revealed a basic understanding of the challenges experienced by teachers to encourage parental involvement. Based on the teachers' perceptions and experiences, parents did not attend parent meetings scheduled by the school and appeared disinterested in schooling activities. The lack of parental involvement in school activities is seemingly assigned to parents inability to take responsibility for the home-school relationship and engaging with the child's education at home (Eccles & Harrold, 1996; Epstein, 2008). There are some instances mentioned by the teachers I interviewed where parents are involved and participated in schooling activities, mostly through serving on the SGB. These parents also support the teachers by reaching out to the uninvolved parents in the community. It is important to note that parental involvement is an intergral component of a learners' life, particularly in the early school years and that the absence of this has implications for effective teaching and learning. For example, parental involvement enhances the school and home connection, assures learners that their parents are interested in their education, and this in turn enhances continued motivation and self-confidence amongst the learners (Adamski, Fraser & Peiro, 2013). Nonetheless, it seems to be the responsibility of the school to ensure that a positive relationship between the parent and the teacher is established and that children's best interests are accommodated. There are, however, serious barriers affecting parental involvement, such as time, literacy levels and lack of education among the parents that negatively impact on parent-school relationship building. As Addi-Raccah and Ainhoren (2009) posits, schools need to work around these issues and implement effective strategies to encourage parental involvement despite the barriers, as parental involvement in the early school years is vital to success in later life.

Based on Eccles and Harrold's (1996) framework, the findings from this study highlighted particular gaps in parents' ability to monitor their children's school-related behaviour and check their progress. Parents who do not even attend parent-teacher meetings to check the progress of their child's academic achievement presented with low levels of commitment assisting their children with school work.

Monitoring also requires parents to contribute to teachers' requests to help with their child's homework, as Mrs Pillay stated that she no longer gives homework because the parents do not or cannot assist their children with completing the homework tasks. The teachers I interviewed all commented on difficulties contacting parents to assist their children to achieve success in school activities, because parents seemingly maintained an aloofness to becoming involved through volunteering or attending any school-related activities. Perhaps due to other challenges not explored in this study, parents in the township and informal settlement feeding areas of the school, could face many other difficulties relating to being involved in school activities.

RECOMMENDATIONS

Collaboration plays a key role, where parents need to work with teachers to assist learners with school activities. It is important that parents understand their roles in as far as their involvement in school is concerned. In striving for parental involvement in schools such as the one in the study reported here, parental orientations to school programs can be introduced, focusing on equipping them with skills, abilities and resources to work with their children at home.

This would be a start to enhance parents' meaningful participation in formal school activities. Schools in all contexts need to recognise that parents require guidance and support and the provision of these needs to be in the form of constant interaction and engagement with school structures. Although this would add more tasks for the teachers, such support from the school is particularly relevant in poor communities such as the township and informal settlement where the school is located. Support from the Department of Education in the province providing, for example, more teachers would probably be a good start.

Workshops capacitating SGBs and SMTs with parental involvement activities need to take priority in schools located in townships and informal settlements. SMTs have responsibilities to work closely with parents and communities to organise events where parents and families are brought together. Examples of these are fun days, open days, sporting activities, music activities, talent shows and recognition meetings. The school needs to identify the parents' strengths and interests and use these to involve them in school activities. In this way, parents will feel important and recognised and this could enhance their participation.

These events need to be organised at times when parents could possibly attend and be effectively communicated to ensure that parents make time to attend. The main objective should be to find ways that would attract parents to the school so that relationships could be established.

Collaborations between schools and stakeholders can give rise to programmes that include activities promoting parenting styles, entrepreneurship activities, health and wellness and other programmes that can benefit the well being of families. These programmes need to focus on strategies that would advance children's success beyond the classroom. Such collaborative activities should take into account the availability of parents and should be scheduled at times when parents could attend (i.e., when not working far away from the community and the school). Communication is key to establishing healthy relationships between the school and the parent community. Various methods could be used, such as newsletters, phone, e-mail, mail, social media and face-to-face meetings. These should take place frequently and in an engaging manner that will make parents feel welcomed at the school despite their own inabilities.

Finally, it is crucial for schools in poverty-stricken communities such as the one where this study was conducted to create a conducive and welcoming atmosphere for engagement. This must be observable upon entrance at the school as well as in the communication with the parents and caregivers. Reception staff also need to be helpful and ready to assist with enquiries in a systematic manner, considering the school ethos, and in an attempt to create an environment likely to encourage parents to be involved in school activities. Peterson et al. (2011) argue that parents-teacher collaborations are important as these contribute towards learners' academic success at school. Therefore, both teachers and parents need to be equipped as stakeholders with deeper insight into the schooling of the youth and in order to create a better future for all involved. When parents are well equipped through engaging in accessible and welcoming school activities, their understanding of such activities will broaden and enhance their ability to contribute positively.

REFERENCES

Adamski, A., Fraser, B. J. & Peiro, M. M. (2013). Parental involvement in schooling, classroom environment and student outcomes. *Learning Environment Research*, *16*, 315-328. doi: 10.1007/s10984-012-9121-7.

Addi-Raccah, A. & Ainhoren, R. (2009). School governance and teachers' attitudes to parents' involvement in schools. *Teaching and Teacher Education*, *25*(6), 805-813. doi:10.1016/j.tate.2009.01.006.

Averill, R., Metson, A. & Bailey, S. (2016). Enhancing parental involvement in student learning. *Curriculum Matters*, *12*, 109-131. Doi: 10.18296/cm.0016.

Bailey, T. (2017). *The Impact of Parental Involvement on Student Success: School and Family Partnership from the Perspective of Students.* Unpublished doctoral dissertation for *Doctor of Education in Teacher Leadership Dissertations*, Kennesaw State University. http://digitalcommons.kennesaw.edu/teachleaddoc_etd/22.

Caño, K. J., Cape, M. G., Cardosa, J. M., Miot, C., Pitogo, G. R., Quinio, C. M. & Merin, J. (2016). Parental involvement on pupils' performance: Epstein's framework. *The Online Journal of New Horizons in Education*, Cebu Normal University, Volume 6 (4), 143-150.

Charamba, M. (2016). *The management of parental involvement at selected secondary schools in the Zeerust District, North West Province.* Unpublished master's thesis for Master degree of Education, University of South Africa.

Cresswell, J. W. (2007). *Qualitative inquiry and research design: choosing among five approaches.* 2nd ed. Thousand Oaks, CA: Sage Publications.

Department of Education. (2015). *Curriculum and Assessment Policy Statement (CAPS)*, Pretoria, South Africa. Retrieved from https://www.education.gov.za.

Department of Education. (2016). *South African Schools Act* (SASA), Pretoria, South Retrieved from Africa. https://www.education.gov.za.

Eccles, J. S. & Harold, R. D. (1996). Parent–school involvement during the early adolescent years. *Teachers College Record*, *94*, 568–587.

El Nokali, N. E., Bachman, H. J. & Votruba-Drzal, E. (2010). Parent involvement and children's academic and social development in elementary school. *Child Development*, *81*(3), 988-1005. doi: 10.1111/j.1467-8624.2010.01447.x.

Epstein, J. K. (2008). Improving family and community involvement in secondary schools. *The Education Digest*, *73*(6), 9-12.

Guo, K. & Kilderry, A. (2018). Teacher accounts of parent involvement in children's education in China. *Teaching and Teacher Education*, *69*, 95-103.

Hirano, K. A. & Rowe, D. A. (2016). A Conceptual model for parent involvement in secondary special education. *Journal of Disability Policy Studies*. *27*(1), 43–53. doi: 10.1177/1044207315583901.

Maluleke, S. G. (2014). *Parental involvement in their children's education in the Vhembe District: Limpopo*. Unpublished master's thesis for the Master of Education degree, University of South Africa.

Murray, K. W., Finigan-Carr, N., Jones, V., Copeland-Linder, N., Haynie, D. L. & Cheng, T. L. (2014). Barriers and Facilitators to School-Based Parent Involvement for Parents of Urban Public Middle School Students. *HHS Public Access. Sage*, Vol 6-1-12. doi: 10.1177/2158244014558030.

Mwirichia, V. M. (2013). *Influence of parental involvement on academic performance of preschool children Kangeta Division, Meru County, Kenya*. Thesis report submitted in partial fulfillment of the requirements for the degree of Masters of Education in Early Childhood Education in the Department of Educational Communication and Technology, University of Nairobi. cees.uonbi.ac.ke.

Neuendorf, K. A. (2002). *The content analysis guidebook*. Thousand Oaks, CA: Sage Publications.

Obayopo, R. O. (2017). *Parental involvement in primary schools: a case study of three socio-economic disparate schools in Ile-Ife, Nigeria*. Dissertation: Master of Education, Education Management, University of South Africa. uir.unisa.ac.za.

O'Donoghue, K. L. (2014). *Barriers to Parental Involvement in Schools: Developing Diverse Programs to Include Unique Demographics*.

Thesis: The College at Brockport: State University of NewYork Digital Commons @Brockport. Education and Human Development Master's Theses Education and Human Development.

Page, R. D. (2016). *The role that parents play in their children's academic progress at a previously disadvantaged primary school in Cape Town.* Thesis submitted in fulfilment of the requirements in Education, University of the Western Cape, South Africa.

Peterson, E. R., Rubie-Davis, C. M., Elley-Brown, M. J., Widdowson, D.A., Dixon, R. S. & Irving, S. E. (2011). Who is to blame? Students, teachers and parents views on who is responsible for student achievement. *Research in Education, 86*(1), 1-12.

Salwiesz, M. C. (2015). *The impact of parent involvement on the education of children: Unlocking the role of the parent involvement in promoting academic achievement among racially diverse kindergarteners.* Dissertation submitted in partial fulfillment of the requirements for Doctor of Philosophy. Case Western Reserve University.

South Africa. (1996b). *The South African Schools Act, No. 84 of 1996.* Pretoria: Government Printers. Retrieved from https://www.gov.za.

Thuba, E., Kathuri, N. J. & Mariene, J. G. (2017). Impacts of Parents' Academic Socialization in Promoting Quality of Education in Public Day Secondary Schools in Meru County – Kenya. *International Journal of Scientific and Research Publications, 7*(8), 2250-3153. ISSN 2250-3153.

Van Schalkwyk, G. J. (2017). Socio-cultural barriers to entry for School-Based Family Counselling. *International Journal of School-Based Family Counseling, 9,* (Special Topic Issue), 1-10.

Yoder, J. R. & Lopez, A. (2013). Parent's Perceptions of Involvement in Children's Education: Findings from a Qualitative Study of Public Housing Residents. *Child and Adolescent Social Work, 30,* 415–433.doi: 10.1007/s10560-013-0298-0.

In: Parental Involvement
Editors: Nurit Kaplan Toren et al.
ISBN: 978-1-53616-828-0
© 2020 Nova Science Publishers, Inc.

Chapter 8

IMMIGRANT TEACHERS IN SCHOOLS: A STRATEGY TO IMPROVE PARENTAL INVOLVEMENT OF IMMIGRANT PARENTS

Florence Nyemba[*], *PhD*
Department of Education, Criminal Justice and Human Services
University of Cincinnati, Cincinnati, Ohio, US

ABSTRACT

This chapter argues for an increased representation of immigrant teachers in schools with high immigrant student populations across all nations. The chapter refers to 'immigrants' as individuals born outside the country where they currently reside. The presence of individuals who share a similar social, cultural and linguistic background with students and their parents would make the school environment more welcoming and increase parental involvement practices. Immigrant teachers act as role models, mentors, and advocates for immigrant parents and their children. By sharing a similar immigrant background, these teachers have a better understanding of the needs of immigrant parents and their children, hence would help bridge the social, cultural and linguistic gap (cultural

---
[*] Corresponding Author's E-mail: florence.nyemba@gmail.com.

translators) between schools and immigrants (Clewell & Villegas, 2001). This chapter suggests for educational legislatures, community leaders and school districts with high immigrant populations to prioritize teacher diversity and develop strategies to attract and retain immigrant teachers of a similar demographic. This step should begin by developing a culturally sensitive teacher education curriculum and teacher preparation programs that attract and help immigrants to teach in their children's schools.

Keywords: culturally responsive pedagogy, parental involvement, immigrant parents, immigrant teachers, teacher education

INTRODUCTION

Parental involvement is defined as when parents are full partners in their children's education and are included, as is appropriate, in decision-making and on advisory committees to assist in the education of their children (Epstein & Jansorn, 2004; Epstein & Sanders, 2006). Schools are tasked with assisting families by helping them create home environments that will allow them to support children as students. Promoting activities that increase the presence of parents in schools such as inviting them to participate in school and classroom volunteer programs, workshops and contributing to school board councils helps parents contribute to their children's learning outcomes (Epstein & Jansorn, 2004; Epstein & Sanders, 2006). Barton (2003), argues that, an increased participation by parents, families, and communities in their children's schooling correlates with a welcoming school environment and higher academic performance. Students have the increased ability to earn higher grades and graduate from school and potentially enroll in higher education when there is a strong partnership between parents and schools (Baker, Wise, Kelley, & Skiba, 2016; Barton, 2003; Jeynes, 2007, 2017; Olivos, 2006).

However, several studies find that although immigrant parents highly value education and hold high educational expectations for their children, they are not highly involved in their children's school activities (Peterson & Ladky, 2007; Sobel & Kugler, 2007; Turney & Kao, 2009). They are less likely "to visit their children's school, participate in or attend school activities and events, help with homework, and talk to teachers and school staff" (Thao, 2009, p. 1). This lack of participation is attributed to several barriers immigrant parents encounter and which are less likely to be experienced by nonimmigrant parents (Hornby & Lafaele, 2011; Thao, 2009). Among the most documented barriers include the inability by some immigrant parents to speak the host languages, lack of knowledge about the host country's educational system and unfamiliarity with the new social way of life (Turney & Kao, 2009). All these barriers created strained relationships between schools and immigrant communities, with parents experiencing negative attitudes from teachers and school staff because of their cultural and linguistic differences (Hornby & Lafaele, 2011). Several studies revealed that some immigrant parents complained that teachers and staff mistreated and disrespected them when they visited schools. They do not have the patience to listen to immigrant parents speaking with foreign accents leading to a complete communication breakdown (Berthelsen & Walker, 2008; Dor & Rucker-Naidu, 2012; Olivos, 2006).

This cultural and linguistic disconnect between schools and immigrant communities' leaves parents without the resources they need to support their children's learning. Parents are most likely motivated to participate when they are confident that they have some degree of control and influence over their children's learning (Hoover-Dempsey, 2011). Furthermore, some immigrant parents stated that if they have strong social support network systems that include interacting with immigrant teachers who are more likely to understand their needs, they would be more involved in school activities. They argued that sometimes they feel like outsiders when they attend school meetings because they do not encounter any school personnel sharing an immigrant background with them. They are also hesitant to seek assistance in fear of the reaction they would get from nonimmigrant teachers and staff.

Parents experience a sense of belonging in their children's schools when teachers display positive attitudes towards them (Hornby & Lafaele, 2011; Waanders, Mendez, & Downer, 2007). Although a few public schools made efforts to provide some of the resources needed to support immigrant students and their families such as school psychologists, counselors, social workers and nurses (Olivos & Mendoza, 2009), the outcry is that there still lacks the socio-cultural support system provided by immigrant teachers desired by immigrant parents and their children to help with educational adjustments. This underrepresentation of immigrant teachers in the classroom is extensively evident in almost all the countries experiencing higher immigrant populations.

THE LACK OF IMMIGRANT TEACHERS IN THE CLASSROOM

With the increased population of immigrant students in the classrooms the question has been, why is the teaching force not as diverse as it needs to be in countries with increasing immigrant populations? Various studies indicate that the struggle remains for most countries in making their educational systems more responsive to the needs required by immigrant students to thrive in school (Ahad & Benton, 2018) and for their parents to be highly involved in school activities. In the United States for example, the K-12 population has become more progressively diverse with immigrant students comprising over one-third of school enrollment, yet the teaching force in public schools is disproportionally made up of nonimmigrant American teachers (mostly white) with only one tenth of minority teachers including immigrants (Carter Andrews, Castro, Cho, Petchauer, Richmond, & Floden, 2019; Dilworth & Coleman, 2014; Figlio & Özek, 2017; McFarland et al., 2018; Musu-Gillette, de Brey, Hussar, Sonnenberg, & Wilkinson-Flicker, 2017; Snyder, Hoffman, & Geddes, 1999; Taie & Goldring, 2017). The most recent data, compiled by the United States Department of Education, Schools and Staffing Survey (SASS), indicate that the growth of minority teaching force, including immigrant teachers, has not improved at all compared to nonimmigrant white American teachers in more than 15 years (Figure 1; National Center for Education Statistics, 2018).

Immigrant Teachers in Schools

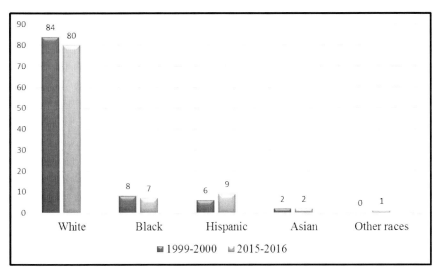

Source: U.S. Department of Education, National Center for Education Statistics, Schools and Staffing Survey (SASS), "Public School Teacher Data File," "Charter School Teacher Data File," "Public School Data File," and "Charter School Data File," 1999–2000; and National Teacher and Principal Survey (NTPS), "Public School Teacher Data File," 2015–16. See *Digest of Education Statistics 2017*.

Figure 1. Percentage Distribution of Teachers in Public Elementary and Secondary Schools, by Race/Ethnicity: School Years 1999–2000 and 2015–16.

As indicated in the data, white teachers continue to make up over 80 percent of the teaching force while minority teachers remained at the bottom without any significant improvements since 1999. Hispanic teachers only improved by three percent, while black teachers, including immigrants from Africa and the Caribbean decreased by one percent, the percentage of Asian teachers does not show any improvement at all and those with two or more races only improved by 1%. This has been concurrent in all the 50 states across the United States.

Further studies also revealed that not only is the teacher's ratio shown in Figure 1 of great concern, but characteristics of public elementary and secondary school principals is also lacking diversity in the United States. Results from the 2015-16 National Teacher and Principal Survey (NTPS) indicates that nonimmigrant white school principals were as high as 77.8 percent followed by Blacks 10,6 percent, Hispanics 8.2 percent and at the bottom Asians with a low 3.4 percent (National Center for Education Statistics, 2018). The shortage of immigrant teachers was also observed in Australia despite its primary and secondary school population is very diverse in terms of ethnic, linguistic and cultural background. Only a fraction (16.75%) of the Australia teaching force was multicultural compared to 81.29% nonimmigrant white Australian teachers in 2007 with no indication to improvement over the next decade (Collins & Reid, 2012).

This growing presence of immigrant children in schools have caused many scholars across the globe to demand a teaching force that reflects the diversity of the students' population and their parents (Adair, Tobin, & Arzubiaga, 2012; Darling-Hammond & Sykes, 1999; Mancilla-Martinez & Lesaux, 2014; Scheetz, 1995; Shure, 2001; Stephens, 1999; Tobin, Arzubiaga, & Adair, 2013). They argue that the lack of diversity in the teaching force negatively impact on immigrant populations in that not only does it affect parental involvement practices as previously discussed, but it also lowers the academic performance by immigrant students.

LOW ACADEMIC PERFORMANCE BY IMMIGRANT STUDENTS

The central question regarding immigrant children in schools is how they are performing compared to nonimmigrant students. The 2015 Organization for Economic Cooperation and Development (OECD) report indicates that in most countries immigrant students perform poorly in school and have high dropout rates compared to nonimmigrant students (Boon & Lewthwaite, 2016). For example, in the United States, school dropout rates were highest among Hispanics, Asians, Africans and Pacific Islander youths compared to nonimmigrant students (American Community Survey, 2017; McFarland et al., 2018). Similarly, apart from Croatia and Switzerland, many European countries also record high percentages of immigrant students dropping out of school early each year. For example, in Malta as high as 20% of immigrant students drop out of school each year; Romania records 19%, Iceland 17%, Greece 13.1%, Italy 13, 7% and Spain 18,6% (Ahad & Benton, 2018). Results on standardized testing scores in the United States also revealed that immigrant students perform worse at all grade levels and in all subject areas (i.e., science, math, and especially reading) and were substantially more likely to score below the nationally ranked 25th percentile (Schleicher, 2015). In Europe, immigrant students also perform lower on international tests causing the majority to drop out before they graduate and limiting their future career opportunities (Ahad & Benton, 2018; Harte, Herrera, Stepanek, & Rand, 2016). The specific concern that emerged from these analyses is the long shortage of skilled teachers to work effectively with immigrant students.

The process of immigration is very stressful for these children and their parents. Most nonimmigrant teachers are not familiar with the kind of issues immigrant children in their classrooms are dealing with, which cause them to skip classes and ultimately dropping out of school. Several scholars raised the argument that nonimmigrant teachers and school principals are not fully prepared for the education and training of immigrant children who have specific needs that must be understood, identified and addressed by educators working with and learning from the students and their parents (Darling-Hammond & Sykes, 1999; Rodriguez-Valls, 2016; Shure, 2001; Stephens, 1999). Immigrant students and their parents bring with them different linguistics cultures, which results in language barriers and a cultural disconnect between schools and immigrant communities. As high as 64% of immigrant students, during the first years in school, speak languages at home that are different from that of the school they attend and cannot read or speak well the predominant language of their host nations. They require abundance of support to familiarize them with the new language and educational system (OECD, 2015; Schleicher, 2015). However, many nonimmigrant teachers lack such skills and competence needed to meet the requirements of these immigrant students and their parents (Ladson-Billings, 2014; Rodriguez-Valls, 2016; Rushton, 2000; Schleicher, 2015; Webster & Valeo, 2011).

A research conducted by Davis (2008) with preservice teachers revealed that their knowledge of diverse cultures in the classroom was marginal. Even experienced educators often employ a pervasive deficit paradigm and blame immigrant students and their families for lower academic achievements and perceived inadequacies (Darling-Hammond, 2010; Davis, 2008; McKoy, MacLeod, Walter, & Nolker, 2017). Results from a 2013 OECD Teaching and Learning Survey (TALIS) across different countries indicated that nonimmigrant teachers needed more professional development in the area of teaching in multicultural settings. On top of the list were nonimmigrant teachers from Latin American countries like Brazil and Chile, as well as from Italy, among others (OECD, 2013). Eres (2016) argued that when teachers cannot comprehend the cultural characteristics of their students, they fail to understand the underlying factors that contribute to students' behavior in the classroom. This usually results in teachers using bad judgements when punishing immigrant students for misconduct in class. On the other hand, teachers complain that these behaviors are new to them but they still use classroom management approaches they are familiar with that may not be suitable to control such behaviors (Eres, 2016; Gershenson, Holt, & Papageorge, 2016; Holt & Gershenson, 2015). Other studies also revealed that, immigrant students are suspended or expelled from schools at disproportionate rates due to failure by nonimmigrant teachers to understand the factors that contribute to their behaviors and come up with alternative intervention strategies. This harsh disciplinary action from teachers place immigrant students at higher risk of academic disengagement and increase the probability that they will drop out of school and resort to risk behaviors for survival (Boser, Wilhelm, & Hanna, 2014).

CULTURALLY RESPONSIVE PEDAGOGY

The increasing gap between the culturally and linguistic diverse students and their teachers drives schools to rethink classroom strategies and family engagement practices to best navigate this cultural divide (Tamer, 2014). If schools are to fully prepare teachers for diverse classrooms, there is the need to redesign teacher education programs to better equip them with the pedagogy and methodology needed to meet the needs of students and their parents (Ford, 2010; Ladson-Billings, 2014; Rodriguez-Valls, 2016; Tamer, 2014). According to Gay (2002), "Through proper training, teachers learn to bridge the gap between instructional delivery and diverse learning styles and establish continuity between how diverse students learn and communicate and how the school approaches teaching and learning" (Krasnoff, 2016, p. 6). Such pedagogical approaches improve teachers' knowledge about their students' cultural backgrounds (i.e., past experiences, home and community culture) with the intent to use that knowledge to design lessons that increase students' academic success and parents engagement (Krasnoff, 2016; Ladson-Billings, 2014; Rodriguez-Valls, 2016; Tamer, 2014).

Culturally Responsive Pedagogy (CRP) is defined as an effective method of teaching in culturally diverse classrooms where teachers are student centered and strives to eliminate barriers to learning and achievement by all students. Culturally responsive teachers open the doors for culturally different students to reach their academic potential (Ford, 2010; Richards, Brown, & Forde, 2007). CRP also cultivates strong relationships that connect home and school cultures, social interactions and expectations for learning and the belief that knowledge is socially constructed and changing (Gay, 2010). It is against this background that CRP is an effective tool to improve parental involvement practices in schools globally. An important step that teachers should take to work successfully with diverse parents is through transforming their socio-cultural consciousness and attitudes towards people who are different from them (Villegas & Lucas, 2002). CRP challenges teachers to undergo a personal transformation through careful self-reflection of their own biases, attitudes, beliefs as well as their beliefs about others (Harro, 2000). Teachers "must recognize discrimination based on ethnicity, social class, and skin color and inspect and confront any negative attitudes they might have toward diverse student groups" (Krasnoff, 2016, p.6). By going through this personal reflection teachers can uncover some experiences in their own lives that shaped the way they view and relate to others (Harro, 2000; Villegas & Lucas, 2002). Discovering why and who they are helps teachers to reconcile their negative views toward specific groups of people with different cultural identities than theirs (Rodriguez-Valls, 2016; Villegas & Lucas, 2002). Once they remove their socio-cultural biases, teachers can respect parents of diverse backgrounds, acknowledge and incorporate the knowledge they bring to schools instead of silencing and alienating them. Teachers will be able to accommodate various culturally centered ways of knowing, thinking, speaking, feeling and behaving.

CRP also challenges schools to implement policies and procedures that promote inclusiveness in the way they deliver services for students and parents. If school principals, teachers and office administrators fail to conform to these, the school environment becomes a battleground for exclusivity (Gay, 2002). The system of privilege and preferences, which is evident in the educational systems in most developed countries, create enclaves of exclusivity in schools in which certain demographic of groups are denied adequate resources to support students' academic achievements and parents' engagement. For example, there is enough evidence to support that schools are reluctant to allocate financial resources to support community engagement practices with immigrant parents. Most schools do not have language translators and training workshops to help immigrant parents understand the host country's school system to improve parental involvement practices. Instead, more resources are channeled towards sport activities than for diversity training and workshops (Zhu, 2017). Furthermore, parents may not participate in school activities if they believe that their children are discriminated against. Several studies revealed the unequal distribution of teachers in schools, with best qualified teachers placed in middle-class school communities, and less qualified teachers placed in poor neighborhoods with higher immigrant populations (Nieto, 1992; Zhu, 2017). The allocation of classes for students is also based on a discriminatory system. Students with an immigrant background are negatively viewed as underperforming, hence cannot compete with nonimmigrant students in high performance classes or resources that are rigorous. This leaves immigrant students' capabilities unnoticed and underdeveloped (Clotfelter, Ladd, & Vigdor, 2006; Darling-Hammond, 2004; Goldhaber, Lavery, & Theobald, 2015). A teacher's responsibility includes holding each student with high expectations and help all students learn (Krasnoff, 2016). If parents believe that their children are treated equally by their teachers, they become motivated to participate in school activities.

Adopting CRP would change this to a more inclusive system and welcome immigrant parents and student to bring their culture-specific knowledge to the fore. Culturally responsive teachers recognize and incorporate into their instructional process the community identity, linguistic variances and beliefs their diverse students bring into the classrooms. By doing so, they build authentic relationships with the students and their communities (Howard, 2007). The curriculum delineates what will be taught, when it will be taught, and the materials that will be used (Ford, 2010). Therefore, culturally responsive teachers must develop curriculum that engages culturally different students and their parents. The curriculum should make connections between what the teachers teach and what culturally different students want to learn. CRP teachers should therefore present a balanced, comprehensive, and multidimensional, view of the topic, issues and events including addressing stereotypes, distortions, and omissions in the curriculum (Banks, 2008; Ford, 2010). Such curriculum creates an inclusive learning environment for students and parents from diverse backgrounds.

IMMIGRANT TEACHERS CAN IMPROVE PARENTAL INVOLVEMENT PRACTICES

Whereas CPR enables teachers to reflect upon their pedagogy and apply modifications to aspects of their teaching to accommodate multiethnic and multiracial students such as immigrants (Boon & Lewthwaite, 2016; Krasnoff, 2016), its weakness is too much focus on implementing the policy with little check to see its full practicality. The issue of discrimination based on nationality and ethnicity for example is a deep-rooted social injustice that some nonimmigrant teachers may not let go easily. For example, Samuel (2018) revealed that existing biases both personal and institutional among nonimmigrant white American teachers results in their decreased commitment or motivation to be culturally responsive thereby unwilling to improve leaning opportunities for black immigrant students as well as engaging with their parents (Samuels, 2018). These preconceived biases narrow their understanding and appreciation of cultures and assets of the students and communities they serve, resulting in a complete disconnect (Samuels, 2018). They fail to examine their own personalities and how they contribute to oppression. It is therefore not surprising that after completing CRP training workshops, some nonimmigrant teachers and principals still regard immigrant children as a burden in the classroom and their parents not knowledgeable enough to contribute to school policy-making (Howard, 2007). Overall, some teachers complain that it is not possible to set aside the vast amount of time required to engage with immigrant parents due to the demands of their intensive curricular tasks and large classes. It is overwhelming for some teachers to accommodate learning opportunities for all populations especially when they have limited time and resources to do so (Samuels, 2018).

It is against this background that schools need immigrant teachers to help improve immigrant parental involvement practices because they do not require extensive CRP training to engage with immigrant families. Compared to nonimmigrant teachers, they have the advantage of pulling existing knowledge from their personal experiences of being immigrants themselves to inspire and connect with immigrant students and their parents (Adair et al., 2012; Broutian, 2016; Griffin, 2018). However, this is not to conclude that they would remove all the barriers faced by immigrant parents and their children in schools; rather, they at least bring different world views, languages and understanding of diversity into schools which helps create inclusive classroom environments (Darling-Hammond & Sykes, 1999; Shure, 2001; Stephens, 1999). Griffin (2018) argues that immigrant teachers bring "a different perspective and a different outlook, a different quality to teaching practice that recognizes, values, and honors the legacy that my kids bring with them every single day. It creates a whole other kind of teacher" (p. 1). Immigrant teachers can improve parental involvement practices through providing, for example, resources in schools pertaining to cultural translation, cultural relevant instruction and role models, as well as support cultural knowledge for engaging with immigrant parents.

Cultural Translators

One of the factors that limit immigrant parents from participating is the different cultural understanding between them and the teachers. Teachers who are themselves immigrants from the same communities of the children and their families are perfectly positioned to bridge this cultural and linguistic gap (Adair, 2009; Adair, Tobin, & Arzubiaga, 2012; Broutian, 2016). Rather than an indication of lacking interest in their child's schooling, linguistic gaps and failure to understand the new educational system prevents some immigrant parents from participating in their children's academic performance. Inability to connect with the parents further contributes to the negative assumptions and attitudes teachers had towards immigrant children and their families (Adair, 2009; Heng, 2014; Olivos, 2006; Olivos & Mendoza, 2009). Immigrant parents would complain that nonimmigrant teachers and staff mistreated and disrespected them because teachers and school personnel lacked the cultural and linguistic understanding of immigrant communities. This negative relationships with schools leaves parents feeling alienated, thus, sometimes unwilling to be involved in school activities fearing rejection by nonimmigrant teachers and school administrators (Olivos, 2006).

Furthermore, most schools do not provide resources to support immigrant parents such as language translators and interpretation services. Parents complain that they encounter challenges when helping with homework because of the unfamiliar educational content or that they do not read or understand the host country's language for instruction (Schleicher, 2015). As cultural translators, immigrant teachers can help parents understand the new educational system, translate information into their home languages and act as liaison between parents and schools. So far, only a few countries such as Austria, Sweden and Finland incorporate immigrant languages into their schools and hire immigrant teachers to teach those languages (Noorani, Baidek, Kremo, & Riihelainen, 2019). Furthermore, immigrant teachers do more than just provide culturally relevant instruction to immigrant students; they also act as advocates for immigrant communities (Flores, 2017; Griffin, 2018).

CULTURAL RELEVANT INSTRUCTION

Immigrant teachers provide a more culturally relevant teaching because they better understand the situations that minority students and their parents encounter (Dilworth & Coleman, 2014; Ladson-Billings, 1995; McCarty & Lee, 2014; McDevitt, 2016). This type of teaching requires expanding the curriculum to include multicultural materials and culturally relevant pedagogy that recognizes and honors the legacy students bring into the classroom (Griffin, 2018). Such culturally relevant instruction that is familiar to parents help them understand the material when they assist with homework. Holeywell (2015) stated that K-12 students enrolled in a Mexican American studies program in Tucson, Arizona experienced higher test scores, better attendance and graduation rates, and had better disciplinary records because the teachers recognized and honored their cultures in their instruction creating a sense of belonging and acceptance at the school. Their parents are also highly engaged in school activities because the instruction is familiar to them. In fact, immigrant teachers are better equipped to incorporate the instructional dimension of CRP compared to nonimmigrant teachers (Holeywell, 2015).

ROLE MODELS

Immigrant parents have confidence that their children will succeed academically in schools with teachers who share similar cultural or ethnic backgrounds with them. Such teachers have a role model effect whereby the students identify with seeing people who resemble them in professional roles. Using their personal reflections of their experiences as immigrants, the teachers can motivate and inspire students and contribute to improvements in academic outcomes (Campbell, 2003; Clewell & Villegas, 2001; Griffin, 2018; Kristjánsson, 2006; Santoro, 2015). For example, the teachers use their personal experiences as immigrants themselves to remove the stereotypes labeled against immigrant students as academically incompetent and inspire them to be successful. A Latino teacher shared her personal experiences as a first-generation immigrant to foreign born students in her class, "By having somebody who looks like you, who's been through the same things as you, that understands that it hasn't been easy here for you. You were promised this dream when you came here, and then the reality of it is around you with helicopters and police sirens all the time" (Griffin, 2018, p. 4). Sharing such personal experiences builds trust and solidarity between teachers, students and their parents (Griffin, 2018).

IMMIGRANT TEACHERS SUPPORT CULTURAL KNOWLEDGE IN SCHOOLS

Increasing teacher diversity also benefits nonimmigrant teachers by increasing their understanding of diverse cultures to connect effectively with immigrant parents. Immigrant teachers bring with them an inherent understanding of the linguistically diverse backgrounds, attitudes and experiences of the students and parents from immigrant communities and therefore could inform nonimmigrant teachers about effective ways to interact with immigrant parents (Dee, 2005). In her study with immigrant teachers, Ross (2014) reveals that nonimmigrant teachers appreciated the help that immigrant teachers provided in dealing with immigrant students during difficult situations. They provide advice where needed, "their stories and knowledge about their cultures have helped us to understand why children may be acting the way they do" (Ross, 2014, p. 91) and provide translations during a conference with parents to discuss the child's behavior (Ross, 2014). Having someone present who understands them better improves parents' participation during such conferences, thus, strengthening home school relationships with immigrant parents (Tobin et al., 2013).

CONCLUSION

In this chapter, I revealed that there is a very strong relationship between parental involvement and children's academic performances. As much as immigrant parents would like to be engaged in their children's school, they are faced with several challenges which limit their participation in school activities. Among the challenges is the lack of immigrant teachers in the schools their children attend. Parents argue that their participation would increase if there is an increased visibility of immigrant teachers to provide the linguistic, social and cultural support they need to help their children adjust to the new educational environment. On the other hand, teaching pedagogical approaches such as CRP to nonimmigrant teachers is important for improving their knowledge of cultural and linguistic diversity, but the gap still remains because reshaping people's inner beliefs about those who are different from them is a complicated process which requires strenuous time and effort. Teachers cannot effectively provide instruction in the absence of a strong connection with students and parents. Therefore, schools and educational stakeholders across all nations need to develop and support working environments aimed at increasing and retaining immigrant teachers in the teaching workforce. This is important also for building a truly diverse workforce capable of serving an increasingly immigrant student population and their communities.

Overall, there is a need to remove the following barriers and increase the visibility of immigrant teachers in schools to support parental involvement practices by immigrant parents.

- *Credentialing:* The educational systems in host countries should accredit immigrant teachers' foreign credentials. Numerous studies have shown that immigrant teachers arrive in host countries with impressive resumes, but their education and training are often overlooked as not equal to those obtained from local colleges and universities (Osaze, 2017; Rabben, 2013). Educational systems in countries such as the United States, Canada and other European countries do not fully recognize K-12 teaching credentials obtained from foreign countries because of the differences in the curriculum and teaching styles (Abramova, 2013). For that reason, immigrants aspiring to pursue a teaching career are required to freshly enroll into teacher preparation programs regardless of the teaching experience they acquired from home countries. Allowing the transferability of foreign academic credentials and their recognition in the host nations will lead to a much-improved integration of immigrant teachers into schools.

- *Access to student loans:* Enrolling in teacher preparation programs to supplement foreign credentials put a heavy financial burden on aspiring immigrant teachers who are already grappling with financial obligations to support their families (Carver-Thomas, 2018). Immigrants cannot finance their education without well-paying jobs and financial aid, which is not available for most undocumented immigrants or those that had not legalized their immigration status. The majority drop out before they finish or never enroll due to financial challenges (Carver-Thomas, 2018; Rabben, 2013). Making financial aid such as student loans and grants available to immigrants enrolled in teacher training programs can help them finish their courses and improve teacher diversity in schools.

- *Mentoring:* Studies indicate that the different standardized exams used in several countries to obtain teacher licensures are never favorable to immigrant teacher candidates who disproportionately fail these standardized exams. Preservice immigrant teachers struggle to pass the exam which they stated was too hard and the line of questioning not familiar to them (McDevitt, 2018). Therefore, host countries should make accessible to immigrant teachers, intensive teacher preparation support programs that offer ongoing mentorship and tutoring to ensure successful completion of preparation programs. Some adjustments must be done to teacher licensure requirements to allow teaching candidates to demonstrate their competency through rigorous but more authentic performance assessments that do not generate the racial disparity in pass rates of traditional multiple-choice exams. Such a shift may encourage more immigrant background students to enter and complete high-quality teacher preparation programs.

- *Language Barriers:* Teacher preparation programs should offer second language training programs to preservice immigrant teachers. Various studies indicate that it is quite challenging for immigrant teachers to be hired because of the failure to fluently speak the language of instruction in schools (Hwang, Baek, & Vrongistinos, 2005; Jhagroo, 2016; Myles, Cheng, & Wang, 2006; Niyubahwe, Mukamurera, & Jutras, 2013). Immigrant teachers are very aware of the gatekeeping role of language and have heard of or experienced cases of discrimination due to lack of proficiency in the majority language (Abramova, 2013; Eres, 2016; Lee, 2010; Lefever et al., 2014; Myles et al., 2006). Speaking with a foreign accent is also considered as a failure to speak the host language well especially for English speaking countries like the United States, Canada and the United Kingdom. The use of foreign languages by teachers even outside the classrooms is prohibited in most schools. A case study in New Zealand with immigrant teachers from Japan, China, Fiji and India revealed such institutional discrimination practices against minority teachers. The teachers were not allowed to use their native languages when talking to each other. Some nonimmigrant parents were not happy with schools employing Indian teachers with heavy accents and often told them to back to their countries (Jhagroo, 2016).
- *Discrimination:* Discrimination in its various forms (race, ethnicity and nationality) in the employment process also contributes to the under representation of immigrant teachers. Therefore, removing discriminatory policies during hiring and induction strategies can help increase immigrant teachers in the classroom. School districts

should partner with local Teacher Training Programs (TTP) and Minority Serving Institutions (MSIs) to coordinate student teaching placements and vet immigrant candidates for hire before they graduate. Hiring committees in schools also need to be diverse to ensure greater fairness in the hiring process. Immigrant teachers complain that it is not easy for schools to employ them when look different, people expect less of you and they think you are less intelligent than them (Hwang et al., 2005). Gay (2005) postulates that stereotypical images of cultures affect our understanding and how we categorize people preventing our seeing a person as an individual. An immigrant teacher, who had to cope with discrimination for over six years working alongside nonimmigrant white teachers in an urban school, repeatedly found her ability and expertise questioned, and were told that she was "too black" (Pizzaro & Kohli, 2018). White teachers ridiculed everything about her including her dress code and "her peers thought that she needed to be watched and handled rather than seen as an in-control professional" and equal (Pizzaro & Kohli, 2018, p. 2). Such constant experiences of racism have psychological impact on the victims in that it fosters doubt and produce anxiety (Pizarro & Kohli, 2018), which ultimately reduces immigrant teachers inspirations to pursue and enjoy teaching in host countries.

In conclusion, immigrant teachers bring with them great knowledge of cultural diversity required in creating culturally responsive learning environment but various discriminatory practices undermine their experience and knowledge (Batalova, Fix, & Creticos, 2008; Carter Andrews et al., 2019; Gay, 2005; Hwang et al., 2005). In this chapter, I advocate for increased representation of immigrant teachers in schools with high immigrant student populations across all nations to serve as role models, mentors, and cultural translators for immigrant parents and their children. By sharing a similar background, these immigrant teachers have a better understanding of the needs of immigrant parents and their children, hence would help bridge the social, cultural and linguistic gap between schools and immigrant communities, making the school environment more welcoming and increase parental involvement practices.

REFERENCES

Abramova, I. (2013). Grappling with language barriers: Implications for the professional development of immigrant teachers. *Multicultural Perspectives*, *15*(3), 152-157.

Adair, J. K. (2009). *Teaching children of immigrants: A multi-sited ethnographic study of preschool teachers in five U.S. cities* (Doctoral Dissertation). Arizona State University. Retrieved from ProQuest Dissertations Publishing, 3360743.

Adair, J. K., Tobin, J. & Arzubiaga, A. E. (2012). The Dilemma of Cultural Responsiveness and Professionalization: Listening Closer to Immigrant Teachers Who Teach Children of Recent Immigrants. *Teachers College Record*, *114*(12), 1-37.

Ahad, A. & Benton, M. (2018). *Mainstreaming 2.0. How Europe's Education Systems can Boost Migrant Inclusion.* Brussels: Migration Policy Institute Europe.

American Community Survey, A. (2017). *Drop out rates status of 16-24 year olds by race/ethnicity and nativity 2016.* Retrieved from http://nces.ed.gov/surveys/sass/.

Baker, T. L., Wise, J., Kelley, G. & Skiba, R. J. (2016). Identifying barriers: Creating solutions to improve family engagement. *School Community Journal*, *26*(2), 161-184.

Banks, J. A. (2008). *Teaching strategies for ethnic studies.* Boston, MA: Allyn & Bacon. ISBN 10-0205594271.

Barton, P. E. (2003). *Parsing the Achievement Gap: Baselines for Tracking Progress.* Educational Testing Services, Princeton, NJ: Policy Information Report. Retrieved from http://www.ets.org/research/pic.

Batalova, J., Fix, M. & Creticos, P. (2008). *UNEVEN PROGRESS: The Employment Pathways of Skilled Immigrants in the United States.* Washington, DC, Migration Policy Institute.

Berthelsen, D. & Walker, S. (2008). Parents' involvement in their children's education. *Family Matters*, (79), 34-41.

Boon, H. J. & Lewthwaite, B. E. (2016). Teacher ethics: the link between quality teaching and multi-ethnic and multiracial education. *Athens Journal of Education*, (3), 331-344.

Boser, U., Wilhelm, M. & Hanna, R. (2014). *The Power of the Pygmalion Effect: Teachers' Expectations Strongly Predict College Completion*. Washington, DC, Center for American Progress.

Broutian, T. R. (2016). *An exploration of the challenges and strategies used by high school immigrant teachers assimilating to the US education system* (Doctoral Dissertation). University of La Verne. ProQuest Dissertations & Theses Global. (1777279038). Retrieved from http://ezproxy.rowan.edu/login?url=http://search.proquest.com/docview/1777279 038?accountid=13605.

Campbell, E. (2003). The ethical teacher. *Philadelphia Open University Press*, *15*(1), 103-106.

Carter Andrews, D. J., Castro, E., Cho, C. L., Petchauer, E., Richmond, G. & Floden, R. (2019). *Changing the Narrative on Diversifying the Teaching Workforce: A Look at Historical and Contemporary Factors That Inform Recruitment and Retention of Teachers of Color*: CA: Los Angeles, CA. SAGE Publications.

Carver-Thomas, D. (2018). *Diversifying the teaching profession: How to recruit and retain teachers of color*. Palo Alto, CA: Learning Policy Institute.

Clewell, B. C. & Villegas, A. M. (2001). *Ahead of the Class: A Handbook for Preparing New Teachers from New Sources. Design Lessons from the DeWitt Wallace-Reader's Digest Fund's Pathways to Teaching Careers Initiative*. Washington, DC,: Urban Institute.

Clotfelter, C. T., Ladd, H. F. & Vigdor, J. L. (2006). Teacher-student matching and the assessment of teacher effectiveness. *Journal of human Resources*, *41*(4), 778-820.

Collins, J. & Reid, C. (2012). Immigrant teachers in Australia. *Cosmopolitan Civil Societies: An Interdisciplinary Journal*, *4*(2), 38-61.

Darling-Hammond, L. (2004). Inequality and the right to learn: Access to qualified teachers in California's public schools. *Teachers College Record*, *106*(10), 1936-1966.

Darling-Hammond, L. (2010). Teacher education and the American future. *Journal of teacher education*, *61*(1-2), 35-47. doi: 10.1177/ 0022487109348024.

Darling-Hammond, L. & Sykes, G. (1999). *Teaching as the learning profession: Handbook of policy and practice*. San Francisco, CA: Jossey-Bass Inc.

Davis, P. E. (2008). Something every teacher and counselor needs to know about African-American children. *Multicultural Education*, *15*(3), 30-34.

Dee, T. S. (2005). A teacher like me: Does race, ethnicity, or gender matter? *American Economic Review*, *95*(2), 158-165. doi: 10.1257/ 000282805774670446.

Dilworth, M. E. & Coleman, M. J. (2014). *Time for a change: Diversity in teaching revisited*. Washington, DC, Nationational Education Associattion.

Dor, A. & Rucker-Naidu, T. B. (2012). Teachers' attitudes toward parents' involvement in school: Comparing teachers in the USA and Israel. *Issues in educational research*, *22*(3), 246-262.

Epstein, J. L. & Jansorn, N. R. (2004). School, family and community partnerships link the plan. *The Education Digest*, *69*(6), 19-23.

Epstein, J. L. & Sanders, M. G. (2006). Prospects for change: Preparing educators for school, family, and community partnerships. *Peabody journal of Education*, *81*(2), 81-120. doi: 10.1207/ S15327930 pje8102_5.

Eres, F. (2016). Problems of the Immigrant Students' Teachers: Are They Ready to Teach? *International Education Studies*, *9*(7), 64-71.

Figlio, D. N. & Özek, U. (2017). Unwelcome guests? The effects of refugees on the educational outcomes of incumbent students. *Journal of Labor Economics*, (37)4, 1-19. doi: 10.1086/703116.

Flores, G. M. (2017). *Latina teachers: Creating careers and guarding culture*: NYU Press.

Ford, D. (2010). Culturally Responsive Classrooms: Affirming Culturally Different Gifted Students. *Multicultural Issues*, *33*(1), 50-53.

Gay, G. (2002). Preparing for culturally responsive teaching. *Journal of teacher education*, *53*(2), 106-116.

Gay, G. (2005). Politics of multicultural teacher education. *Journal of Teacher Education*, *56*(3), 221-228.

Gay, G. (2010). *Culturally Responsive Teaching. Multicultural Education Series*. New York: Teachers College Press.

Gershenson, S., Holt, S. B. & Papageorge, N. W. (2016). Who believes in me? The effect of student–teacher demographic match on teacher expectations. *Economics of Education Review*, (52), 209-224. doi: 10.1016/j.econedurev.2016.03.002.

Goldhaber, D., Lavery, L. & Theobald, R. (2015). Uneven playing field? Assessing the teacher quality gap between advantaged and disadvantaged students. *Educational Researcher*, *44*(5), 293-307. doi: 10.3102/0013189X15592622.

Griffin, A. (2018). *Our Stories, Our Struggles, Our Strengths: Perspectives and Reflections from Latino Teachers*. Washington, DC: Education Trust.

Harro, B. (2000). The cycle of liberation. In W. J. B. M. Adams, R. Castaneda, H. W. Hackman, M. L. Peters, & X. Zuniga (Ed.), *Readings for diversity and social justice: An anthology on racism, anti-Semitism, sexism, heterosexism, ableism, and classism*, (Vol. 2, pp. 79-82). New York: Routledge.

Harte, E., Herrera, F., Stepanek, M. & Rand, E. (2016). *Education of EU Migrant children in EU member states*: RAND Cooperation: Santa Monica, California., and Cambridge, UK.

Heng, T. T. (2014). The nature of interactions between Chinese immigrant families and preschool staff: How culture, class, and methodology matter. *Journal of Early Childhood Research*, *12*(2), 111-127. doi: 10.1177/1476718X13515423.

Holeywell, R. (2015). New study shows benefits of two-way, dual-Language education. Retrieved from https://kinder.rice.edu/ blog/ holeywell 060315/.

Holt, S. & Gershenson, S. (2015). *The impact of teacher demographic representation on student attendance and suspensions.* IZA Discussion Paper No. 9554. Retrieved from https://ssrn.com/abstract=2708367.

Hoover-Dempsey, K. (2011). Self-efficacy: Up to the challenge. In S. Redding, M. Murphy, & P. Sheley (Ed.), *Handbook on family and community engagement,* (pp. 61-68). Charllote, NC: Information Age Publicing, Inc.

Hornby, G. & Lafaele, R. (2011). Barriers to parental involvement in education: An explanatory model. *Educational Review, 63*(1), 37-52. doi: 10.1080/00131911.2010.488049.

Howard, G. R. (2007). As diversity grows, so must we. *Educational Leadership, 64*(6), 16-22.

Hwang, Y. S., Baek, E. O. & Vrongistinos, K. (2005). Immigrant Hispanic/Latinos Teachers' Perception of Education. *Teaching Education, 16* (4), 325-336.

Jeynes, W. H. (2007). The relationship between parental involvement and urban secondary school student academic achievement: A meta-analysis. *Urban education, 42*(1), 82-110. doi: 10.1177/0042085906293818.

Jeynes, W. H. (2017). A meta-analysis: The relationship between parental involvement and Latino student outcomes. *Education and Urban Society, 49*(1), 4-28. doi: 10.1177/0013124516630596.

Jhagroo, J. R. (2016). "You Expect Them to Listen!": Immigrant Teachers' Reflections on Their Lived Experiences. *Australian Journal of Teacher Education, 41*(9), 48-57. doi: 10.14221/ajte.2016v41n9.3.

Krasnoff, B. (2016). *Culturally responsive teaching: A guide to evidence-based practices for teaching all students equitably.* Portland, OR: Education Northwest, Region X Equity Assistance Center.

Kristjánsson, K. (2006). Emulation and the use of role models in moral education. *Journal of Moral Education, 35*(1), 37-49. doi: 10.1080/03057240500495278.

Ladson-Billings, G. (1995). Toward a theory of culturally relevant pedagogy. *American educational research journal, 32*(3), 465-491. doi: 10.3102/00028312032003465.

Ladson-Billings, G. (2014). Culturally relevant pedagogy 2.0: aka the remix. *Harvard Educational Review*, *84*(1), 74-84. doi: 10.17763/ haer. 84.1.p2rj131485484751.

Lee, J. (2010). *What is it like to be an immigrant teacher in the US schools?* Unpublished Doctoral Dissertation, University of Georgia. Retrieved from https:// getd.libs.uga.edu/ pdfs/ lee_jeehae_201012_phd.pdf.

Lefever, S., Paavola, H., Berman, R., Guðjónsdóttir, H., Talib, M. T. & Gísladóttir, K. R. (2014). Immigrant teachers in Iceland and Finland: Successes and contributions. *IJE4D Journal*, *3*, 65-85.

Mancilla-Martinez, J. & Lesaux, N. K. (2014). Promoting shared cultural and linguistic backgrounds among children and families in Early Head Start/Head Start programs. *NHSA Dialog: A Research-to-Practice Journal for the Early Childhood Field*, *17*(3), 1-14.

McCarty, T. & Lee, T. (2014). Critical culturally sustaining/revitalizing pedagogy and Indigenous education sovereignty. *Harvard Educational Review*, *84*(1), 101-124. doi: 10.17763/haer.84.1.q83746nl5pj34216.

McDevitt, S. E. (2016). Rediscovering and reconnecting funds of knowledge of immigrant children, families, and teachers. *Childhood Education*, *92*(6), 470-475. doi: 10.1080/00094056.2016.1251796.

McDevitt, S. E. (2018). *Border Lives: Exploring the Experiences of Immigrant Teachers Teaching and Caring for Young Immigrant Children and Families* (Doctoral Dissertation). Columbia University. Retrieved from https://academiccommons.columbia.edu/doi/ 10.7916/ D85M7P4H.

McFarland, J., Hussar, B., Wang, X., Zhang, J., Wang, K., Rathbun, A. & Mann, F. B. (2018). T*he Condition of Education 2018*. *NCES 2018-144*. Washington, DC, National Center for Education Statistics Institute of Education Services. Retrieved from http://nces.ed.gov/ pubsearch/ pubsinfo.asp?pubid=2018144.

McKoy, C. L., MacLeod, R. B., Walter, J. S. & Nolker, D. B. (2017). The impact of an in-service workshop on cooperating teachers' perceptions of culturally responsive teaching. *Journal of Music Teacher Education*, *26*(2), 50-63. doi: 10.1177/1057083716629392.

Musu-Gillette, L., de Brey, C., McFarland, J., Hussar, W., Sonnenberg, W. & Wilkinson-Flicker, S. (2017). *Status and Trends in the Education of Racial and Ethnic Groups.* Washington, DC: U.S. Department of Education, National Center for Education Statistics. Retrieved from http://nces.ed.gov/pubsearch.

Myles, J., Cheng, L. & Wang, H. (2006). Teaching in elementary school: Perceptions of foreign-trained teacher candidates on their teaching practicum. *Teaching and Teacher Education, 22*(2), 233-245. doi: 10.1016/j.tate.2005.09.001.

National Center for Education Statistics, N. (2018). *2017-18 National Teacher and Principal Survey (NTPS 2017-18).* Washington, DC, U.S Department of Education. Retrieved from https://nces.ed.gov/surveys/ntps/question1718.asp.

Nieto, S. (1992). *Affirming diversity: The sociopolitical context of multicultural education*: White Plains, NY: Longman.

Niyubahwe, A., Mukamurera, J. & Jutras, F. (2013). Professional integration of immigrant teachers in the school system: A literature review. *McGill Journal of Education/Revue des sciences de l'éducation de McGill, 48*(2), 279-296.

Noorani, S., Baidek, N., Kremo, A. & Riihelainen, J. (2019). Eurydice Brief: Intergrating Students from Migrant Backgrounds into Schools in Europe: National Policies and Measures. *Education, Audiovisual and Culture Executive Agency,* 1-28.

OECD. (2013). *Teaching and Learning International Survey, TALIS 2013: Conceptual Framework.* OECD; Paris.

OECD. (2015). *Immigrant Students at School: Easing the Journey towards Intergration.* OECD Reviews of Migrant Education; Paris.

Olivos, E. M. (2006). *The power of parents: A critical perspective of bicultural parent involvement in public schools*, (Vol. 290), New York: Peter Lang.

Olivos, E. M. & Mendoza, M. (2009). Immigration and educational inequity: An examination of Latino immigrant parents' inclusion in the public school context. *Journal of Latino/Latin American Studies, 3*(3), 38-53. doi:10.18085/llas.3.3.k12913266121047h.

Osaze, E. D. (2017). *The Non-Recognition or Devaluation of Foreign Professional Immigrants Credentials in Canada: The Impact on the Receiving Country (Canada) and the Immigrants.* Retrieved from http://hdl.handle.net/10315/34314.

Peterson, S. S. & Ladky, M. (2007). A Survey of Teachers' and Principals' Practices and Challenges in Fostering New Immigrant Parent Involvement. *Canadian Journal of Education, 30*(2), 881-910.

Pizarro, M. & Kohli, R. (2018). "I Stopped Sleeping": Teachers of Color and the Impact of Racial Battle Fatigue. *Urban Education.*, 1-25. doi:10.1177/0042085918805788.

Rabben, L. (2013). *Credential recognition in the United States for foreign professionals.* Washington, DC: Migration Policy Institute.

Richards, H. V., Brown, A. F. & Forde, T. B. (2007). Addressing diversity in schools: Culturally responsive pedagogy. *Teaching Exceptional Children, 39*(3), 64-68. doi: 10.1177/004005990703900310.

Rodriguez-Valls, F. (2016). Pedagogy of the immigrant: A journey towards inclusive classrooms. *Teachers and Curriculum, 16*(1), 41-48.

Ross, F. (2014). *Newcomers entering teaching: The possibilities of a culturally and linguistically diverse teaching force.* In C. E. Sleeter, L. I. Neal, & Kumashiro, K. K. *Diversifying the Teacher Workforce*, (pp. 95-106): New York: Routledge. doi: 10.4324/9781315818320.

Rushton, S. P. (2000). Student teacher efficacy in inner-city schools. *The Urban Review, 32*(4), 365-383. doi: 10.1023/A:102645980.

Samuels, A. J. (2018). Exploring Culturally Responsive Pedagogy: Teachers' Perspectives on Fostering Equitable and Inclusive Classrooms. *SRATE Journal, 27*(1), 22-30.

Santoro, N. (2015). The drive to diversify the teaching profession: narrow assumptions, hidden complexities. *Race Ethnicity and Education, 18*(6), 858-876. doi:10.1080/13613324.2012.759934.

Scheetz, L. P. (1995). *Recruiting Trends, 1995-96. Education Supplement. A Study of 294 Elementary and Secondary School Systems Employing New Teacher Education Graduates.* Michigan State University: Career Services St Placement. Retrieved from https://archive.org/stream/ERIC_ED391787/ERIC_ED391787_djvu.txt.

Schleicher, A. (2015). *Helping Immigrant Students to Succeed at School and Beyond.* OECD, PISA, 2012 Database. Retrieved from https://www.oecd.org/education/Helping-immigrant-students-to-succeed-at-school-and-beyond.pdf.

Shure, J. L. (2001). Minority teachers are few and far between. *Techniques: Connecting Education and Careers,* 76(5), 6-10.

Snyder, T. D., Hoffman, C. M. & Geddes, C. M. (1999). *Digest of Education Statistics, 1998*: Washington, DC. National Center for Education Statistics.

Sobel, A. & Kugler, E. G. (2007). Building partnerships with immigrant parents. *Educational Leadership,* 64(6), 62-66.

Stephens, J. E. (1999). Wanted: Minority teachers for U.S. Schools. *School Business Affairs.* 65 (5), 37-42.

Taie, S. & Goldring, R. (2017). *Characteristics of Public Elementary and Secondary School Teachers in the United States: Results from the 2015-16 National Teacher and Principal Survey. First Look. NCES 2017-072.* National Center for Education Statistics, Jessup, MD: ED Publications.

Tamer, M. (2014). *The education of immigrant children: As the demography of the U.S.continues to shift, how can schools best serve their changing population.* Havard Graduate School of Education.

Thao, M. (2009). *Parent Involvement in School: Engaging Immigrant Parents. Snapshot.* Saint Paul, Minnesota: Wilder Research.

Tobin, J., Arzubiaga, A. E. & Adair, J. K. (2013). *Children Crossing Borders Immigrant Parent and Teacher Perspectives on Preschool for Children of Immigrants.* New York: Russell Sage Foundation.

Turney, K. & Kao, G. (2009). Barriers to school involvement: Are immigrant parents disadvantaged? *The Journal of Educational Research, 102*(4), 257-271. doi: 10.3200/JOER.102.4.257-271.

Villegas, A. & Lucas, T. (2002). Preparing culturally responsive teachers: Rethinking the curriculum. *Journal of Teacher Education,* 53(1), 20-32. doi: 10.1177/0022487102053001003.

Waanders, C., Mendez, J. L. & Downer, J. T. (2007). Parent characteristics, economic stress and neighborhood context as predictors of parent involvement in preschool children's education. *Journal of School Psychology*, *45*(6), 619-636. doi: 10.1016/ j.jsp.2007.07.003.

Webster, N. L. & Valeo, A. (2011). Teacher preparedness for a changing demographic of language learners. *TESL Canada Journal*, *28*(2), 105-128. doi: 10.18806/tesl.v28i2.1075.

Zhu, G. (2017). We can't teach what we don't know: White teachers, multiracial schools., *Multicultural Education Review*, (9)*4*, 289-292. doi: 10.1080/2005615X.2017.1383814.

ABOUT THE EDITORS

Nurit Kaplan Toren
University of Haifa, Haifa, Israel and
Oranim Academic College of Education, Tivon, Israel
E-mail: ntoren@edu.haifa.ac.il

Nurit Kaplan Toren received her PhD in Education and Human Development from the University of Haifa, Israel (2005). She started her career as a high school educational counselor and teacher and currently teaches Educational Psychology at the University of Haifa and Oranim Academic College of Education MA program. Her research examines the structure of parents' educational involvement and its effect on students' school functioning, with particular focus on antecedents of parents' educational involvement in the context of culture, age and gender. She is the senior editor of the International Journal for School-Based Family Counseling and member of the executive committee of Oxford Symposium in School-Based Family Counseling.

Gertina J. van Schalkwyk

E-mail: gjvsumac@gmail.com

Gertina J. van Schalkwyk, DPhil, is Adjunct Associate Professor of Psychology at the University of Macau in Macau (SAR), China. She trained and has worked at the University of Pretoria in South Africa. She has published several book chapters, encyclopaedia entries and journal articles in refereed international journals. Her interests are focused in developmental psychology (across the lifespan), education, family counseling, cross-cultural psychology, and qualitative methods. She is Editor-in-chief of the international Journal of School & Educational Psychology and an Associate Fellow and Executive Member of the Oxford Symposium for School-Based Family Counseling.

About the Contributors

Amin Nyna is associate professor in curriculum studies, university distinguished teacher, and an NRF-rated researcher at the University of KwaZulu-Natal in South Africa. A former Fulbright scholar, she teaches discourses and research methodologies in education to Masters students, and co-ordinates support for doctoral candidates. She has published papers in the fields of higher education curriculum, medical education, teacher education, and gender, and has co-edited a special issue in the journal 'Alternation' on teaching and learning in higher education each year since 2012. She is co-founder and co-editor of the journal, 'African Perspectives of Research in Teaching and Learning' and co-edited the book, "Disrupting higher education curriculum: Undoing cognitive damage".
E-mail: amin@ukzn.ac.za.

Arcidiacono Francesco is Professor and Director of the Research Department at the University of Teacher Education BEJUNE, Biel/Bienne (Switzerland). His area of specialization is the study of social interactions and development in educational settings. He is interested in studying how people, individually and collectively, co-construct their participation within everyday situations in formal and informal contexts of action.
E-mail: francesco.arcidiacono@hep-bejune.ch.

Averill Robin is an Associate Professor in the Faculty of Education,Te Whānau o Ako Pai, at Victoria University of Wellington, Te Herenga Waka, in Aotearoa New Zealand. Robin's research focusses on ways to improve equity of access to achievement particularly in relation to Indigenous Māori and Pasifika students, in particular through the areas of culturally responsive and culturally sustaining pedagogies, mathematics educaiton, and initial teacher education. With experience in secondary school teaching, professional development facilitation, and national assessment and moderation, Robin now teaches in initial teacher education and postgraduate programmes. With an extensive background in mathematics education, Robin is widely published including through teacher texts and resources, edited books, journal articles, research articles for teachers, and contract evaluation research.

E-mail: robin.averill@vuw.ac.nz.

Gaunt Ruth is a Reader in Social Psychology at the University of Lincoln, UK. She received her PhD in Psychology at Tel-Aviv University, and has held post-doctoral fellowships at both University of Louvain and Harvard University, and the Marie Curie Fellowship at University of Cambridge. Her research applies a social psychological approach to the study of gender, families and employment.

E-mail: rgaunt@lincoln.ac.uk.

González-Martínez Esther is Professor at the University of Teacher Education BEJUNE, Biel/Bienne (Switzerland). Her area of specialization is the analysis of social interactions in institutional settings. Her research adopts an ethnomethodological perspective as well as conversation and multimodal analysis, supplemented by ethnographic fieldwork.

E-mail: e.gonzalezmartinez@hep-bejune.ch.

Kumar Revathy is professor of educational psychology at the University of Toledo. She is a Fulbright Specialist Scholar, past associate editor for Developmental Psychology, past historian and current secretary for Division 15 of the American Psychological Association, and Provost

Faculty Fellow for the academic years 2018-2020. She earned a Ph.D. in Education and Psychology from the Combined Program in Education and Psychology, University of Michigan and was an adjunct assistant research scientist at the Institute for Social Research's Survey Research Center, University of Michigan. Her research focuses on social and cultural processes involved in constructing a sense of self and identity among adolescents and young adults in culturally diverse societies. Of particular interest are the role of teachers, teacher-education programs, schools, communities, and families in facilitating minority and immigrant adolescents' development, learning, and motivation. She was a recipient of the Spencer Foundation Major Grant and is Co-Principal Investigator on two grants funded by the National Science Foundation. She also received internal grants from the University of Toledo to conduct mindfulness intervention projects with elementary school students and preservice teachers.

E-mail: Revathy.Kumar@utoledo.edu.

Lerkkanen Marja-Kristiina is a Professor of Education at the University of Jyväskylä, Department of Teacher Education, Finland, and Professor II at the University of Stavanger, Norway. She has been interested in developmental trajectories of young children's reading and math skills, and the effects of motivation and engagement, teacher stress and wellbeing, teacher-student interaction and teacher-parents partnership and trust to child's learning.

E-mail: marja-kristiina.lerkkanen@jyu.fi.

Nyemba Florence holds a PhD in Educational Studies from the University of Cincinnati (2014). Her current research focus is in the field of global education and educational inequalities among minority populations, migration, gender and African politics. She broadly focuses on the experiences of immigrant women and children, poverty, inequality, access and participation in higher education, social and cultural foundations in education. Dr. Nyemba has experience in qualitative methodologies, action research and participatory action research.

E-mail: florence.nyemba@gmail.com.

Pakarinen Eija is an Associate Professor at the University of Jyväskylä, Department of Teacher Education, Finland. Her research foci include teacher-child interactions, teacher-student relationships, home-school collaboration, and teacher and student stress and well-being.
E-mail: eija.k.pakarinen@jyu.fi

Penttinen Viola is a doctoral student at the University of Jyväskylä, Department of Teacher Education, Finland. She studied parental involvement and trust in her masters' thesis in education. In her doctoral thesis, she is focusing on teachers' stress and teacher-child interaction.
E-mail:viola.h.a.penttinen@jyu.fi

Pinho Mariana is a Research Fellow at the Eleanor Glanville Centre (EGC), University of Lincoln, UK. She holds a PhD in Psychology and prior to that she received her MSc in Psychology from the University of Porto (Portugal). Her research interests include social psychology of the family, gender ideologies and work and family.
E-mail: mpinho@lincoln.ac.uk

Sethusha Mantsose Jane is a senior lecturer in the Early Childhood Education Department based in the College of Education at the University of South Africa (UNISA). She is also one of the middle managers in the office of Teaching Practice at UNISA. She is a teaching practice supervisor and conducts workshops for internal and external supervisors and school based mentors across the country and in the SADC regions. She has also conducted numerous ECD workshops for the UNISA Chance to Advance Community Outreach Programme across the country. She is a recipient of the Vision Keepers Award from the Research Directorate at UNISA and visited the University of Texas, San Antonio as required by this award. Her research areas are teaching practice, early childhood teaching and learning and classroom assessment. She has published in Perspectives in Education journal, Journal of Educational Studies, and co-published in the Journal of Literacy Research. She has contributed three book chapters in Early Childhood Education and Teaching Practice.
E-mail: sethumj@unisa.ac.za

Reviewers:

Amin Nyna, University of KwaZulu-Natal, South Africa
Bodvin Kathleen, University of Antwerp, Belgium
Cooper Catherine R., University of California, USA
Ho Yi SIT Holly, University of Macau, Macau
Terence Edwards, Educational Psychologist, New Zealand

INDEX

A

academic motivation, 116, 136
academic performance, 57, 67, 96, 144, 168, 173, 175, 183, 191, 194, 198, 205, 208
academic progress, 3, 11, 12, 192
academic success, v, xi, 86, 144, 163, 174, 189, 201
access, ix, 40, 151, 162, 177, 226, 227
accommodation, 6, 7, 10
accountability, 173, 183
action research, 145, 168, 227
adaptive functioning, 109
administrators, v, 176, 202, 205
adolescent boys, 100
adolescents, xi, 24, 92, 98, 100, 101, 102, 103, 104, 105, 106, 108, 112, 113, 116, 136, 164, 227
Africa, xiii, 45, 146, 147, 166, 168, 172, 176, 190, 197
age, x, xi, 7, 38, 40, 71, 92, 94, 100, 111, 118, 122, 125, 129, 130, 131, 132, 134, 177, 223
anger, 153, 157, 158, 161
anthropologists, 159
anthropology, 24, 38

anxiety, 211
assessment, 15, 85, 113, 139, 175, 213, 226, 228
assets, 23, 31, 204
assignment completion, 34, 35
attitudes, x, 40, 91, 92, 93, 94, 106, 107, 109, 115, 120, 121, 123, 126, 128, 131, 134, 139, 145, 154, 190, 201, 205, 207, 214
autonomy, 4, 17, 31, 34
awareness, 10, 11, 98, 107, 136

B

barriers, v, x, 2, 5, 17, 18, 19, 84, 114, 136, 173, 176, 187, 192, 195, 201, 204, 208, 212
barriers to entry, 114, 192
basic services, 160
beginning teachers, 10
behavioral problems, 116
behaviors, 164, 168, 200
beneficial effect, xi, 105
benefits, vi, 2, 21, 66, 116, 120, 135, 146, 160, 161, 162, 174, 207, 215
black tea, 197

blame, 113, 152, 153, 155, 192, 200
breakdown, 195
breastfeeding, 130

C

candidates, 114, 209, 211, 218, 225
caregivers, 173, 181, 189
case study, 163, 166, 172, 177, 191, 210
category a, 117
Catholic school, 89
causality, 135
challenges, v, vi, ix, xii, xiii, 1, 3, 6, 8, 13, 14, 18, 23, 36, 37, 56, 92, 108, 147, 155, 156, 160, 162, 172, 173, 174, 176, 179, 180, 182, 183, 186, 188, 201, 202, 205, 208, 209, 213
child development, 69, 137, 139, 140
childcare, vii, 34, 39, 82, 115, 116, 117, 118, 119, 120, 121, 122, 123, 124, 125, 127, 128, 129, 130, 131, 132, 133, 134, 135, 136, 137, 138
childhood, xi, 8, 85, 89, 114, 181, 228
Christians, 100
classes, 21, 153, 159, 177, 178, 182, 199, 202, 204
classroom, 9, 10, 12, 14, 17, 20, 21, 22, 31, 58, 68, 69, 71, 80, 82, 86, 93, 155, 161, 164, 172, 180, 182, 189, 190, 194, 196, 199, 200, 204, 206, 210, 228
classroom management, 161, 182, 200
classroom practices, 164, 172
close relationships, 88
collaboration, 3, 46, 65, 71, 73, 75, 76, 77, 78, 79, 80, 81, 83, 85, 89, 160, 167, 180, 181, 228
communication, 4, 9, 12, 67, 70, 81, 82, 87, 94, 98, 100, 107, 108, 149, 161, 165, 166, 172, 174, 175, 184, 186, 189, 195
communication patterns, 94

community, xiii, 3, 4, 8, 12, 17, 18, 21, 22, 23, 24, 25, 26, 29, 30, 31, 69, 84, 85, 89, 103, 107, 110, 111, 138, 146, 147, 148, 153, 154, 155, 158, 159, 160, 161, 162, 163, 164, 165, 167, 168, 171, 172, 173, 175, 177, 181, 182, 186, 187, 189, 191, 194, 198, 201, 202, 203, 212, 214, 216, 228
community psychology, 111
compulsory formal education, 71
conceptual model, 111
cooperation, 37, 70, 84, 93, 181
correlation, 74, 124, 127, 156
critical thinking, 6
cross-cultural comparison, 121
crown, 7
cultural competencies, 7, 9, 10, 11, 29
cultural differences, xi, 21, 70, 91, 92, 97, 103, 105, 108
cultural heritage, 6, 8, 22
culturally responsive and sustaining practice, 2, 3, 6
culturally responsive pedagogy, x, 5, 194, 219
culturally sustaining pedagogy, 2, 5, 30
culturally sustaining teaching, 5, 7
culture, v, 6, 10, 12, 16, 18, 103, 149, 159, 163, 201, 203, 214, 215, 223
curricula, 1, 5, 17, 155, 171, 172
curriculum, vii, xii, 1, 2, 3, 4, 6, 8, 12, 13, 15, 17, 18, 19, 20, 21, 22, 23, 24, 28, 31, 60, 72, 95, 144, 160, 162, 175, 180, 184, 190, 194, 203, 206, 209, 219, 220, 225
curriculum development, xii

D

dance, 20, 31
data collection, 37, 38
decision-making process, 174
deficit, 152, 200

Index   233

delinquency, 114, 174
Delta, 26, 85
demographic characteristics, 128
demography, 220
Department of Education, xiii, 25, 111, 152, 153, 157, 164, 172, 180, 181, 188, 190, 191, 193, 196, 197, 218
depression, 137
deprivation, 147, 160
developed countries, 202
developmental psychology, 224
direct observation, 135
disadvantaged students, 215
discrimination, 201, 203, 210, 211
distribution, 40, 85, 115, 118, 148, 162, 202
distribution function, 148
diversity, x, xii, xiii, 8, 13, 15, 26, 35, 92, 109, 161, 165, 166, 194, 197, 198, 202, 204, 207, 208, 209, 211, 215, 216, 218, 219
division of labor, 120, 126, 137, 138

E

earnings, 118, 121, 139
ecology, 24, 114
economic, xiii, 2, 7, 10, 15, 40, 57, 92, 93, 101, 115, 116, 117, 119, 121, 131, 132, 136, 137, 138, 140, 143, 147, 151, 158, 159, 160, 161, 173, 176, 191, 198, 214, 220
economic status, 7, 176
education, x, xi, xii, xiii, 2, 3, 4, 6, 7, 8, 9, 10, 11, 12, 13, 17, 21, 23, 25, 26, 27, 28, 29, 30, 31, 35, 38, 39, 61, 71, 81, 84, 85, 86, 88, 89, 91, 92, 93, 94, 97, 98, 101, 105, 106, 107, 109, 111, 113, 114, 116, 118, 120, 121, 123, 128, 129, 130, 131, 134, 138, 145, 148, 152, 154, 155, 157, 160, 162, 163, 165, 167, 171, 172, 173, 175, 177, 180, 181, 185, 187, 190, 191, 192, 194, 199, 200, 208, 209, 213, 214, 215, 216, 217, 220, 221, 224, 225, 226, 227, 228
education policy, 2, 13, 100
educational attainment, 116
educational opportunities, 101
educational policy, vi, ix, 13
educational process, 106
educational psychology, 226
educational research, 61, 214, 216
educational settings, xiii, 225
educational system, 195, 196, 199, 202, 205, 208
educators, v, vi, ix, xii, xiii, 3, 8, 9, 26, 100, 107, 136, 164, 199, 200, 214
elementary school, 67, 71, 85, 86, 88, 112, 164, 191, 218, 227
employment, 115, 121, 125, 135, 139, 150, 156, 162, 182, 210, 226
engagement, 8, 11, 14, 15, 18, 22, 25, 26, 27, 30, 69, 84, 86, 87, 122, 140, 145, 156, 157, 164, 167, 188, 189, 200, 202, 212, 216, 227
environment, 11, 19, 106, 108, 113, 161, 173, 180, 189, 193, 194, 202, 208, 212
environmental influences, 86
environmental sustainability, 6
Estonia, 68, 86, 87, 89, 95
ethnic background, 206
ethnic groups, 7
ethnicity, 7, 85, 201, 203, 210, 212, 214
ethnographic study, 212
ethnography, 61, 144, 163, 165, 168
everyday life, xii, 1, 34, 37, 63
evidence, x, 2, 13, 23, 24, 31, 67, 115, 117, 135, 144, 184, 185, 202, 216
evidence-based practices, 216
exercise, 41, 44, 45, 46, 54, 55, 153

F

facilitators, 136
factor analysis, 73, 98, 99, 125
families, ix, xii, 3, 8, 9, 10, 12, 14, 15, 22, 27, 29, 30, 32, 33, 34, 35, 36, 37, 38, 39, 40, 41, 55, 57, 58, 61, 63, 64, 69, 72, 73, 81, 87, 97, 108, 120, 123, 135, 138, 141, 145, 151, 157, 165, 168, 175, 185, 188, 189, 194, 196, 200, 204, 205, 209, 215, 217, 226, 227
family characteristics, 87
family connection, 12, 62
family history, 38
family involvement in school learning, 3
family members, 34, 36, 38, 117
family system, 115, 116, 117, 119, 121, 130, 134
family systems theory, 115, 116, 117, 119, 121, 130, 133, 134
fear, 138, 186, 195
feelings, 9, 94, 119
financial, 126, 135, 140, 202, 209
financial resources, 202
first dimension, 67
food, 58, 124, 148, 161
force, 121, 196, 197, 198, 219
foreign language, 39, 210
formal education, 148
foundations, xii, 96, 162, 164, 227
funding, 22, 72, 147, 150, 160, 163

G

gender differences, x, xi, 66, 68
gender ideologies, 115, 116, 120, 121, 126, 130, 133, 134, 135, 136, 228
gender ideology, xi, 115, 117, 119, 120, 121, 126, 129, 130, 132, 133, 136
gender role, 128
geography, 12, 45

geometry, 20, 45
global education, 227
globalization, ix, 163
governance, 11, 14, 98, 109, 146, 157, 165, 166, 172, 173, 190
governor, 165
grades, 53, 65, 69, 72, 77, 80, 82, 84, 86, 93, 156, 194
grants, 148, 162, 209, 227
group activities, 20
group membership, 101, 104, 105
guidance, 13, 93, 173, 188

H

harmony, 155
health, 111, 180, 189
high expectations, 4, 202
high school, 67, 71, 72, 73, 94, 123, 163, 173, 213, 223
higher education, 67, 128, 158, 194, 225, 227
history, 11, 49, 91, 117, 145, 150, 158
home-based and school-based, ix, x, xi, 92, 98, 100, 108, 109
homes, 2, 14, 34, 36, 37, 39, 60, 62, 151, 158, 161
home-school partnerships, 12, 25, 168, 175
homework, vii, xi, 4, 13, 14, 16, 25, 31, 32, 33, 34, 35, 36, 40, 41, 42, 43, 44, 45, 46, 47, 49, 50, 51, 53, 54, 55, 56, 57, 60, 61, 62, 63, 64, 71, 94, 97, 101, 152, 153, 154, 157, 164, 174, 175, 185, 187, 195, 205, 206
host, xii, 195, 199, 202, 205, 208, 209, 210, 211
hostility, 158
human, 121, 130, 140, 213
human capital, 121, 130, 140

I

ideals, 6, 22
identification, 150, 172
identity, 36, 203, 227
ideology, xi, 121
images, 47, 49, 53, 211
immigrant experiences, 145
immigrant parents, xii, 193, 194, 195, 196, 202, 203, 204, 205, 206, 207, 208, 211, 218, 220
immigrant teachers, 193, 194, 195, 196, 198, 204, 205, 206, 207, 208, 209, 210, 211, 212, 213, 217, 218
impotence, 157
improvement strategies, 172
income, ix, 38, 84, 85, 118, 120, 123, 126, 128, 129, 130, 134, 137, 148
indigenous, xii, 2, 7, 8, 13, 22, 23, 27, 28, 30, 31, 217, 226
individuals, 41, 43, 58, 66, 193
inequality, 117, 146, 148, 227
inequity, 218
institutions, 37, 148, 151, 158, 162
instructional activities, 41, 46, 62
integration, 209, 218
interaction effect, 105
interpersonal factors, 119
interpersonal relationships, 149, 166
intervention, 28, 88, 160, 172, 178, 181, 182, 200, 227
intervention strategies, 172, 178, 200
isolation, 146
Israel, v, vi, x, xi, xii, xiii, 89, 91, 92, 93, 94, 98, 100, 101, 102, 106, 109, 110, 111, 112, 121, 122, 123, 139, 214, 223
issues, xi, 13, 41, 42, 44, 69, 92, 93, 94, 101, 158, 187, 199, 203
Italy, 37, 63, 112, 199, 200
iteration, 23, 24, 31

J

Japan, 210
Jews, xi, 92, 94, 99, 100, 101, 102, 103, 106, 111
junior high school, 71, 96, 98

K

Kenya, 191, 192
kindergarten, 59, 68, 71, 72, 86, 87, 88, 93, 94
kindergartens, 94
Korea, 60

L

labor force, 121
labor market, 136
lack of opportunities, 176
language barrier, 173, 183, 199, 212
languages, 18, 100, 195, 199, 204, 205, 210
later life, xi, 175, 181, 187
lead, 23, 56, 103, 163, 173, 174, 209
leadership, 11, 12, 15, 16, 17, 21, 23, 31
learner achievement, 23, 174
learners, 1, 2, 5, 6, 7, 8, 9, 10, 11, 13, 18, 20, 21, 22, 23, 25, 29, 89, 147, 152, 171, 172, 173, 174, 175, 177, 180, 181, 182, 183, 185, 187, 188, 189, 221
learning disabilities, 25
learning environment, 203, 211
learning outcomes, 11, 194
learning task, 11, 57, 60, 61
level of education, 36, 89, 97
liberation, 138, 215
light, xi, 3, 6, 21, 91, 92, 134
Likert scale, 96
linguistics, 38, 199
literacy, 116, 141, 184, 185, 186, 187

Index

living conditions, 92, 145, 158
longitudinal study, 32, 89, 111

M

magazines, 185
majority, 133, 149, 156, 174, 199, 209, 210
management, 37, 126, 151, 166, 167, 172, 190
marginalised learners, 6, 13
marriage, 126, 128, 134
materials, 16, 17, 34, 42, 43, 45, 46, 49, 56, 69, 177, 203, 206
maternal employment, 120, 121, 137
mathematics, 20, 23, 24, 25, 27, 28, 30, 31, 32, 53, 67, 114, 226
mathematics education, 25, 30, 226
mental health professionals, v
messages, 17, 93
meta-analysis, 14, 25, 26, 216
methodology, xi, 200, 215
middle-class families, 39
Ministry of Education, 4, 7, 8, 9, 10, 11, 16, 18, 21, 22, 23, 24, 25, 26, 27, 28, 29, 31, 93, 94, 109, 110, 113
minority groups, xii, 3
models, 75, 115, 116, 119, 130, 131, 137, 146, 193, 205, 211, 216
motivation, 2, 8, 69, 187, 204, 227
motivation to learn, 2, 8, 69
multicultural education, 218
multidimensional, 87, 97, 203
multi-ethnic, x, 91, 100, 109, 213
multimodal conversation analysis, 34, 57
multiple regression analyses, 131

N

narratives, 172, 178, 179
National Center for Education Statistics, 196, 197, 198, 217, 218, 220

national curricula, 17
nationality, 203, 210
negative attitudes, xiii, 195, 201
negative outcomes, 173
negative relation, 205
neglect, 180
North America, 25, 38
nurses, 196
nurturing parent, 15, 18
nutrition, 180

O

obedience, 146
obstacles, x, 92, 164
open-mindedness, 161
operations, 97
opportunities, 5, 7, 20, 21, 35, 70, 82, 83, 108, 146, 147, 178, 199, 204
oppression, 204
organize, 37, 56
overlap, 115, 118, 131, 134, 135

P

paradigm shift, 6
parent involvement, v, 14, 16, 20, 24, 31, 64, 85, 86, 87, 100, 111, 143, 144, 145, 146, 147, 149, 153, 154, 155, 156, 157, 159, 160, 161, 162, 163, 164, 165, 166, 167, 168, 174, 175, 176, 191, 192, 218, 221
parental attitudes, 173
parental care, xi, 127, 128, 180, 181
parental knowledge, 97, 98, 100, 102, 103, 105, 114
parental participation, 97, 117
parental school involvement, 66, 69, 71, 72, 83
parental support, 12, 25

Index

parental trust, 65, 66, 67, 68, 71, 72, 74, 75, 80, 82, 83, 84
parent-child interaction, xi, 33, 34, 55, 64
parent-child relationship, 68, 114
parenting, xi, 3, 14, 69, 101, 103, 110, 119, 120, 135, 136, 138, 139, 140, 158, 175, 181, 182, 189
parent-teacher relationships, v, x, 86, 88, 92, 94, 108, 113
parent-teacher trust relationships, 96
participation, 7, 9, 14, 15, 38, 55, 61, 62, 65, 73, 75, 76, 77, 78, 79, 81, 82, 83, 85, 88, 97, 117, 122, 124, 137, 144, 145, 150, 153, 166, 173, 174, 188, 194, 195, 208, 225, 227
partnership, xii, 7, 9, 14, 15, 22, 27, 28, 29, 62, 84, 86, 95, 96, 107, 110, 114, 167, 175, 190, 194, 227
path model, 65, 75, 77, 78, 79, 82, 113
pedagogy, x, 2, 5, 23, 28, 30, 31, 63, 194, 200, 203, 206, 216, 217, 219
performance, 5, 20, 35, 57, 67, 87, 96, 107, 113, 117, 125, 134, 144, 145, 153, 165, 168, 171, 172, 173, 174, 175, 181, 183, 190, 191, 194, 198, 202, 205, 210
performers, 144
personal development, 21
personality, 123
policy makers, 83
policymakers, 91, 93, 100, 135
population, xiii, 7, 100, 102, 148, 196, 198, 208, 220
positive attitudes, 95, 116, 171, 175, 195
positive relationship, 20, 94, 172, 187
poverty, 140, 143, 147, 148, 154, 156, 160, 162, 167, 168, 174, 189, 227
prejudice, 156, 158, 159, 160, 161
preschool, 70, 71, 87, 191, 212, 215, 221
preschool children, 191, 221
primary school, xi, xii, 30, 36, 59, 65, 66, 70, 71, 72, 75, 76, 77, 78, 79, 80, 81, 83, 141, 163, 165, 166, 172, 177, 179, 181, 191, 192
principles, 7, 20, 165
probability, 200
professional development, 18, 21, 22, 28, 200, 212, 226
professionalization, 168
professionals, 8, 84, 152, 154, 155, 219
project, 5, 18, 31, 37, 38, 39, 72, 143, 149, 150
prosocial behavior, 67
psychological health, 140
psychology, 38, 40, 63, 224
psychopathology, 112
public education, 94
public schools, 165, 166, 195, 196, 214, 218
pupil achievement, 25

Q

questioning, 55, 209
questionnaire, 72, 73, 75, 85

R

race, 140, 145, 146, 150, 154, 164, 168, 210, 212, 214
reading, 4, 27, 44, 50, 67, 69, 89, 97, 150, 185, 199, 227
reading skills, 69, 89
real time, 36
reciprocal relationships, 10, 16
recognition, 188, 209, 219
recommendations, v, xiii, 2, 145, 160, 179
recruiting, 175
reducing barriers to learning, 2
reflexivity, 60, 178
reformation, 6, 7, 10
refugees, 214
regions of the world, xii
regression, 131, 133

regression equation, 131, 133
reproduction, 162, 163
requirements, 33, 57, 151, 191, 192, 199, 210
researchers, v, vi, ix, xi, xiii, 38, 179
resistance, 37, 151, 160
resources, 2, 11, 13, 17, 22, 23, 33, 43, 56, 89, 108, 118, 121, 130, 136, 158, 160, 174, 175, 177, 185, 188, 195, 202, 204, 205, 226
response, 6, 7, 47, 51, 57, 88, 93, 102, 103, 184
responsiveness, 2, 6, 10, 12, 68
rewards, 162
rhetoric, 94, 143, 156
role-playing, 108
rural schools, 166

S

safety, 180
scarce resources, 162
scarcity, 158
school achievement, 28, 36, 116, 144
school activities, 4, 35, 39, 81, 93, 95, 108, 173, 174, 176, 182, 183, 184, 186, 187, 188, 189, 194, 195, 196, 202, 205, 206, 208
school community, xiii, 17, 21, 146, 155, 161, 162, 171, 175
school culture, 15, 16, 201
school improvement, 67, 173
schooling, v, ix, xii, xiii, 2, 5, 19, 23, 26, 29, 81, 84, 88, 110, 146, 164, 165, 167, 172, 173, 174, 175, 176, 177, 178, 179, 182, 186, 189, 190, 194, 205
science, 30, 31, 51, 63, 167, 199
secondary schools, 28, 110, 143, 149, 150, 160, 167, 190, 191
self-confidence, 116, 187
self-esteem, 74, 104, 116, 171

self-reflection, 201
self-worth, 102, 103, 104, 105, 109
semi-structured interviews, 38, 143, 144, 172, 178
sensitivity, 144, 145, 161
services, iv, 151, 175, 202, 205
settlements, xiii, 176, 177, 188
showing, 47, 55, 96, 109, 115
social activities, 70, 98
social development, 85, 88, 116, 191
social interaction, 159, 201, 225, 226
social interactions, 201, 225, 226
society, 3, 12, 13, 80, 91, 93, 100, 103, 163
socioeconomic status, 24, 36, 101, 168, 176
sovereignty, 28, 217
special education, 88, 111, 191
specialization, 182, 225, 226
spheres of influence, 3
spirituality, 16
stakeholders, 20, 67, 70, 106, 174, 189, 208
standardized testing, 199
state, 26, 63, 146, 148, 151, 152, 155, 158, 160, 162
stereotyping, 143, 158, 159, 160
stress, 70, 134, 220, 227, 228
structural models, 115, 116, 119, 131
structure, 16, 102, 148, 181, 223
student achievement, 16, 26, 67, 88, 113, 155, 192
student motivation, 21
support services, 160
Sweden, 37, 63, 205
Switzerland, 33, 198, 225, 226
synthesis, 2, 23, 24, 31, 60, 179

T

talent, 188
target, 22, 122
teacher attitudes, 173

Index

teacher education, 18, 23, 155, 165, 194, 200, 214, 215, 225, 226
teacher effectiveness, 213
teacher perspectives, 144, 158
teacher preparation, 194, 209
teacher relationships, v, x, 86, 88, 92, 94, 106, 108, 113
teacher training, 108, 164, 209
teacher-student relationship, 68, 228
teaching and learning, 3, 7, 9, 22, 108, 172, 174, 177, 179, 180, 184, 187, 201, 225, 228
teaching experience, 209
telephone, 42, 51, 123
temperament, 144, 161
textbooks, 44, 57, 58, 151
theoretical approach, 115, 121, 133
theoretical approaches, 115, 121, 133
training, 11, 108, 144, 161, 199, 201, 202, 204, 208, 210
training programs, 210
transcripts, 40, 152, 178
transformation, ix, 6, 7, 10, 150, 160, 201
tutoring, 82, 209

U

under-resourced school, 144, 146, 156, 157, 161, 162
unemployment rate, 148, 162
universality, v
urban, 84, 85, 86, 102, 144, 148, 149, 164, 168, 173, 176, 211, 216
urban areas, 148, 176
urban school, 84, 102, 144, 149, 211

V

validation, 89
variables, 74, 101, 135
varimax rotation, 125
victims, 211
video ethnography, 34, 38, 62
video-recording, xi, 38
violence, 95
vulnerability, 160

W

Washington, 212, 213, 214, 215, 217, 218, 219, 220
waste, 152
weakness, 135, 203
wealth, 145, 147
wellbeing, ix, xi, 11, 21, 22, 95, 105, 116, 117, 227
work activities, 39
workforce, 208
working conditions, 158
working families, 37
working hours, 82, 130, 131
workload, 156
workplace, 42, 135
worldview, 159
wrongdoing, 155

Z

Zimbabwe, 163

Related Nova Publications

CHILDREN'S RIGHTS: GLOBAL PERSPECTIVES, CHALLENGES AND ISSUES OF THE 21ST CENTURY

EDITOR: Samuel M. Lange

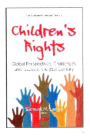

SERIES: Family Issues in the 21st Century

BOOK DESCRIPTION: The opening chapter of *Children's Rights: Global Perspectives, Challenges and Issues of the 21st Century* argues that an alternative praxis, one that honours constructivist and post humanist theoretical approaches to teaching and learning, is a rights-based praxis.

SOFTCOVER ISBN: 978-1-53615-565-5
RETAIL PRICE: $82

UNDERSTANDING EARLY ADOLESCENCE: PERSPECTIVES, BEHAVIOR AND GENDER DIFFERENCES

EDITOR: Felicien Martin

SERIES: Family Issues in the 21st Century

BOOK DESCRIPTION: The authors research developmental differences in effortful control, sensation seeking and risk-taking behavior between adolescents and young adults. Additionally, gender and socioeconomic status differences in all three variables were investigated.

SOFTCOVER ISBN: 978-1-53615-105-3
RETAIL PRICE: $82

To see a complete list of Nova publications, please visit our website at www.novapublishers.com

Related Nova Publications

WHAT MUM TAUGHT US: VALUABLE LESSONS AND OUTSTANDING HOSPITALITY, INCLUDING PRECIOUS MESOPOTAMIAN RECIPES

AUTHORS: Theodora Issa, Ph.D., Touma Issa, Ph.D., Tomayess Issa Ph.D., Tamara Issa Raphael and Theodore Issa, FCPA, CA

SERIES: Family Issues in the 21st Century

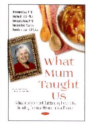

BOOK DESCRIPTION: This book is dedicated to the authors' mother, Bathqyomo Marine Khoury-Issa, with her unique characteristics as a spouse, mother and matriarch of the Issa Family. Her care put continues to exist in the food she used to cook (both main dishes and sweets), the care she gave to the garden, the way she faced life and the way she welcomed people into her home and family.

SOFTCOVER ISBN: 978-1-53614-586-1
RETAIL PRICE: $120

To see a complete list of Nova publications, please visit our website at www.novapublishers.com